The Pragmatic Programmer for Machine Learning

Machine learning has redefined the way we work with data and is increasingly becoming an indispensable part of everyday life. This book discusses how modern software engineering practices are part of this revolution both conceptually and in practical applications.

Comprising a broad overview of how to design machine learning pipelines as well as the state-of-the-art tools we use to make them, this book provides a multi-disciplinary view of how traditional software engineering can be adapted to and integrated with the workflows of domain experts and probabilistic models.

From choosing the right hardware to designing effective pipeline architectures and adopting software development best practices, this guide will appeal to machine learning and data science specialists, whilst also laying out key high-level principles in a way that is approachable for students of computer science and aspiring programmers.

Chapman & Hall/CRC Machine Learning & Pattern Recognition

A First Course in Machine Learning
Simon Rogers, Mark Girolami

Statistical Reinforcement Learning: Modern Machine Learning Approaches
Masashi Sugiyama

Sparse Modeling: Theory, Algorithms, and Applications
Irina Rish, Genady Grabarnik

Computational Trust Models and Machine Learning
Xin Liu, Anwitaman Datta, Ee-Peng Lim

Regularization, Optimization, Kernels, and Support Vector Machines
Johan A.K. Suykens, Marco Signoretto, Andreas Argyriou

Machine Learning: An Algorithmic Perspective, Second Edition
Stephen Marsland

Bayesian Programming
Pierre Bessiere, Emmanuel Mazer, Juan Manuel Ahuactzin, Kamel Mekhnacha

Multilinear Subspace Learning: Dimensionality Reduction of Multidimensional Data
Haiping Lu, Konstantinos N. Plataniotis, Anastasios Venetsanopoulos

Data Science and Machine Learning: Mathematical and Statistical Methods
Dirk P. Kroese, Zdravko Botev, Thomas Taimre, Radislav Vaisman

Deep Learning and Linguistic Representation
Shalom Lappin

Artificial Intelligence and Causal Inference
Momiao Xiong

Transformers for Machine Learning: A Deep Dive
Uday Kamath, Kenneth L. Graham, Wael Emara

Entropy Randomization in Machine Learning
Yuri S. Popkov, Alexey Yu. Popkov, Yuri A. Dubno

Introduction to Machine Learning with Applications in Information Security, Second Edition
Mark Stamp

The Pragmatic Programmer for Machine Learning: Engineering Analytics and Data Science Solutions
Marco Scutari and Mauro Malvestio

For more information on this series please visit: https://www.routledge.com/
Chapman--HallCRC-Machine-Learning--Pattern-Recognition/book-series/
CRCMACLEAPAT

The Pragmatic Programmer for Machine Learning
Engineering Analytics and Data Science Solutions

Marco Scutari
Mauro Malvestio

CRC Press
Taylor & Francis Group
Boca Raton London New York

CRC Press is an imprint of the
Taylor & Francis Group, an **informa** business
A CHAPMAN & HALL BOOK

Cover design by Carlo Sandonà

First edition published 2023
by CRC Press
6000 Broken Sound Parkway NW, Suite 300, Boca Raton, FL 33487-2742

and by CRC Press
4 Park Square, Milton Park, Abingdon, Oxon, OX14 4RN

CRC Press is an imprint of Taylor & Francis Group, LLC

© 2023 Marco Scutari and Mauro Malvestio

Library of Congress Cataloging-in-Publication Data

Names: Scutari, Marco, author. | Malvestio, Mauro, author.
Title: The pragmatic programmer for machine learning : engineering analytics and data science solutions / Marco Scutari, Mauro Malvestio.
Description: Boca Raton : CRC Press, [2023] | Series: Machine learning & pattern recognition | Includes bibliographical references and index. | Summary: "The book provides a guide for data scientists and data analysts on modern software engineering to plan, implement, and improve the use of machine learning models. The book will also be useful to academics working in quantitative subjects where reliable software is required to obtain reproducible results and to increase the impact of research. It includes best practices on how best to implement models into code, how to document and troubleshoot code to ensure correctness, and how to deploy code into production. The book also explores how best practices are put to use in computing environments, using real-world examples and two case studies"-- Provided by publisher.
Identifiers: LCCN 2022043088 (print) | LCCN 2022043089 (ebook) | ISBN 9780367263508 (hardback) | ISBN 9780367255060 (paperback) | ISBN 9780429292835 (ebook)
Subjects: LCSH: Machine learning. | Software engineering. | Statistics--Data processing.
Classification: LCC Q325.5 .S38 2023 (print) | LCC Q325.5 (ebook) | DDC 006.3/1--dc23/eng20230111
LC record available at https://lccn.loc.gov/2022043088
LC ebook record available at https://lccn.loc.gov/2022043089

ISBN: 978-0-367-26350-8 (hbk)
ISBN: 978-0-367-25506-0 (pbk)
ISBN: 978-0-429-29283-5 (ebk)

DOI: 10.1201/9780429292835

Typeset in Merriweather
by KnowledgeWorks Global Ltd.

Publisher's note: This book has been prepared from camera-ready copy provided by the authors.

To my Oxford M.Sc. students: this is the book I would have liked to have to teach you Statistical Programming. Sorry that it took me a while to write it!

To my childhood best friend, the unbeatable C64.

Contents

Preface   xiii

1 What Is This Book About?   1
   1.1 Machine Learning   1
   1.2 Data Science   4
   1.3 Software Engineering   6
   1.4 How Do They Go Together?   8

I Foundations of Scientific Computing   11

2 Hardware Architectures   13
   2.1 Types of Hardware   14
        2.1.1 Compute   15
        2.1.2 Memory   20
        2.1.3 Connections   24
   2.2 Making Hardware Live Up to Expectations   26
   2.3 Local and Remote Hardware   28
   2.4 Choosing the Right Hardware for the Job .   30

3 Variable Types and Data Structures   35
   3.1 Variable Types   36
        3.1.1 Integers   36
        3.1.2 Floating Point   40
        3.1.3 Strings   47
   3.2 Data Structures   48
        3.2.1 Vectors and Lists   49
        3.2.2 Representing Data with Data Frames   51
        3.2.3 Dense and Sparse Matrices   53
   3.3 Choosing the Right Variable Types for the
        Job   56

3.4 Choosing the Right Data Structures for the
     Job   61

4 Analysis of Algorithms   63
4.1 Writing Pseudocode   63
4.2 Computational Complexity and Big-O
     Notation   66
4.3 Big-O Notation and Benchmarking . . .   70
4.4 Algorithm Analysis for Machine Learning   72
4.5 Some Examples of Algorithm Analysis . .   73
     4.5.1 Estimating Linear Regression Models   74
     4.5.2 Sparse Matrices Representation . .   80
     4.5.3 Uniform Simulations of Directed Acyclic
            Graphs   84
4.6 Big-O Notation and Real-World
     Performance   90

**II Best Practices for Machine Learning
    Pipelines   93**

5 Designing and Structuring Pipelines   95
5.1 Data as Code   95
5.2 Technical Debt   98
     5.2.1 At the Data Level   99
     5.2.2 At the Model Level 101
     5.2.3 At the Architecture (Design) Level . 104
     5.2.4 At the Code Level 106
5.3 Machine Learning Pipeline 107
     5.3.1 Project Scoping 111
     5.3.2 Producing a Baseline Implementation 115
     5.3.3 Data Ingestion and Preparation . . 116
     5.3.4 Model Training, Evaluation and
            Validation 118
     5.3.5 Deployment, Serving and Inference   121
     5.3.6 Monitoring, Logging and Reporting   123

6 Writing Machine Learning Code   129
6.1 Choosing Languages and Libraries 130

6.2 Naming Things 133
6.3 Coding Styles and Coding Standards . . . 136
6.4 Filesystem Structure 139
6.5 Effective Versioning 143
6.6 Code Review 146
6.7 Refactoring 151
6.8 Reworking Academic Code: An Example . 153

7 Packaging and Deploying Pipelines 163
7.1 Model Packaging 163
    7.1.1 Standalone Packaging 164
    7.1.2 Programming Language Package
         Managers 164
    7.1.3 Virtual Machines 165
    7.1.4 Containers 167
7.2 Model Deployment: Strategies 172
7.3 Model Deployment: Infrastructure 176
7.4 Model Deployment: Monitoring and Logging 177
7.5 What Can Possibly Go Wrong? 179
7.6 Rolling Back 182

8 Documenting Pipelines 185
8.1 Comments 186
8.2 Documenting Public Interfaces 189
8.3 Documenting Architecture and Design . . 199
8.4 Documenting Algorithms and Business
    Cases 205
8.5 Illustrating Practical Use Cases 209

9 Troubleshooting and Testing Pipelines 213
9.1 Data Are the Problem 214
    9.1.1 Large Data 215
    9.1.2 Heterogeneous Data 217
    9.1.3 Dynamic Data 218
9.2 Models Are the Problem 219
    9.2.1 Large Models 219
    9.2.2 Black-Box Models 220
    9.2.3 Costly Models 221

9.2.4 Many Models 222
9.3 Common Signs That Something Is Up . . 223
9.4 Tests Are the Solution 226
9.4.1 What Do We Want to Achieve? . . . 227
9.4.2 What Should We Test? 228
9.4.3 Offline and Online Data 230
9.4.4 Testing Local and Testing Global . . 234
9.4.5 Conceptual and Implementation
Errors 237
9.4.6 Code Coverage and Test Prioritisation 239

III   Tools and Technologies   245

10 Tools for Developing Pipelines   247
10.1 Data Exploration and Experiment Tracking   247
10.2 Code Development 251
10.2.1 Code Editors and IDEs 252
10.2.2 Notebooks 254
10.2.3 Accessing Data and Documentation   257
10.3 Build, Test and Documentation Tools   . . 257

11 Tools to Manage Pipelines in Production   263
11.1 Infrastructure Management   263
11.2 Machine Learning Software Management   266
11.3 Dashboards, Visualisation and Reporting . 271

IV   A Case Study   275

**12 Recommending Recommendations: A Recom-
mender System Using Natural Language Understanding   277**
12.1 The Domain Problem 278
12.2 The Machine Learning Model 281
12.3 The Infrastructure 285
12.4 The Architecture of the Pipeline 288
12.4.1 Data Ingestion and Data Preparation   289
12.4.2 Data Tracking and Versioning . . . 293
12.4.3 Training and Experiment Tracking . 294

12.4.4 Model Packaging 297
12.4.5 Deployment and Inference 298

Bibliography **303**

Index **337**

Preface

Pitching new ideas by prefacing them with quotes like "Data scientist: the sexiest job of the 21st century" [142] or "Data is the new oil" [357] has become such a cliché that any audience (in business and academia alike) will collectively roll their eyes in exasperation. And for good reason. Likewise, we do not believe radiologists or lorry drivers will be replaced by artificial intelligence and out of a job for the foreseeable future, and we are not alone in realising the limits of machine learning [358].

Even so, it is difficult to understate the impact that machine learning is having on many aspects of our lives. It has taken the pre-existing trends of using data and analytics (under the banner of "data mining", "big data" and similar buzzwords) to inform business decisions and drive scientific discovery, and made them ubiquitous. Machine learning has combined the mathematical rigour of information theory and statistics, the computational aspects of computer science and the goal-driven flexibility of optimisation theory, redefining how we work with data.

The flip side of trying to distil parts of so many different disciplines has been the clash between their respective cultures, which has been well summarised by Leo Breiman in "Statistical Modeling: The Two Cultures" [54]. On top of that, there is a tension between machine learning practice in the industry and academia: the latter strongly values producing novel models and theoretical results, while the former is driven by the need to produce practical results that have business value. With so many different perspectives, it is a wonder that a rough consensus on what machine learning is has actually evolved! (Personally, our red line is conflating deep learning with machine learning. There is life beyond deep neural networks!)

In this melting pot of ideas, we feel that software engineering has played a remarkably small role compared to other disciplines. Machine learning, after all, is "a technique that allows computer systems to improve with experience and data" [122]. Therefore, there is a presumption that one will interact with a computer system, which in turn happens by engineering a piece of software that communicates to the computer system what it is supposed to do. The quality of this engineering is crucial in both academia and industry. In academia, software quality issues are one of the underlying causes of the "reproducibility crisis" [234, 340]. In industry, poor engineering leads to lower practical and computational performance [177], to a quick accumulation of technical debt [313] and sometimes to catastrophic failures with costs in the millions [317, 319, 368, 394]. There is, of course, a sizeable body of accumulated wisdom on how to architect and write software in foundational books like *The Pragmatic Programmer* [369] and *A Philosophy of Software Design* [252]. However, these books are written with business software in mind, and we find that they do not capture or touch only tangentially on key practices that go a long way towards successfully implementing and deploying machine learning models. Analysis of algorithms; matching data and algorithms with appropriate hardware; embracing data as part of the software; testing and documenting algorithms and their implementations; modularising and building pipelines; and, last but not least, naming variables. From our experience in academia and in the industry, engineering software and teaching software engineering to students and new staff alike, these topics are often not given the importance they deserve. We hope to convince the readers of this book that the viability of any software that analyses data, whether you call it machine learning, data science or business analytics, depends crucially on putting careful thought into these engineering practices. We do not aim to be prescriptive: the individual practices that we discuss will be more or less relevant in different settings, and can be implemented with a variety of software tools. On the contrary, we want our readers to think about what we wrote in the context of their own experience and to figure out which parts apply and which do not!

The book starts with a brief introduction to machine learning and software engineering, to set out how we view them and how we think that they should interact in practical applications. The remainder is structured in four parts, from foundational to practical:

1. **Foundations of Scientific Computing:** covering key topics that are foundational for the *planning, analysis* and *design* of machine learning software, such as: the trade-offs of using different hardware configurations; the characteristics of different data types and of suitable data structures; and the analysis of algorithms to determine their computational complexity.

2. **Best Practices for Machine Learning and Data Science:** revisiting best practices in software engineering from the point of view of a machine learning engineer, from *writing, troubleshooting* and *deploying code* to production (that is, serving models) to *writing technical documentation*.

3. **Tools and Technologies:** discussing *broad classes of tools* that shape how we think about what is feasible to do with machine learning pipelines, with examples from the state of the art and the trade-offs they make.

4. **A Case Study:** putting the recommendations in the previous chapters into practice by *discussing and prototyping a machine learning pipeline* for natural language understanding from the work of Lipizzi et al. [195].

All the material in this book, including the book itself, is available online at

https://ppml.dev

and will be updated to fix assorted typos and code problems as they become known to us.

Finally, we would like to thank all the people who supported us and made this book possible. First of all, our families who put up with our long working hours. The colleagues who gave us feedback on early drafts of the book: Vincenzo Manzoni, Fabio Stella and Ron Kenett. And, last but not least, our editor Randi Cohen who bore with us through the many delays this book suffered during the Covid pandemic.

Lugano, Switzerland   *Marco Scutari*
Milano, Italy   *Mauro Malvestio*
August 2022

1

What Is This Book About?

The modern practice of data analysis is shaped by the convergence of many disciplines, each with its own history: information theory, computer science, optimisation, probability and statistics among them. Machine learning and data science can be considered their latest incarnations, inheriting the mantle of what used to be called "data analytics". Software engineering should be considered as a crucial addition to this list. Why do we need it to implement modern data analysis efficiently and effectively?

1.1 Machine Learning

There are many definitions of machine learning. Broadly speaking, it is a discipline that aims to create computer systems and algorithms that can learn a structured representation of reality without (or with less) human supervision in order to interact with it [305]. At one end of the spectrum, we can take this to be a narrow version of artificial general intelligence in which we want our computer systems to learn intellectual tasks independently and to generalise them to new problems, much like a human being would. At the other end, we can view machine learning as the ability to learn probabilistic models that provide a simplified representation of a specific phenomenon to perform a specific task [110] such as predicting an outcome of interest (supervised learning) or finding meaningful patterns in the data (unsupervised learning). Somewhere in between these two extremes lie expert systems [60], which "capture the ability to think and reason about as an expert would in a particular domain" and can provide "a meaningful answer to a less than fully specified question."

Broadly speaking, in order to do this:

1. We need a working model of the world that describes the task and its context in a way that a computer can understand.
2. We need a goal: how do we measure the performance of the model? Because that is what we optimise for! Usually, it is the ability to predict new events.
3. We encode our knowledge of the world, drawing information from training data, experts or both.
4. The computer system uses the model as a proxy of reality and, as new inputs come in, to perform inference and decide if and how to perform the assigned task.

The exact form these elements take will depend on the domain we are trying to represent and on the model we will use to represent it. Machine learning is, at its core, a collection of models and algorithms from optimisation, statistics, probability and information theory that deal with abstract problems: from simple linear regression models [398], to Bayesian networks [314], to more complex models such as deep neural networks [122] and Gaussian processes [288]. These algorithms can be applied to a variety of domains from healthcare [381] to natural language processing [2] and computer vision [393], with some combinations of algorithms and domains working out better than others.

In classical statistics (Figure 1.1, bottom right), analysing data required the modeller to specify the probabilistic

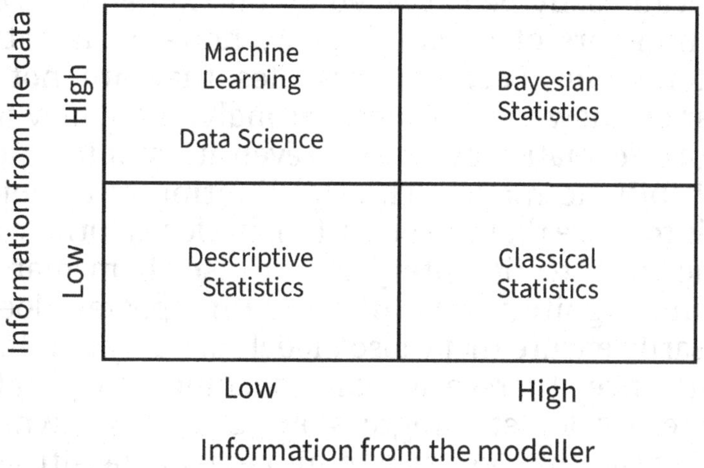

		Information from the modeller — Low	Information from the modeller — High
Information from the data	**High**	Machine Learning Data Science	Bayesian Statistics
	Low	Descriptive Statistics	Classical Statistics
		Low	High

Information from the modeller

FIGURE 1.1 Different approaches to data analysis grouped by their sources of information: the data or the assumptions made by the modeller.

model generating them in order to draw inferences from a limited number of data points. Such models would necessarily have a simple structure for two reasons: because the modeller had to manually interpret their properties and their output, and because of the lack of any substantial computing power to estimate their parameters. This approach would put all the burden on the modeller: most of the utility that could be had from the model would come from the ability of the modeller to distil whatever he was modelling into simple mathematics and to incorporate any available prior information into the model structure. The result is the emphasis on closed-form results, low-order approximations and asymptotics that characterises the earlier part of modern statistics.

There are, however, many phenomena that cannot be feasibly studied in this fashion. Firstly, there are limits to a human modeller's ability to encode complex behaviour when manually structuring models. These limits can easily be exceeded by phenomena involving large numbers of variables or by non-linear patterns of interactions between variables that are not very regular or known in advance. Secondly, there may not be enough information available to even attempt to structure a probabilistic model. Thirdly, limiting our choice of models to those that can be written in closed form to allow the modeller to fit, interpret and use them manually, without a significant use of computing power, does not necessarily ensure that those models are easy to interpret. For instance, there are many documented pitfalls in interpreting logistic regression [226, 287], which is arguably the simplest way to implement classification.

Classical applications of Bayesian statistics (Figure 1.1, top right) address some of these limitations. The modeller still has to structure a model covering both the data and any prior beliefs on their behaviour, but the posterior may be estimated algorithmically using Markov Chain Monte Carlo (MCMC).

In contrast [54], algorithmic approaches shift the burden from the modeller to data collection and computer software (Figure 1.1, top left). The modeller's role in constructing the probabilistic model is limited, and is largely replaced by a computer system sifting through large amounts of data: hence the name "machine learning". The structure of the model is learned from the data, with few limitations in what it may look like. Neural networks and Gaussian processes are universal approximators, for instance. Almost all the information comes from the data, instead of being prior information that is mediated by the modeller, which is why machine learning approaches are data-hungry.

1.2   Data Science

Data science is similarly data-driven (Figure 1.1, top left), but focuses on extracting insights from raw data and presenting them graphically to support principled decision making. Kenett and Redman [179] describe it as follows: "the real work of data scientists involves helping people make better decisions on the important issues in the near term and building stronger organizations in the long term". It requires strong involvement from the data scientist in all areas of business, shifting the focus from computer systems to people. Nevertheless, data scientists use statistical and machine learning models as the means to obtain those insights.

Compared to classical statistics, when data are abundant (Big Data! [178]) we do not really need to construct their generating process from prior knowledge. The data contain enough information for us to "let them speak for themselves" and obtain useful insights, which are what we are mainly interested in. Of course, prior information from experts is still useful: models that incorporate it tend to be better at producing insights that can be acted upon.

As a result, data science puts a strong focus on the quality of the data, which is often problematic when dealing with data aggregated from multiple sources (data fusion) or with non–tabular data (natural language processing and computer vision). Often, data are poorly defined, simply wrong or ultimately irrelevant for the purpose they were collected for. Expert knowledge is crucial to assess them, to integrate them and to fix them if possible. Machine learning is widely applied to both text and images as well, but focused mostly on modelling their hidden structure until recently, when explainability became a hot topic [see, for instance, 191, 325].

Computer systems are key to data science, albeit with a different role than in machine learning. Storing and accessing large amounts of data, exploring them interactively, building the software pipelines that analyse them, handling the resulting spiky workloads: these are all tasks that require a sophisticated use of both hardware and software.

1.3 Software Engineering

Software engineering is the systematic application of sound engineering principles to all phases of the software life cycle: design, development, maintenance, testing and evaluation [385]. Its central tenet is mastering the complexity inherent to developing large pieces of software that are reliable and efficient; that are usable and can be evolved over time; and that can be developed and maintained in a viable way in terms of both cost and effort [252].

Early definitions of software engineering suggested that we should treat it as if it were a traditional engineering discipline like, say, civil engineering. The result is the *waterfall model* [300], which lays out software development as a sequence of steps starting from collecting requirements and finishing with the deployment of the finished product. Modern practices recognise, however, that this model is flawed in several ways. Firstly, civil engineering arises from and is bound by the laws of physics, whereas we make up our own world with its own rules when we develop software. These rules will change over time as our understanding of the problem space evolves; the laws of physics do not. Secondly, the task the software is meant to perform will change over time, and our working definition of that task will change as well. Civil engineering mostly deals with well-defined problems that stay well-defined for the duration of the project. Finally, modifying a large building after its construction is completed is very difficult, but we routinely do that with software. Most

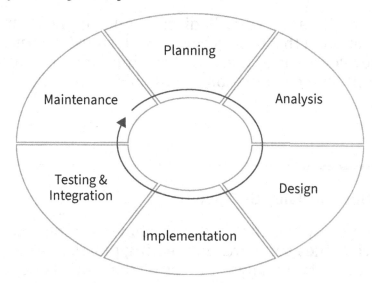

FIGURE 1.2 A schematic view of the phases of the software development life-cycle.

of the overall effort in the software lifetime is usually in maintaining and evolving it.

Current software engineering practices take the opposite view that software development is an open-ended ("software is never done"), iterative (the "software life-cycle") process: this is the core of the "Agile Manifesto" [36]. At a high level, it is organised as shown in Figure 1.2: a perpetual cycle of planning, analysis, design, implementation, testing and maintenance. The design of the software is heavily influenced by the domain it operates in [domain-driven development, 96]. It uses tests [test-driven development, 35], refactoring [105] and continuous integration [86] to incorporate new features, to fix bugs in a timely manner and to keep the code "in shape". Admittedly, all of these approaches have been touted as silver bullets to the point they have become buzzwords, and their practical implementation has often distorted them to the point of making software development worse. However, the key ideas of agile have merit, and we will discuss and apply them in moderation in this book. They are well suited to structure the development of machine learning pipelines, which are built on a combination of mutable models and input data.

1.4   How Do They Go Together?

The centrality of computing in machine learning and data science makes software engineering practices essential in modern data analysis: most of the work is done by computer systems, which are powered by software.[1] Encoding the data, storing and retrieving them efficiently, implementing machine learning models, tying them together and with other systems: each of these tasks is complex enough that only sound engineering practices can ensure the overall correctness of what we are doing. This is true, in different ways, for both academic research and industry applications. As Kenett and Redman [179] put it, using a car analogy:

> "If data is the new oil, technology is the new engine. The engine powers the car and, without technological advancements, a data- and analytics-led transformation would not be possible. Technologies include databases, communications systems and protocols, applications that support the storage and processing of data, and the raw computing horsepower (much of it now in the cloud) to drive it all."

In academia, there is a widespread belief that the software implementations of novel methods can be treated as

---

[1]This is not to discount the role of hardware, just to set the focus of the book. Processing units tailored to machine learning use are an active research and engineering field as exemplified by Nvidia [244], Google [59] and other companies [295].

"one-off scripts". "We only need to run it once to write this paper, there is no point in refactoring and re-engineering it." is a depressingly common sentiment. As is not sharing code to "stay ahead of the competition". However, research and application papers using machine learning rely crucially on the quality of the software they use because:

1. The models themselves are often black boxes whose mathematical behaviour is not completely understood (Section 9.2).
2. The data are complex enough that even experts in the domains they come from struggle to completely explain them (Section 9.1).

If we do not understand both the data and the models completely, it becomes very difficult to spot problems in the software we use to work on them: unexpected behaviour arising from software bugs may be mistaken for a peculiarity in either of them. It is then crucial that we minimise the chances of this happening by applying all the best engineering practices we have at our disposal. Present and past failures to do so have led to a widespread "reproducibility crisis" in fields as diverse as drug research [272, 20–25% reproducible], comparative psychology [332, 36% reproducible], finance [61, 43% reproducible] and computational neuroscience [224, only 12% of papers provide both data and code]. Machine learning and artificial intelligence research is in a similarly sorry state: that "when the original authors provided assistance to the reproducers, 85% of results were successfully reproduced, compared to 4% when the authors didn't respond" [261] *does* suggest that there is margin for improvement. Fortunately, in recent years scientists have widely accepted this is a problem [234], and the machine learning community has reached some consensus on how to tackle it [340].

In industry, poor engineering leads to lower practical and computational performance and a quick accumulation of technical debt [313, and Section 5.2]. Badly engineered data may not contain the information we are looking for in a usable form; models that are not well packaged may be slow to deploy and difficult to roll back; data may contain biases or may change over time in ways that make models fail silently; or the machine learning software may become an inscrutable black box whose outputs are impossible to explain, making troubleshooting impossible.

To conclude, we believe that solid machine learning applications and research rest on three pillars:

1. The foundations of machine learning (mathematics, probability, computer science), which provide guarantees that the models work.
2. Software engineering, which provides guarantees that the implementations of the models work (effectively and efficiently).
3. The quality of the data in terms of features, size, fairness, and in how they were collected.

In this book, we will concentrate on the software engineering aspect, touching briefly on some aspects of the data. We will not discuss the theoretical or methodological aspects of machine learning, which are better covered in the huge amount of specialised literature published to date [such as 109, 122, 147, 288, 305, and many others].

Part I

Foundations of Scientific Computing

2

Hardware Architectures

Building a compute system to run machine learning software requires careful planning. How well it will perform depends on choosing the right hardware; a set of machine learning algorithms that can attack efficiently and effectively the task we want to perform; and how to represent the data we will use, the models and their outputs. For the purpose of this book, we define a "compute system" as a computer system, not necessarily server-class, that will perform one or more of the tasks required to learn or use machine learning models. We will often call it a "machine learning system" as well to highlight its purpose. Other types of systems, such as those focusing on storage (database servers, data lakes, object storage) or delivery (human-readable dashboards, computer-readable API endpoints) will be mentioned only in passing.

In this chapter we focus on the hardware, moving to the data in Chapter 3 and to the algorithms in Chapter 4. After covering the key aspects of a compute system (Section 2.1), we discuss how to use it to the best of its potential (Section 2.2), the trade-offs involved in integrating remote systems (Section 2.3) and how to design it based on our requirements (Section 2.4). Modern machine learning libraries try to make these decisions for us, but they have limits that become apparent in many real-world applications: in such cases, being able to reason about the hardware is an invaluable skill.

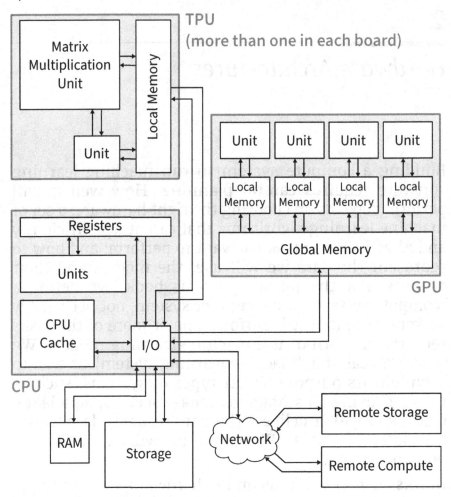

FIGURE 2.1 A schematic view of the key components that may appear in a modern compute system (not necessarily all at the same time). Sizes and distances are not to scale.

2.1 Types of Hardware

Compute systems come in a variety of configurations whose components are summarised in Figure 2.1. Broadly speaking, we can say that they vary along three axes:

1. *compute*, the processors that perform the operations required to learn and run our machine learning models;
2. *memory* to store the data, the models and their outputs as variables and data structures; and the
3. *connections* that we use to move the data and the models around.

These dimensions are admittedly somewhat arbitrary, but they are well-suited to discuss the topics we will cover in this book. In this context, choosing the right hardware means choosing a trade-off in terms of compute, memory and connections that allows the machine learning system to achieve the goals it is designed for while fitting the available budget. To quote one of the universal truths from RFC 1925 [55]:

"(7a) Good, Fast, Cheap: Pick any two (you can't have all three)."

2.1.1 Compute

The three types of processors we can commonly find in machine learning systems are:

1. *Central processing units* (CPUs), usually either an x86-64 processor from AMD or Intel or an ARM processor.
2. *Graphics processing units* (GPUs) from NVidia or AMD.
3. *Tensor processing units* (TPUs), usually from Google. Other specialised hardware to accelerate machine learning certainly exists [295] but, for practical purposes, fulfils the same role as TPUs.

CPUs, GPUs and TPUs represent different trade-offs in terms of speed, capabilities and versatility. Trading one off for another is unavoidable: the end of the "easy" performance improvements granted by Moore's law (transistors per chip double each year or two) and by Dennard's law (power density is constant as transistors get smaller, that is, we get more transistors) mean that we cannot expect general-purpose processors to become faster at the rate we were used to. Transistors cannot get any smaller without breaking the laws of physics. Current and voltage cannot drop any further while keeping transistors dependable, so we cannot easily double transistors per chip anymore. The only way out of this conundrum is domain-specific architectures that use their transistor- and power-budgets to the fullest for specific types of operations [168]. Hence the rise of GPUs and, more recently, TPUs in machine learning applications.

CPUs are the most versatile type of compute: they can perform a wide range of operations by means of the instructions they implement; they can perform multiple operations in parallel to some extent (whether on different cores or on different threads on the same core); and they can efficiently handle any type of data. At the same time, CPUs contain *logical units* that implement specialised single-instruction multiple-data (SIMD) instruction sets such as the Streaming SIMD Extensions (SSE1 to SSE4 on x86, Neon on ARM) and the Advanced Vector Extensions (AVX, AVX2, AVX512 on x86, SVM on ARM) to perform numerical computations efficiently and simultaneously on multiple variables.[1] The speed-ups that can be obtained by their use can be substantial, ranging from 10–15% to a factor of 10 [see, for instance, 103, 412]. The main limitation of SIMD instructions is that they can only operate on the contents of the *registers*, the smallest and fastest memory inside the CPU. For instance, on x86-64 CPUs each register can

---

[1]For the moment, we will use "data" and "variables" interchangeably. How data are actually represented in different types of variables will be the topic of Chapter 3.

hold 2–16 floating point numbers, and there are 16 (SSE, AVX, AVX2) or 32 (AVX512) registers for each core.

Another type of instruction that performs multiple operations in parallel are *fused operations* such as FMA ("fused add and multiply"), which perform predefined sets of operations on multiple variables and in approximately the same time it would take to perform a single operation. They also have the added benefit of performing just one floating point rounding to precision after the last operation, thus eliminating many rounding issues (more on this in Section 3.1.2).

GPUs specialise in parallel computations over large amounts of data. They are fundamentally different from CPUs: they behave like asynchronous devices in which we load data, we wait for data to be processed and then we collect the results. For practical purposes, modern GPUs can be viewed as multithreaded, multicore vector processors [392] designed to operate on one-dimensional arrays of data. The data is internally subdivided into blocks that will be processed by hundreds of independent, identical *units*.[2] Each unit is extremely simple: it is close to a CPU's SIMD/FMA logical unit in terms of functionality. It has its own set of registers and a local memory cache, but it can only apply a single type of operation at a time and is completely driven by the GPU scheduler. The GPU scheduler takes care of keeping the units busy by assigning them tasks in such a way as to maximise *occupancy* (the overall load of the GPU) and by keeping them fed with data from the global memory of the GPU.

This level of parallelism makes them potentially much faster than CPUs: a CPU has at most a few tens of cores,

---

[2]Naming conventions vary by vendor. In Nvidia GPUs, they are called "streaming units" organised in "streaming multiprocessors"; in AMD GPUs they are called "compute units" and "workgroup processors"; in Intel GPUs "execution units" and "execution cores".

whereas a GPU has hundreds of units that are equally capable of using SIMD instructions. This allows the GPU scheduler to handle tasks of unequal sizes and with different latencies, limiting their impact on the efficiency of parallel computations. Furthermore, each GPU unit has more registers[3] than a CPU core and can work on a much larger amount of data at extremely low latencies.

On the other hand, the hardware design that makes all of this possible restricts what a GPU can do. Units are optimised to work on 32-bit floating point and integer numbers; modern hardware also supports 16-bit and 64-bit floating point numbers well, but working with other types of variables is difficult. Getting data to the units requires copying them first to the GPU global memory, where they will be stored in one or more memory banks. Different units cannot read different data from the same memory bank at the same time, so we should carefully optimise the layout of the data in memory. Furthermore, data are assumed to be organised into one-dimensional arrays: further structure is disregarded. Support for branching (that is, if-then-else programming constructs) is limited to the GPU scheduler: units have no concept of conditional execution at all. Finally, units are organised in groups of 32 to 64, and the GPU scheduler can only allocate tasks to groups. Any task whose size is not a multiple of the group size will result in under-utilised groups and decrease occupancy.

TPUs are even more specialised: they are expressly built for training and performing inference on deep neural network models with the best possible average and tail performance. The architecture of TPU cores[4] rests on five design decisions [168]:

---

[3]For instance, each unit in an Nvidia RTX 2060 has 256kB of registers [243], while a CPU only has $32 \times 16 = 512$ bytes worth of AVX512 registers for each core (hence the name of the instruction set).

[4]In describing TPUs, we follow Google's naming conventions

- including a single, very simple core per processor;
- concentrating most computing power in a large, two-dimensional matrix-multiply unit;
- organising memory in a mesh network that allows for asynchronous, lockless communications between cores;
- implementing hardware support for integers and floats with limited precision, which use less memory;
- dropping all the features that are not strictly needed for working with deep neural networks.

This single-minded focus on deep learning makes TPUs the best hardware to use for this kind of models, with documented speed-ups on the order of 20-30 times over GPUs in terms of performance per watt [168]. In particular, [167] reports that TPUs are 50 times faster per watt for inference and 5 to 10 times faster for training. These improvements are largely driven by the fact that TPU cores are much smaller than GPU or CPU cores (38 times less area), so they consume (13 times) less energy and leave a larger share of the available transistors to the matrix-multiply unit. Another important factor is the memory layout, which allows deadlock-free communications between TPU cores at 500Gb per second and removes the need to synchronise them periodically. Intuitively, we can expect these performance improvements to carry over to other types of machine learning models that require similar patterns of mathematical operations, and particularly to those that can be completely formulated in terms of matrix manipulations.

The price we pay for this level of performance is the complete lack of flexibility and versatility of TPUs, which are really good only at multiplying matrices. TPU cores cannot perform any instruction scheduling, do not support multithreading, and in general have none of the

_____

because, at the time of this writing, that is the only TPU in wide use in machine learning.

sophisticated features we can find in CPUs and GPUs. They are completely driven by the CPU of the compute system they are attached to. To make up for that, code can be compiled with Google's XLA compiler [343] to require no dynamic scheduling and to maximise data- and instruction-level parallelism, combining operations to use SIMD/FMA instructions and to ensure that the matrix-multiplication unit is always busy. XLA has complete visibility into the structure of Tensorflow and PyTorch models and can optimise across operations much better than a traditional compiler or the CPU and GPU schedulers. It is effective to the point that it can achieve sustained 70% peak performance [167]. TPUs are also heavily optimised for a single type of variable, Google's "brain" floating point format ("bfloat"), and are slower for variables in the industry-standard IEEE 754 floating point format [253]. (More in Section 3.1.2.) Furthermore, they are designed specifically for 16-bit ("bfloat16") floating point operations over 32-bit operations. Both formats are empirically good enough for working deep neural networks and are eight times more efficient to operate on than IEEE formats [167].

2.1.2 Memory

The practical performance of CPUs, GPUs and TPUs is limited by the fact that we need to provide them data to operate on. Each processor can only access the memory it is directly attached to: the registers and the internal cache for CPUs, the on-board global and local memory for GPUs and TPUs (see Figure 2.1). This translates to delivering input data from system RAM to their dedicated memory and copying the outputs they produce back to system RAM for further processing.

Moving data between different memories costs time, as does moving them within each type of memory, although less so. Ideally, we want to have as much data as close as possible to the processor that will work on it. Furthermore, we want that processor to keep working on that data in place for as long as possible to amortise the cost of moving data over a large number of operations. This aspiration is limited by three factors:

1. the *amount* of memory available to and directly accessible by each type of processor;
2. the *latency* of accessing different types of memory;
3. and the *bandwidth* of our connections to different types of memory, which determines how quickly data can be transferred after it is accessed.

In other words, latency is the time spent waiting for the memory copy to start, and the bandwidth is the maximum amount of memory we can copy per second.

Clearly, each type of processor will be fastest in accessing its dedicated memory because it is physically located next to or inside it. Distance plays a key role in determining the latency of memory accesses: the propagation speed of electrical signals limits how quickly we can reach for that memory. The need to process these signals along the way, for instance, to translate the addresses of memory locations in different formats, may further delay accesses as well. CPU registers, the local memory of GPU units and the local memory of TPUs are directly attached to the respective processors to minimise distance and to make them directly addressable. This reduces latency from microseconds (10^{-6} seconds) or tens of microseconds (10^{-5} seconds) to a few hundred or tens of microseconds (10^{-9} to 10^{-7} seconds). To quote RFC 1925 once more:

"(2) No matter how hard you push and no matter what the priority, you can't increase the speed of light."

The latency of accessing particular types of memory is usually inversely proportional to their size and is bound below by the frequency of the processor accessing it. We

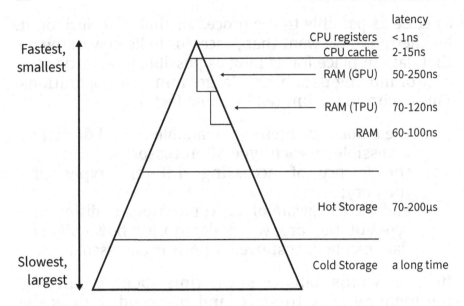

FIGURE 2.2 A schematic view of the different types of memory, their size and their latency (the time it takes for the CPU to access them). Times are expressed as nanoseconds ($1ns = 10^{-9}s$) or microseconds ($1?s = 10^{-6}s$).

illustrate this point in Figure 2.2, focusing on the CPU, but our considerations hold for GPUs and TPUs as well. CPU registers and the various CPU caches are the smallest because their size is limited by the physical size of the CPU. For instance, the three levels of cache (L1, L2, L3) on a Sandy Bridge Intel CPU are 32kB (L1), 256kB (L2) and 20MB (L3) in size and can be accessed in 4, 12 and 29 cycles respectively [412]. In contrast, registers can only store a few hundreds of bytes, but it only takes a single cycle to access them. For practical purposes, we can take a CPU cycle to be the reciprocal of the CPU's clock frequency. Say that we have a 2GHz CPU:

$$1 \text{ cycle} / (2 \times 10^9 \text{Hz}) = 5 \times 10^{-10}s = 0.5ns.$$

With this equation we can derive the latencies shown in Figure 2.2: accessing registers takes 0.5ns and accessing the CPU cache takes between 2ns and 14.5ns. It is easy to see that performance degrades quickly if the CPU is forced to wait for several nanoseconds to fetch the data from the CPU cache for every 0.5ns it spends doing computations. The degradation may be less noticeable for instructions that take longer than 1 cycle to complete, such as division, trigonometric and transcendental functions, simply because the time spent on the computations is larger compared to that spent waiting.

Next in the memory hierarchy are different sets of RAM: the system RAM accessible from CPUs, the video RAM on the GPU boards and that in TPU boards. As we can see from Figure 2.2, the latency of accessing RAM can be in the hundreds of nanoseconds, making it slower than CPU caches by a factor of at least 10. The GPU and TPU RAM, called "global memory" in Figure 2.1, can be even slower because GPUs and TPUs are connected to the CPU through a PCI Express bus (PCIe),[5] which adds to the latency. However, RAM is much larger than CPU caches, ranging from a few gigabytes (GPU and TPU RAM) to a few terabytes (for system RAM).

The latency of RAM is such that we want to read data from it as few times as possible, and to read as much data as possible each time. For example, consider accessing 10MB of data in RAM to apply a set of 10 FMA instructions.

- If we transfer the data to the CPU as a single batch, we have to wait 60–100ns in order to access it, and then 5ns performing computations.
- If we transfer data in 200 50kB batches, we have to wait 12000–10000ns (12–20?s) to spend the same 5ns on computations.

---

[5]PCIe is in use in both x86-64 and ARM systems, and comes in several revisions and speeds. At the time of this writing, the current one is PCIe 4.0 which uses up to 16 channels in parallel to transfer up to 64GB/s.

The transfer itself takes the same time since it only depends on the bandwidth of the PCIe connection between the CPU and the RAM: 10MB take 216?s at 64GB/s. However, in the first case the latency introduced by the memory transfer is negligible, while in the second case it increases the overall time by about 20%. This is why both GPUs and TPUs are initialised by copying all the data from system RAM in a single batch, making the memory transfer (often called "kernel launch") a fixed overhead cost that will be amortised over the whole computation.

At the bottom of the memory hierarchy we have hot and cold storage. Hot storage is meant to contain data that we need to access often and right away, and will comprise hard drives (mostly solid-state drives) that are locally attached to the compute system. Cold storage is for data that we access less frequently and that do not require fast access times. It comprises a combination of tape, slower hard drives and network-attached storage. Hot storage usually has a size of several tens of terabytes, with less redundancy; cold storage can potentially scale to the petabytes, and often has more redundancy because it contains data that should be preserved in the long term. Hot storage is local, so it is limited by the latency and the bandwidth of PCIe; cold storage may be remote, so it is limited by network latencies and bandwidth. The storage medium is rarely a limiting factor: it almost always has more bandwidth than the connection we use to access it, which becomes the bottleneck.

2.1.3 Connections

The last, crucial part of a compute system is the connections that allow the data to move between different processors and types of memory. The performance of memory is necessarily limited by how it is connected to various processors. Memory directly connected to a particular processor (CPU caches and registers, the memory built in GPU and TPU boards) is always the fastest to access for that particular processor because it works at its full native speed. This means that latency is minimised and that bandwidth is maximised. For example, TPU memory has a throughput of 500Gb/s [167] and GPU memory has a throughput of 500–1000Gb/s (Nvidia Quadro cards [227]). The latency is negligible for both.

However, GPUs cannot access the system RAM directly; nor can CPUs access the memory on the GPU boards. This means that any data that is transferred to a GPU for processing must be copied from the system RAM to the on–board memory. Speed is then limited by the bandwidth of the PCIe bus that connects the GPU to the system and latency increases to the levels shown in Figure 2.2. The same is true for TPUs.

This is the reason why *data locality*, keeping the data "close" to the processor that will work on it, matters: direct connections have the best possible latency and bandwidth, while indirect ones are limited by the PCIe bus. Furthermore, transferring data between different types of memory typically involves copying it to system RAM as an intermediate step, which degrades performance even further.

Hot and cold storage are different from other types of memory in several respects. Firstly, they do not have any compute capabilities and therefore we cannot avoid transferring the data they contain to system RAM to work on it. Secondly, neither type of storage will necessarily saturate its connection to the system RAM: the connection does not introduce any bottleneck in itself. Hot storage is typically connected to the compute system via PCIe, but its sustained read–write speed (8GB/s for SATA 3 to 4GB/s for NVMe) is comfortably smaller than PCIe. Cold storage is even slower, or is only available through a network connection such as 100Gb/s Ethernet.

2.2 Making Hardware Live Up to Expectations

All these hardware types have powerful capabilities, each in their own way, but in order to use them effectively we need either compilers that can leverage them (if we can compile software from source) or libraries that have been built to do so (if we cannot). This means using compilers that understand the memory layout of the system and what specialised hardware instructions are available, or software built on optimised libraries like CUDA [244] (for NVidia GPUs) or Intel's Math Kernel Library (MKL) [156] (for CPUs). Some popular machine learning frameworks and libraries such as PyTorch [259] go even further and abstract all hardware–specific optimisations away, adapting automatically to the characteristics of the hardware they run on.

The key to getting the best possible performance out of modern compute systems is to recognise that they have many processors (specialised or otherwise) and that we want to keep all those processors busy as much as possible. In other words, we need *parallelism*:

- At the *instruction level*, we want software to use hardware instructions that can be executed simultaneously.
- At the *data level*, we want tasks with modular inputs and outputs so that we can operate on each of their elements independently, without having to wait for other operations to complete.
- At the *thread level*, we want different parts of our machine learning software to depend on each other's outputs as little as possible so that we can run them in separate threads or processes across different cores, processors or even systems.

To what extent thread–level parallelism is possible depends on what algorithms we are using and on how they are implemented (see Section 4.6). The same is true for data-level parallelism: whether data points and random variables can be considered to be independent, whether parameters can be estimated independently, and whether predictions can be computed independently depends on what machine learning model we are using and on how we learned it. Instruction-level parallelism, on the other hand, depends crucially on the software using the appropriate hardware instructions (SIMD and FMA in CPUs and GPUs, matrix-multiplication units in TPUs). This is true for data-level parallelism as well because being able to operate on multiple data points simultaneously is useless if the software does not tell various processors to do that.

Taking advantage of parallelism requires us to feed data to all the processors involved in the computations so that they have something to operate on. How we do that determines the *operational intensity* of the software: the number of operations per byte of RAM accessed during execution. Data locality is then key to improving that: loading data has a much higher latency than operating on data that are already in the local memory of the processor, so the processor will end up sitting idle while waiting for the data to arrive. This is bound to happen every time we load data from a different level in the hierarchy in Figure 2.2, as we discussed in Section 2.1.3. It is also bound to happen, to some extent, as we get close to running processors at full capacity. For instance, the CPU will often sit idle while waiting to receive results from GPUs and TPUs. And the closer we get to full occupancy, the less room we have for optimising load across and within processors. By the law of diminishing returns, we eventually end up decreasing their overall performance as the gains from increasing occupancy are outweighed by the overhead of managing different threads and processes contending for resources.

In other words, increasing operational intensity means reducing the number of memory accesses. Performing data transformations in place is a way to do that: it reduces the number and the volume of high–latency data transfers to and from RAM while maximising the usage of faster local memory. In doing so, we prevent the processors from stalling while waiting for data (they are "starving") and we allow them to operate continuously (we "keep them fed" with data). The price is that memory use is likely to increase because we need to rearrange the data in memory and possibly to keep multiple copies around. Depending on the algorithm, it is sometimes possible to get most of the intensity without sacrificing space complexity, as in [103].

When we are eventually forced to read from RAM, large RAM reads are better than many small RAM reads: we should lay out data continuously in RAM to allow for that. If we do not do that, most algorithms will become memory–bound. (More on that in Chapter 3.) Limiting memory usage in the first place will also help in this respect. Hence the interest in numeric formats with smaller precisions such as 16–bit floating point numbers and integers [167, 168]; and in reducing the number of parameters of machine learning models by compressing them or by making the models sparser [148].

2.3 Local and Remote Hardware

The discussion of the key aspects of compute systems in Sections 2.1 and 2.2 implicitly assumes that all hardware is part of a single system. That is unlikely to be the case: machine learning systems typically comprise different systems with specific purposes because different tasks run best on different hardware, and it is expensive to maximise memory, storage and compute in a single system all at the same time. Having different systems makes it possible to specialise them and to make them perform better while reducing costs. We can think of them as *remote storage* and *remote compute*, as they are labelled in Figure 2.1, connected by either a local or a geographical network.

Remote systems that are in the same local network are typically connected by a high-speed Ethernet connection. 50Gb Ethernet is good enough even at the scale of Facebook operations [148], so throughput is not a limiting factor for smaller machine learning systems. Latencies are more of a problem: the networking equipment that routes the traffic in the network is likely to introduce several microseconds of delay in establishing a new connection.

For remote systems that are in a different geographical location, both latency and bandwidth are limiting factors. A prime example is *cloud instances*, virtual servers that we can quickly create ("provision") or destroy ("decommission") and that run on hardware that we own (a private cloud) or that we rent from a public cloud provider such as Amazon Web Services (AWS), Microsoft Azure or Google Cloud Computing Services (GCP). Latency arises from the physical time it takes for signals to go through several layers of networking equipment to reach a system that is possibly in a different country. For instance, if we are located on the west coast of the United States the latency of a connection to the east coast is 40ms, to the United Kingdom is 81ms, and to Australia is 183ms [135]. If the remote system is activated on demand, we must also wait for it to boot before we can start processing any data: this can take between 1s and 40s depending on the type of virtualisation underlying the instances (Sections 7.1.3 and 7.1.4). Compared to the latencies in Figure 2.2, accessing data on a remote system is therefore 3–6 orders of magnitude slower than the storage of a local system. This is the case, for instance, for AWS spot instances: while they are cheaper to run, they must be booted up every time they are used and they may be shut down without warning.

On the one hand, we want to preserve locality as much as possible: colocating the data and all the compute systems that will work on it to avoid large, repeated data transfers across different locations. Designing the topology of the local network connecting different systems can minimise the impact of data transfers within the network and can make it feasible to spread the load of training complex models across different systems [148]. This approach is known as *distributed* or *federated learning* [192]: as an example, see the research done at DeepMind for distributed deep reinforcement learning [94] and Google's systems architecture for federated learning from mobile devices [47]. The latter is an instance of *edge computing* [181], which addresses data privacy, security, and latency constraints by pushing data processing to low-power devices closer to where the data originates (Section 5.3.1).

On the other hand, it is desirable to keep geographical spread for the purpose of disaster recovery. Keeping multiple copies of the data and of the models in different locations makes it unlikely that a hardware failure will result in the loss of crucial resources: a time-honoured strategy to achieve that is the "3-2-1 backup rule" (3 copies of your data, your production data and 2 backup copies, on 2 different types of storage with 1 copy off-site). It also helps with locality, but requires some care in synchronising the data and the models at different locations to ensure that the correct version is used everywhere.

2.4 Choosing the Right Hardware for the Job

No single compute system(s) configuration is best overall: practical performance is the result of complex interactions between the type(s) of algorithms, the models and the type(s) of hardware. Engineering the best possible performance should then begin by defining what the objectives of the machine learning system are (Section 5.3.1) and then choosing the software and the hardware required to achieve them. A comprehensive discussion on this topic can be found in [135], which explores all the different aspects of hardware, operating systems, protocols, benchmarking and profiling. In what follows, we will focus on the interactions between the machine learning models, the software stack that underlies them and the hardware. Numeric libraries such as BLAS [41], LAPACK [17] and GSL [106], frameworks like TensorFlow [341] and PyTorch, and low–level libraries such as XLA and CUDA essentially act as compilers for the models and translate them into the best available set of hardware instructions for the most suitable processor(s).

Some tasks are better suited to particular types of hardware. Consider, for instance, deep neural networks. There are important computational differences between training and inference: the latter is less parallelisable, has higher memory requirements, and requires wider data to keep enough precision and avoid catastrophic errors in the final model [167]. Hence training is best performed on compute systems generously equipped by GPUs and TPUs, while inference performs well even on CPUs [148]. After all, GPUs and TPUs are not magic "go fast" devices! They only benefit certain classes of problems that are embarrassingly parallel and mostly consist of vector (GPU) or matrix (TPU) operations. How many of each should we buy? That depends on the relative scale and frequency with which we perform each task. Typically, model training is performed every few days, while inference runs in real–time, possibly millions of times per day. For instance, 90% of the overall compute cost at Amazon is inference [14]: at that scale, using GPUs becomes a necessity again. But since GPUs are poorly suited for inference, an ad hoc software scheduler [162] is required to use them efficiently and with consistent, predictable performance. At smaller scales, compute systems with many CPU cores will be sufficient and simpler to set up.

Specific machine learning models may be feasible to use only on some types of hardware. Models that make heavy use of matrix operations naturally perform better on GPUs and TPUs but they are limited in size by the amount of on-board memory that the GPUs and TPUs can access. The whole model must fit and, at the same time, there must be enough memory left to store the data the model will operate on. Furthermore, we want to operate on data in batches as large as possible to increase occupancy: performance may be disappointing if we are forced to process data in small batches because the model uses up most of the on-board memory. This problem is not mitigated by putting multiple GPUs or TPUs in the same compute system because models are not shared between them. If memory requirements are beyond the capabilities of GPUs and TPUs, we are limited to running models on CPUs and system RAM, which has a much larger capacity but is slower. CPUs, however, may perform better for models or tasks that are not very parallelisable because different cores can perform completely different operations.

Finally, a note from our future selves: we should plan for more hardware than we strictly need right now to accommodate what are likely to be growing compute, memory and storage needs (*capacity planning*). Compute requirements for training machine learning models grew by a factor of 10 between 2012 and 2018 [167]. In addition, automated model selection techniques (also known as "hyperparameter tuning" for some types of models) such as AutoML [149] are becoming increasingly common and use, on average, 50 times more compute power than what is needed to learn the type of model they select. The amount of data [178] and the size of models [66, 421] are likewise constantly growing over time, requiring more hot storage and more memory (of all types) to store and use them [34].

Cloud computing may reduce the need for capacity planning: if instances are relatively inexpensive and if they can be quickly created and destroyed, we may buy less hardware up–front and scale it as needed. In fact, dynamic scaling algorithms can do that automatically in most cloud services. Furthermore, all major cloud providers offer instances with GPUs and, in the case of Google, TPUs for use in applications that require them. However, cloud computing is not a universal solution to capacity planning. Firstly, the cloud instances we rent from public cloud providers are billed based on how long they are in use and on how much/how quickly they allow us to scale in response to sudden changes in our needs. Therefore, it may be cheaper to buy the hardware outright if we foresee using them often enough or for long enough periods of time and if we have predictable workloads and network traffic patterns. Secondly, cloud computing can only give us *horizontal scalability* (increasing the number of systems we can use) and is ill–suited to achieve *vertical scalability* (increasing the computing power in individual systems). Horizontal scalability may not improve the performance of machine learning models that are not modular or parallelisable to at least some extent, and may not help at all if we need to work with large blocks of data that must be kept in memory. Thirdly, cloud instances are more difficult to profile and trace, making it more difficult to understand their behaviour (the *observability* of the system is limited) and to diagnose any issue they may have. (More on this in Section 5.3.6.)

3

Variable Types and Data Structures

In exploring the components that machine learning systems are built on, we stressed that different types of hardware are optimised to work with data and models stored in specific formats. Both are complex entities comprising a variety of elements that are organised into *data structures* such as data frames (representing tabular data) or standardised model formats like ONNX [247]. The individual elements inside these data structures are *variables* of specific *types* such as integer numbers, floating point numbers and strings.

In this chapter we revisit the variable types we mentioned in Chapter 2, as well as string representations, and we discuss possible reasons to choose one over another for different classes of data (Section 3.1). We then give some notable examples of how variables are organised in data structures such as vectors and lists (Section 3.2.1), data frames (Section 3.2.2) and matrices (Section 3.2.3). Different choices of variable types (Section 3.3) and data structures (Section 3.4) represent different trade-offs both in terms of hardware support, as we saw in Chapter 2, and in terms of the computational complexity of the machine learning algorithms that will operate on them, as we will discuss in Chapter 4.

3.1 Variable Types

Machine learning software primarily deals with numbers that are the mathematical representation of the data we are modelling. Images can be represented using the values of the colour channels of each of their pixels; text can be encoded into strings, which are then converted to frequencies for particular words; sensor data are recorded as a time series. We can store each of them with different types of variables, each with pros and cons that we will discuss in Section 3.3.

3.1.1 Integers

Integer variables can be used to represent natural ($\mathbb{N}$) or integer numbers ($\mathbb{Z}$). They are often used to represent Boolean variables as *indicators* (also known as *dummy variables*) as follows.

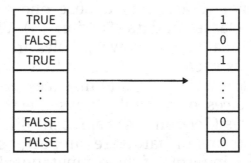

More generally, they can be used to give a numeric representation to finite sets by mapping each element to a different integer number.

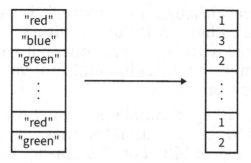

Enumerations in C or factors in R are constructed exactly in this way to minimise memory usage. However, this numeric representation is not suitable for modelling discrete variables because it makes parameter estimates dependent on the specific mapping between elements and integer numbers.[1] Instead, we map discrete variables to their *one-hot encoding*:[2] each element in the set is assigned an indicator variable that takes a value of 1 if the element is observed, and 0 otherwise.

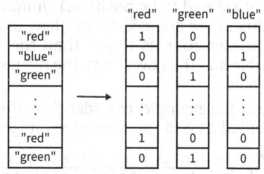

The number of elements we want to represent determines how many bits of memory each integer will use: n bits allow for 2^n distinct values. A single bit is enough for a

---

[1] If we use the colour in a regression model, the effect of "green" on the response will be twice that of "red", which clearly does not make any sense since the numbers associated with the colours are arbitrary.

[2] One-hot encoding is a particular case of what are known as *contrasts* in statistics. Since they are collinear, we usually drop one before using them in a model.

Boolean value, although, in practice, it is usually stored using at least 1 byte. A finite set with k elements can be represented with $\log_2 k$ bits: one-hot encoding side-steps this limitation by using indicator variables at the cost of using more memory.

Natural and integer numbers cannot be completely represented by integer variables: that would require an infinite number of bits. For this reason, programming languages provide integer variables of different *sizes* such as 8, 16, 32 and 64 bits. These sizes are all multiples of 8 bits because processors are optimised to work on bytes. The size of an integer variable determines the largest number it can represent. For instance, the largest (*unsigned*) natural number we can represent in 32 bits is $2^{32} - 1 \approx 4.29 \times 10^9$, and the largest (*signed*) integer number is $\pm 2^{31} - 1 \approx \pm 2.14 \times 10^9$ because 1 bit is reserved for encoding the sign. (If that bit is set to zero, the number is considered to be positive.) Numbers that are outside of this range are said to *overflow*, meaning that their bit representation is larger than the size of the integer variable and thus overflows the memory reserved for that variable.

For the sake of the example, consider the natural number 3134 represented as a 16-bit unsigned integer variable.

2^{15}	2^{14}	2^{13}	2^{12}	2^{11}	2^{10}	2^9	2^8	2^7	2^6	2^5	2^4	2^3	2^2	2^1	2^0
0	0	0	0	1	1	0	0	0	0	1	1	1	1	1	0

Most significant bits   Least significant bits

It's easy to check that this representation is equivalent to the "natural" one, they just use different bases:

$$2^1 + 2^2 + 2^3 + 2^4 + 2^5 + 2^{10} + 2^{11} = 3134.$$

The largest number that can be represented in 16 bits is $2^{16} - 1 = 65535$, and 3134 is comfortably smaller than that: we can easily see that the 4 *most-significant bits* that represent the 4 largest powers of 2 (2^{15}, 2^{14}, 2^{13} and 2^{12}) are all equal to zero. Now consider a much larger number: 247586.

2^{17}	2^{16}	2^{15}	2^{14}	2^{13}	2^{12}	2^{11}	2^{10}	2^{9}	2^{8}	2^{7}	2^{6}	2^{5}	2^{4}	2^{3}	2^{2}	2^{1}	2^{0}
1	1	1	1	0	0	0	1	1	1	0	0	1	0	0	0	1	0

Overflow   Most significant bits   Least significant bits

Again, we can easily check that

$$2^1 + 2^5 + 2^8 + 2^9 + 2^{10} + 2^{14} + 2^{15} + 2^{16} + 2^{17} = 247586.$$

Unfortunately, 247586 is larger than 65535 and cannot be represented in 16 bits. If we try to store it in 16 bits, we overflow: the integer variables will contain only the 16 *least-significant bits* representing the powers from 2^0 to 2^{15}. The bits corresponding to 2^{16} and 2^{17} will be silently dropped, and the integer variable will contain the number

$$2^1 + 2^5 + 2^8 + 2^9 + 2^{10} + 2^{14} + 2^{15} = 50978.$$

In the case of signed integers, the bits that overflow will overwrite the sign bit, and result in the integer variable storing a number that may be incorrect in both sign and absolute value. Consider again the number 247586, this time represented as a 16–bit signed integer variable.

2^{17}	2^{16}	2^{15}	2^{14}	2^{13}	2^{12}	2^{11}	2^{10}	2^{9}	2^{8}	2^{7}	2^{6}	2^{5}	2^{4}	2^{3}	2^{2}	2^{1}	2^{0}
1	1	1	1	0	0	0	1	1	1	0	0	1	0	0	0	1	0

Overflow   Sign   Most significant bits   Least significant bits

The first 15 bits of the binary representation are stored correctly, the bit corresponding to 2^{15} overwrites the sign bit, and the last two bits corresponding to 2^{16} and 2^{17} are again silently dropped. As a result, the integer variable will contain the number

$$-(2^1 + 2^5 + 2^8 + 2^9 + 2^{10} + 2^{14}) = -18210.$$

As an exception to the rule, R represents a missing integer value (NA) with the largest negative signed integer for a given precision. In Python, Pandas uses masked arrays for the same purpose and keeps a separate Boolean variable that indicates whether the integer is a missing value (denoted pandas.NA). NumPy does not support missing values for integer variables.

Range limitations aside, integer variables allow *exact computer arithmetic*: their bit representation coincides with the mathematical representation of integer and natural numbers in base 2, so there is no rounding or loss of precision.

3.1.2 Floating Point

Floating point variables are used to represent real ($\mathbb{R}$) and complex numbers ($\mathbb{C}$), the former with a single variable and the latter with two (one for the real part, one for the imaginary part). Each variable is composed of four parts: the *sign* S, the *bias* or *offset* O, an *exponent* E and a *mantissa* M. The floating point representation of a real number x is then

$$x = (-1)^S * (1 + M)2^{E+O}.$$

The overall size of the variable in bits is typically one of 16, 32, and 64 bits, often called *half-precision, single-precision, double-precision*. The number of bits assigned to each of the exponent (after adding the offset) and the mantissa depends on what encoding is used; the sign is always stored in a single bit. The variables defined in the IEEE 754 standard [253] reserve:

precision	exponent	mantissa
half (16 bit)	5 bits	10 bits
single (32 bit)	8 bits	23 bits
double (64 bit)	11 bits	52 bits

The value of the offset is determined as $O = 2^{|E|-1} - 1$ where $|E|$ is the size of the exponent in bits.

The alternative "brain" format devised by Google in the process of developing TPUs (see Section 2.1.1) typically has size 16 bits and is known as "bfloat16". It works in the same way as the IEEE 754 floating point, so we will not discuss it further; the only difference is that it allocates 8 bits to the exponent and 7 bits to the mantissa.

What does this mean in terms of binary representation? Consider the number 435.25. In the usual scientific notation, which is in base 10, we can write it as 4.3525×10^2. If we do the same in base 2, the scientific notation becomes 1.7001953125×2^8. The exponent is 8, and the mantissa is 0.7001953125. As a half−precision floating point variable, 435.25 then has the following binary representation:

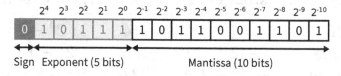

The exponent is stored after adding the offset:

$$8 + (2^{5-1} - 1) = 23 = 2^0 + 2^1 + 2^2 + 2^4.$$

The resulting number is treated as unsigned, regardless of whether the original exponent was positive or negative. If the sign is stored in the most significant bit of the variable, the exponent is adjusted with the offset, and the mantissa is stored in the least significant bits, we can compare floating point numbers just by ranking their binary representations, which can be done efficiently with hardware instructions.

The mantissa is

$$2^{-1} + 2^{-3} + 2^{-4} + 2^{-7} + 2^{-8} + 2^{-10} = 0.7001953,$$

which differs from 0.7001953125 by 1.25×10^{-8}. This difference is known as the *floating point error* arising from the limits in the precision that can be achieved with the number of bits of the mantissa. The only numbers that can be represented exactly are those that factorise into the powers of 2 available in the exponent and in the mantissa. This obviously excludes all numbers with an infinite number of digits, such as π, e or $1/3$.

What is the range of floating point numbers? The largest number (positive or negative) that we can represent is limited by the size of the exponent: with $|E|$ bits we can represent up to $2^{|E|}$ exponents. The offset ensures that the available exponents are equally divided between positive and negative numbers ranging from $-2^{|E|-1} - 2$ to $2^{|E|-1} - 1$ due to the offset.

precision	smallest exponent	largest exponent
half	$-(2^4 - 2) = -14$	$2^4 - 1 = 15$
single	$-(2^7 - 2) = -126$	$2^7 - 1 = 127$
double	$-(2^{10} - 2) = -1022$	$2^{10} - 1 = 1023$

This range is smaller than the theoretical $2^{|E|}$ values it could potentially contain because some combinations of bits are reserved for special classes of numbers:

- Zero is encoded with the exponent field and the mantissa filled with 0s.
- Positive and negative infinity (+Inf, -Inf) are encoded with the exponent field filled with 1s and a mantissa filled with 0s.
- Irrepresentable numbers (usually denoted NaN) are encoded with the exponent field filled with 1s and at least one non-zero bit in the mantissa. Different patterns of bits in the mantissa are used for different types of irrepresentable numbers: the most common is the missing value identifier NA. Typically, NaN arises

from dividing a number by zero or by trying to apply a mathematical function to a value outside its domain, for instance, taking the logarithm of a negative number.

- Subnormal numbers, that is, numbers that are too small to be written in binary scientific notation with the available exponents. In other words, their leading exponent is smaller than the smallest available exponent. They are encoded with the exponent field filled with 0s. These numbers have reduced precision because they effectively use only part of the mantissa. As an example, $2^{-10} \times 2^{-14} \approx 5.96 \times 10^{-8}$ is represented as follows in half precision:

	2^4	2^3	2^2	2^1	2^0	2^{-1}	2^{-2}	2^{-3}	2^{-4}	2^{-5}	2^{-6}	2^{-7}	2^{-8}	2^{-9}	2^{-10}
0	0	0	0	0	0	0	0	0	0	0	0	0	0	0	1

Sign Exponent (5 bits)   Mantissa (10 bits)

How coarse is floating point rounding? For any given precision, that depends on the magnitude of the number. As we saw in the example above, the mantissa can encode only so many significant decimal digits: $\log_{10}(2^{10}) \approx$ 3 digits for half-precision, $\log_{10}(2^{23}) \approx 7$ for single precision, $\log_{10}(2^{51}) \approx 16$ for double precision. This effectively creates a grid of values that can be represented exactly, and any other number is rounded to the nearest number that can be represented exactly or to `+Inf/-Inf`. The grid becomes coarser, in absolute terms, as the exponent becomes larger. Consider a number like 0.0002 that is small for a half-precision variable:

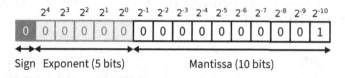

	2^4	2^3	2^2	2^1	2^0	2^{-1}	2^{-2}	2^{-3}	2^{-4}	2^{-5}	2^{-6}	2^{-7}	2^{-8}	2^{-9}	2^{-10}
0	0	0	0	1	0	1	0	1	0	0	0	1	1	1	0

Sign Exponent (5 bits)   Mantissa (10 bits)

The exponent is

$$-13 + (2^{5-1} - 1) = 2^1$$

and the mantissa is

$$2^{-1} + 2^{-3} + 2^{-7} + 2^{-8} + 2^{-9} = 0.638671875,$$

which gives

$$1.638671875 \times 2^{-13} \approx 0.000200033.$$

Increasing this number by the least possible amount by adding 2^{-10} and decreasing it by the same amount shows that the nearest numbers that can be represented in half precision are $\approx 0.000200033 \pm 1.19 \times 10^{-7}$.

Now consider a relatively large number (for half precision) like 10002:

	2^4	2^3	2^2	2^1	2^0	2^{-1}	2^{-2}	2^{-3}	2^{-4}	2^{-5}	2^{-6}	2^{-7}	2^{-8}	2^{-9}	2^{-10}
0	1	1	1	0	0	0	0	1	1	1	0	0	0	1	0

Sign Exponent (5 bits)   Mantissa (10 bits)

The exponent is

$$13 + (2^{5-1} - 1) = 28 = 2^2 + 2^3 + 2^4$$

and the mantissa is

$$2^{-3} + 2^{-4} + 2^{-5} + 2^{-9} = 0.220703125,$$

which gives $1.220703125 \times 2^{13} = 10000$. The closest numbers that can be represented in half precision are 9992 and 10008: all the numbers in between are rounded. This leaves an interval of ± 8 around 10000. For large enough numbers, floating point variables cannot even represent integer numbers without rounding!

How can we keep the errors introduced by floating point rounding in check? Errors compound across operations, and machine learning models typically perform large numbers of operations compared to the size of their inputs. (More on that in Chapter 4.) Fortunately, probability theory and statistics have historically standardised computations to work on the logarithmic scale to make closed–form mathematical derivations easier. Working with the logarithmic transforms of floating point numbers reduces the chances that large numbers will overflow to +Inf/-Inf or that small numbers will be rounded down to zero. In the case of numbers with subnormal floating point representations, we also retain better precision because their logarithm will not be subnormal. This is particularly important in the common case of summing up large numbers of log–probabilities. Working with numbers on the same scale (that is, they have similar exponents) also helps in avoiding catastrophic losses in precision. When operations involve numbers on very different scales, the difference in the granularity of the floating point rounding may cause the result to have unacceptably large errors even though all the operands are accurate. As an extreme example, consider adding 10002 and 0.0002: the result would be 10000, the closest floating point number in half precision! A similar issue is *catastrophic cancellation*, which may happen when subtracting two floating point numbers that are very close to each other.

Unlike integer arithmetic, floating point arithmetic is not exact because of the impact of floating point rounding. The results of operations involving floating point variables can differ in many ways from the mathematical operations they implement, even in common scenarios. It is easy to demonstrate with a simple recurrence such as

$$x_0 = 4, x_1 = 4.25, x_{n+1} = 108 - \left(815 - \frac{1500}{x_{n-1}}\right)\frac{1}{x_n},$$

which converges to 100 in double precision even though the true limit in $\mathbb{R}$ is 5 [304]. This can happen even if all the operands are exactly representable, as proved in [303]. Some effects of this discrepancy are:

- Numbers that should be equal are not equal. We should always compare numbers with a tolerance that is a function of the floating point precision we are using. The default in R is the square root of the smallest representable number, obtainable as sqrt(.Machine$double.eps).

```r
sqrt(2) * sqrt(2) == 2                                                        R
## [1] FALSE

all.equal(sqrt(2) * sqrt(2), 2, tol = sqrt(.Machine$double.eps))
## [1] TRUE
```

- Conversely, numbers that should not be equal may end up being equal.

```r
1e99 == 1e99 + 1                                                             R
## [1] TRUE

1 - 1e-20 == 1
## [1] TRUE
```

- The order in which operations are performed matters, even when the mathematical operations or functions they implement are commutative and/or associative. Structuring code so that key computations are implemented only once and therefore ensuring that operations are always performed in the same sequences is the best way to prevent this issue.

```r
print(0.6 + 0.7 + 0.8, digits = 20)                                         R
## [1] 2.0999999999999996447

print(0.8 + 0.7 + 0.6, digits = 20)
## [1] 2.1000000000000000888
```

- The order in which operations are performed matters also because intermediate results may underflow to zero or overflow to +Inf/-Inf unless we reorder operations to prevent that from happening.
- Working on a log-scale is the best option when dealing with the small probabilities that often arise from multivariate distributions or from a large number of

data points. Otherwise, the final result is likely to underflow to zero.

```
probs = runif(10^2, min = 10^-6, max = 10^-3)
sqrt(prod(probs))
## [1] 0

exp(0.5 * sum(log(probs)))
## [1] 1.27e-170
```

3.1.3 Strings

Strings are sequences of characters encoded in binary form and stored into variables. Their binary format varies, but it typically is UTF-8 on Linux and MacOS X and UTF-16 on Windows. Both are Unicode standards [378] that use between 1 and 4 bytes to encode each character and support many alphabets, mathematical symbols and pictograms such as emoji.

In the context of machine learning software, character strings are typically only encountered as input data in natural language processing (NLP) applications. In other settings, they are used as human-readable labels for the items in a set and can be represented using integers as we saw in Section 3.1.1. In fact, they are eventually given a numerical representation even in NLP in order to feed them to algorithms such as word2vec [299], GLOVE [260] and BERT [78]. In NLP, strings are also preprocessed taking into account their meaning and their grammatical and syntactical properties to facilitate later analyses. For instance:

- Common words that do not add meaning to a sentence, often called *stopwords*, are removed to reduce the dimensionality of the data.
- Words may be *stemmed*, that is, different words may be reduced to their common stem after removing suffixes and prefixes to identify which are in fact the same word.
- Words may be *tagged* with their syntactic role.

- Words may be *normalised* by making all characters lower-case and sometimes by removing accents and diacritics as well. Complex, composite characters can be encoded in different ways in both UTF-8 and UTF-16, and transforming them into their *canonical form* is essential to identify unique words correctly.
- Extraneous characters such as punctuation, hyphenation and numbers may be removed as non-informative. Abbreviations and acronyms may be expanded to make explicit the words they correspond to. Similarly, emoji may be replaced by a textual description.

A detailed treatment of these topics is beyond the scope of this book, and we refer the reader to monographs such as [2] and to the documentation of relevant software libraries such as Spacy [97] and NLTK [240].

3.2 Data Structures

Data structures are particular ways of organising variables of one or more types for effective and efficient processing. Different data structures will be most effective for different operations or different algorithms. We will discuss both aspects further in Section 3.4 and later in Chapter 4, characterising memory and computational efficiency in terms of space and time complexity. Here we will only cover those data structures that are foundational for machine learning software, referring the reader to other excellent resources [50, 68] for a broader coverage of the topic.

Why use data structures? Firstly, they make code more compact by allowing us to abstract away basic variable manipulations that would otherwise be repeatedly implemented in different places. Our code will be clearer and most likely have fewer bugs as a result. Secondly,

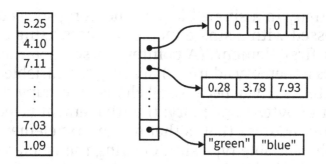

FIGURE 3.1 A schematic view of the logical structure and the memory layout of vectors (left) and lists (right).

data structures tell the software how particular groups of variables belong together, both in terms of how they are laid out in memory and how we operate on them. This makes it possible for the software we write to be compiled or interpreted (see Section 6.1) to operate efficiently on the variables contained in the data structures. Thirdly, the information that particular groups of variables belong together will be useful to developers working on our code. Those variables may describe the parts of a single mathematical object or real–world entity, they may have the same semantic meaning or they may have attached metadata that can be used for interpretation and debugging purposes: all facts that are useful to know when reading and developing code.

3.2.1 Vectors and Lists

The most fundamental data structures in machine learning software are *vectors* and *lists*. Both can contain any type of variable, and are defined by their *length* (the number of elements they contain). Their conceptual structure is shown in Figure 3.1.

Vectors are *homogeneous* data structures holding sequences of variables of the same type. The variables are stored sequentially in a single block of memory, so vectors can be accessed with a single memory access using a *pointer* to their first element. (A pointer is itself a variable that contains a memory address.) Reading the variables stored in a vector is trivial because all elements occupy the same number of bytes in memory: the ith element is located at a memory address that is that of the first element plus i times the variable type size. Copying the whole vector is also trivial, since it is stored as a single block of memory. The same is true for subsets of variables that are adjacent to each other within a vector.

Lists, on the other hand, are *heterogeneous* data structures that can contain different kinds of elements. They essentially act as vectors of pointers to arbitrary data structures or variable types. Therefore, each element in a list can be anything: a single variable of some type, a vector of any length, a second list, a matrix, etc. However, this means that accessing the elements of a list is less trivial since we need to locate each element and access it separately. However, copying the list and subsetting it can be easier: if we do not need to modify the contents of its elements, we can just copy (all or a subset of) the pointers to the elements to create a new list. This is called a *shallow copy*, and can significantly reduce memory use. However, we must duplicate the elements as well if we need to modify them later in the new list in order to avoid altering the original list they are attached to. Copying both the list and its elements is called a *deep copy*. In contrast, subsetting vectors requires a deep copy in the general case. Shallow copies are only possible when copying a whole vector or when subsetting a slice of adjacent elements.

Storing variables into vectors makes *vectorised* computations possible: a function can be applied independently to each element of the vector, potentially leveraging hardware's SIMD and FMA instructions to achieve instruction- and data-level parallelism as we discussed in Section 2.2.

If the return value of the function is a scalar, the results can be saved in a second vector of the same length. Otherwise, the results can be saved in a dense matrix (Section 3.2.3) or in a data frame (Section 3.2.2) in which each row or column contains the return values for a single input element. Vectorised computations are also possible for lists using thread–level parallelism, assuming that the function can handle all the types of variables stored in the list. Its outputs would then be stored in a second list regardless of whether each of them is a scalar or not.

3.2.2 Representing Data with Data Frames

A data frame is a *heterogeneous* two-dimensional data structure with columns of potentially different types. Its primary task is storing tabular data and the associated metadata, such as column– and row– names. The implementations in Julia (DataFrame.jl) and Python (Pandas and Scikit–Learn [311]) have been heavily inspired by R data frames: they only have minor differences in their semantics. The most notable is that operations on two data frames will match cells by position in R and Julia (regardless of row– and column–names) and by row– and column–names in Python (regardless of the cell positions).

The fundamental structure of a data frame is that of a list: each column in the tabular data is a vector that is stored as an element along with its own metadata as shown in Figure 3.2. Therefore, each column is stored in a separate block of memory, and there are no constraints on the types of variables that can be stored in different columns. In addition, a data frame typically contains its dimensions and the labels of the rows and of the columns as metadata, making it possible to access its contents as we would with a table. The dimensions are the number of rows and columns of the data frame. The labels of the

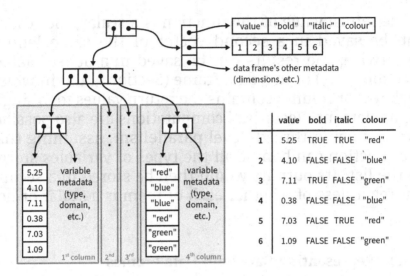

FIGURE 3.2 A schematic view of tabular data (bottom right) encoded as a data frame (left, top).

columns (called "column names" in R) can be used to access them by their names instead of by their positions in the data frame, which improves the readability of code and thus our ability to debug it. It makes the code invariant to the data layout as well. The labels of the rows ("row names" in R) serve the same function but are not used as often: they usually have no practical use in the common case in which we assume that data points are independent and identically distributed.

Data frames make it efficient to operate on columns. Creating a new data frame with a subset of columns is like subsetting a list, with the additional step of carrying over row and column labels as needed. Copying it can be done efficiently with a shallow copy. Adding a column to a data frame is similar: we perform a shallow copy into a new data frame with an empty slot in which we can insert the vector storing the column's values. Applying a function to each column of a data frame can be vectorised and performed in parallel, and the appropriate method can be called for each column in the case of generic functions.

However, operating on rows is not efficient in most cases. Adding or removing data points involves modifying the length of each column, which will likely involve copying the chosen data points to newly-allocated vectors of the appropriate length.

3.2.3 Dense and Sparse Matrices

A matrix is a *homogeneous* two-dimensional data structure holding a grid of variables of the same type arranged into rows and columns. It is the programming construct that represents the mathematical objects of the same name studied in linear algebra. Matrices can be *dense* or *sparse*. Most of the elements of dense matrices are informative (that is, non-zero cells) and therefore must be stored in the data structure. On the other hand, most of the elements of sparse matrices are equal to zero so we can save considerable amounts of memory by storing only the locations and the values of the few non-zero elements. We will cover the trade-off between speed and memory use for these two types of matrices in Section 4.5.2 while discussing computational complexity.

In Python, dense matrices are implemented in NumPy as a special case of multidimensional arrays along with vectors [141]. The same is true in R. In both cases, the data structure encoding a multidimensional array comprises the *pointer* to the first element of the array; the *variable type* of the elements; and the *dimensions of the array*, which determine its shape (Figure 3.3). The dimensions and the variable type of the elements determine the *strides*: the number of bytes skipped in memory to proceed to the next element along a given dimension. They are pre-calculated and stored in NumPy but not in R.

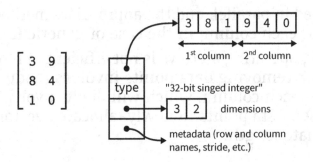

FIGURE 3.3 A schematic view of a dense matrix (left) encoded as a multidimensional array with variables stored in column-major format (right).

On the other hand, R arrays contain labels for their dimensions (row and column names in the case of matrices). The elements are stored as a vector, typically in *column-major order*: the columns of the matrix are concatenated starting from the left-most one.

Storing dense matrices as a list of columns, or as a list of rows, is typical in C and C++ but it is less common in higher-level languages, where we can use data frames for the same purpose.

The fact that multidimensional arrays store their dimensions as metadata allows three types of operations on their elements. The first is vectorised operations in which a function is applied individually to each element. The second is what is called *broadcasting* in Python and Julia and *recycling* in R: when a function operates on two arrays with different dimensions, the shorter array is repeated (that is, virtually concatenated to itself) to make the shapes of the operands match. The third is *marginalisation* or *reduction*: aggregating elements across one or more dimensions of an array, for instance, by summing or averaging them, to produce a second array with fewer dimensions.

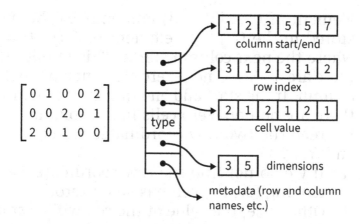

FIGURE 3.4 A schematic view of a sparse matrix (left) and its compressed sparse column (right) format representation.

Sparse matrices are supported in R through the Matrix package [30] and in Python through the SciPy package [388]. For brevity, we will only illustrate in detail the *compressed sparse column* data structure that is the most widely used in both packages. Consider the sparse matrix shown in Figure 3.4 along with its compressed representation from the Matrix package. The three vectors in the data structure contain, from top to bottom: the *start* and *end indexes* of each column (C), the *row* of each non-zero cell in the matrix (R) and its *value* (V). This representation assumes that the non-zero cells are stored in position order, starting from the top-left cell, moving down within each column, and considering columns from left to right.

Say, for instance, that we would like to read the value of the cell $(2, 3)$ in the matrix from the data structure. The required steps are:

1. Use the column delimiters in C to find which subset of R and V to read. The ith column of the matrix starts at the index stored in the ith

element of C ($C[3] = 3$) and ends by the index stored in the $(i + 1)$th element of C ($C[4] = 5$), where the next column starts. This implies that there are $5 - 3 = 2$ non-zero elements in the third column. If the start and end indexes are identical, there are no non-zero cells in the column.

2. We read the two row coordinates stored in $R[3]$ and $R[4]$.

   a. If we do not find the row coordinate we are looking for, the cell has value zero.

   b. Otherwise, the value of the cell will be stored in the element of V that has the same index as the row coordinate. In our case, the row coordinates of the non-zero elements of the third column are $R[3] = 2$ and $R[4] = 3$. Row coordinate 2 is in $R[3]$, so we can read the corresponding cell value from $V[3]$.

Other data structures for sparse matrices include the *compressed row column*, which is identical to the above save that the roles of R and C are reversed and the *coordinate list* (called the "triplet format"), which stores row and column coordinates directly in R and C.

3.3 Choosing the Right Variable Types for the Job

The floating point format used to represent real numbers in Section 3.1.2 has a more complex structure than the fixed point format for integer variables in Section 3.1.1. Intuitively, this might suggest that the same operation is more efficient on integer variables than on floating point variables. This is not usually the case for two reasons. Firstly, high-level languages like Python and R have additional checks to deal with integer overflow. In R, integers are stored using 32 bits and they are either replaced with NaN or transformed into double-precision floating point variables when they overflow. In base Python, integers are stored with *arbitrary precision*: their size is extended as needed to prevent them from overflowing. Pandas [207] integer variables have size 64 bits, and NumPy [141] provides integer variables in sizes 8, 16, 32 and 64 bits: both can overflow and, unlike in R, are not replaced with NaN. Consider the following vector inner product benchmark in R:

```R
library(microbenchmark)
floats.vec1 = rnorm(2 * 10^7)
floats.vec2 = rnorm(2 * 10^7)
integers.vec1 = sample(10, 2 * 10^7, replace = TRUE)
integers.vec2 = sample(10, 2 * 10^7, replace = TRUE)


microbenchmark(integers.vec1 %*% integers.vec2,
               floats.vec1 %*% floats.vec2, times = 200)
```

On average, the inner product takes 196.7% longer with integer vectors than it does with double-precision floating point vectors on a 7th-generation Intel Core processor. The same benchmark in Python and NumPy is shown below, and the results are similar: the inner product takes 40.5% longer with integer vectors.

```Python
import timeit
import numpy as np


ITERATION = 200


float_vector1 = np.random.normal(0, 1, 2 * pow(10, 7))
float_vector2 = np.random.normal(0, 1, 2 * pow(10, 7))


int_vector1 = np.random.choice(10, size=2 * pow(10, 7))
int_vector2 = np.random.choice(10, size=2 * pow(10, 7))


def product_int():
    np.dot(int_vector1, int_vector2)
```

```
def product_float():
    np.dot(float_vector1, float_vector2)

print("Inner product with int by", ITERATION, "iteration, avg:",
    np.mean(timeit.repeat(
        repeat=ITERATION,
        stmt=product_int,
        number=1)))

print("Inner product with float by", ITERATION, "iteration, avg:",
    np.mean(timeit.repeat(
        repeat=ITERATION,
        stmt=product_float,
        number=1)))
```

Secondly, it should be apparent from Section 2.1.1 that in recent years much effort has been put into improving hardware support for floating point numbers. CPUs, GPUs and TPUs have all been optimised to handle single- and double-precision floating point variables with SIMD and FMA instructions as much as they have been optimised to handle integer variables, if not more. Therefore, depending on the available hardware and on the ability of compilers to leverage it, using floating point variables may lead to faster code when using low-level languages. However, whether that will be the case for a specific machine learning software depends on the exact combination of hardware and software used and can only be ascertained by benchmarking it. Matching software and hardware was a key point in Section 2.2 and Section 2.4.

The size of the variables also matters: we saw in Section 2.1.2 how faster forms of memory are smaller, and how copying data between different types of memory can impact operational intensity. We should always choose the smallest size of integer or floating point variables that we can handle with SIMD and FMA hardware instructions, and that has a large enough range to represent the numbers we are working with. The effect on performance is noticeable even in the simple Python benchmark above: reducing the size of the floating point and integer variables in the vectors from 64 bits (the default) to 32 bits and then to 16 bits produces interesting patterns in the normalised running times.

variable type	64 bits	32 bits	16 bits
floating point	100%	54.1%	887.1%
integer	100%	62.2%	61.6%

Reducing the size of both floating point and integer variables from 64 to 32 bits improves the speed of the inner product by a factor of 1.5–2, as we would expect. Reducing the size of the variables further to 16 bits provides only marginal benefits for integer variables but, surprisingly, slows floating point variables by a factor of nearly 9. That is a strong indication that we are unable to leverage SIMD and FMA instructions as we do for integers of the same size!

Size matters even more in the case of floating point variables. As we noted in Section 3.1.2, the smaller the precision, the larger the floating point errors are likely to be. They also propagate with each operation and compound each other. This can become a critical issue with variables that are involved in most of the steps of an algorithm, such as the *accumulator variables* used to calculate a sum or product of a series of values, and with those that are rescaled to predefined ranges with other computed quantities. An example from classical statistics is computing the empirical correlation between two vectors:

1. We compute the average of each vector, which we store in two accumulator variables.
2. We compute the variance of each vector by summing up the squared differences from its average, which we store in two more accumulator variables.
3. We do the same with the cross-product of the differences to compute the covariance, which is an additional accumulator variable.
4. We divide the covariance by the square root of the product of the variances.

Each of these steps can potentially build up an error large enough to produce a correlation coefficient that is either greater than 1 or less than -1. Floating point errors compound and propagate from the means to the variances and the covariances, affecting the final division through the accumulator variables that store them. In such a situation, we should store accumulator variables with a higher precision than the variables they are accumulating to limit the magnitude of the errors of the individual operations: for instance, we should store the average of numbers stored in single precision as a double precision variable. Using FMA instructions may also help because, as we noted in Section 2.1.1, they operate at higher precision and only round their final result. Choosing the scale of the numbers being accumulated may also help by keeping all variables in a range that is not prone to overflow or underflow. Keeping all variables on the same scale also prevents catastrophic loss of precision, particularly in multiplications and divisions. This is the reason why so much numeric software works with quantities on log-scales: large numbers are reduced in magnitude and do not overflow or lose precision easily, and small numbers become large negative numbers instead of underflowing or losing precision.

Last but not least, floating point rounding may be unacceptable for legal reasons in some applications, particularly in finance and accounting. Fixed point integers may be used instead, with the convention that the smallest possible amount of currency (say, 1/100th of £0.01) is taken as the unit value. A rare open-source example of this approach in the commercial world is Oanda's libfixed [245] library.

3.4 Choosing the Right Data Structures for the Job

The choice of data structures can have an even larger impact than that of variable types because it determines memory access patterns. Operational intensity depends crucially on efficient memory use and access, as we argued in Sections 2.1.2 and 2.2.

Lists can be more memory efficient than vectors if we need to repeatedly subset them, for example, because we need to work on combinations or permutations of their values. If shallow copies are acceptable, lists are faster to duplicate as well because we do not have to allocate memory for and copy their elements. If shallow copies are not acceptable, then vectors are faster to copy because all their elements are stored as a single block of memory and can be copied with a single operation. And they are not less memory efficient, since their size is determined by their length. In fact, lists use more memory than vectors because they contain pointers to each element in addition to the elements themselves: the difference can be significant if the elements are small overall. These considerations are important for optimising performance given the effects on memory latency discussed in Sections 2.1.2 and 2.2.

We can make similar considerations for data frames and matrices, since data frames essentially behave as lists whose elements are the columns storing the variables in the tabular data.

Ideally, we should choose which data structures to use in our code taking into account what data structures are used in the libraries and in the other software that are part of the machine learning pipeline. If different parts of the pipeline encode data and models in different ways, we will be forced to convert between them, which is inefficient and increases memory use. For instance, R typically imports data as data frames. However, the underlying BLAS and LAPACK code that powers many models (all linear regressions among them) requires data to be stored as dense matrices in column–major format. Converting a data frame into a matrix requires copying all the data into a single memory block, column by column, which doubles memory use and wastes processor time.

We should also choose data structures based on how the algorithms that use them access their contents. Data that are processed together should be stored together to allow algorithms to perform as few separate memory accesses as possible. For instance, if we mostly process whole columns in tabular data, then a data frame is ideal because a single column can be efficiently read from memory as a single memory block. However, a data frame makes memory access very inefficient if we need to process individual rows in various combinations because each variable in a row is stored in a separate memory block and because we need to access all variables to read each row. If the data are homogeneous, storing them in a dense matrix with cells stored in row–major order is a better choice.

4

Analysis of Algorithms

In the previous chapters we discussed how the hardware architectures we use (Chapter 2), the nature of the data we analyse and how we represent data with data structures (Chapter 3) contribute to the performance of a machine learning pipeline. The last major piece of this puzzle is the algorithmic complexity of the algorithms that power the machine learning models.

Algorithmic complexity is defined, in the abstract, as the amount of resources required by an algorithm to complete. After using pseudocode to write a high–level description of the machine learning algorithm we would like to implement (Section 4.1), we can determine the complexity of its components and how they contribute to the complexity of the algorithm as a whole. We represent and reason about complexity in mathematical terms with big–O notation (Section 4.2). Quantifying it (Section 4.3) presents several issues that are specific to machine learning (Section 4.4), which we will illustrate with three examples (Section 4.5).

4.1 Writing Pseudocode

The first step in reasoning about an algorithm is to write it down using *pseudocode*, combining the understandability of natural language and the precision of code to facilitate our analysis and the subsequent implementation in software. Natural language is easier to read, but it is also ambiguous. Code, on the other hand, is too specific: it forces us to think about implementation details and programming-language conventions thus making it harder to focus on the overall picture.

Pseudocode is meant to offset the weaknesses of natural language and code while preserving their strong points. Ideally, it provides a high-level description of an algorithm that facilitates its analysis and implementation by making the intent of each step clear while suppressing those details that are irrelevant for understanding the algorithm. There is no universal standard on how to write pseudocode, although some general guidelines exist (see, for instance, Chapter 9 in "Code Complete" [206]). The three key guidelines that are commonly accepted are:

- Each step of the algorithm should be a separate, self-contained item in an enumeration.
- Pseudocode should combine the styles of good code and of good natural language to some extent. For instance, it may fall short of full sentences. It should avoid idioms and conventions specific to any particular programming language, using a lax syntax for code statements. For the same reason, variable names should come from the domain of the problem the algorithm is trying to solve rather than from how they will be implemented (for instance, in terms of data structures). We will return to this point in Section 6.2.
- Pseudocode should ignore unnecessary details and use short-hand notation when possible, leaving the context to more in-depth forms of documentation. In other words, the level of detail should be that of a high-level view of the overall structure of the algorithm so that we can focus on its intent.

Admittedly, these recommendations are vague because the best way of conveying a high-level view of an algorithm to the reader depends on a combination of the pseudocode style and the reader's background. As usual, knowing the audience is key in communicating effectively.

Writing good pseudocode for machine learning algorithms, or for machine learning pipelines spanning multiple algorithms, has two additional complications: the role played by the data and the need to integrate some amount of mathematical notation.

Firstly, if we are to treat data as code (Section 5.1), we may want to include more details about them in the pseudocode than we would in other settings. Such information may include, for example, the dimensions of the data and those characteristics of its features that are crucial for the algorithm to function. In a sense, this is similar to including some type information about key objects, and it is useful in clarifying what the inputs and the outputs of the algorithm are as well as in giving more context to key steps.

Secondly, mathematical notation may be the best tool to describe key steps in a clear and readable way, so we may want to integrate it with natural language and code to the best effect. In order to do that, we should define all the variables and the functions used in the notation while leaving additional details to a separate document. For practical purposes, mentioning the meaning of each symbol when introducing new mathematical notation (for instance, "the prior Beta distribution $\pi(\alpha, \beta) \sim Be(\alpha, \beta)$" as opposed to just "$\pi(\alpha, \beta) \sim Be(\alpha, \beta)$") is often enough to give context (what are properties of π, how it will be used, etc.). Complex formulas, derivations and formal proofs would reduce the readability of pseudocode by making it overlong and forcing the reader to concentrate on understanding them instead of looking at the overall logic of the algorithm.

Describing all algorithms used in a machine learning pipeline using pseudocode has some further advantages we will touch on in later chapters:

· it makes code review easier (see Section 6.6);
· it facilitates iterative refinement because pseudocode is easier to modify than code (see Section 5.3.1);
· it provides design documentation in a form that is easy to maintain (see Section 8.3).

4.2   Computational Complexity and Big-O Notation

Computational complexity is a branch of computer science that focuses on classifying computational problems according to their inherent difficulty across three different dimensions:

· as a function of input size (say, the sample size or the number of variables);
· as a function of how much resources will be used, in particular time (say, CPU time spent) and space (memory or storage use);
· on average (how long it will typically take), in the best case or in the worst case (how long it can possibly take).

In other words, we would like to infer how much resources an algorithm will use just from its specification: this is called *algorithm analysis*. Typically, the specification takes the form of pseudocode. As for the resources, we must first choose our unit of measurement. In the case of space complexity, the choice is usually obvious: either an absolute memory unit (such as MB, GB) or a relative one (such as the number of double-precision floating point values) for various types of memory (RAM, GPU memory, storage). In the case of time complexity, we must choose a set of fundamental operations that we consider to have a theoretical complexity of 1. Such operations can range from simple (arithmetic operations) to complex (models trained) depending on the level of abstraction we would like to work at. On the one hand, the lower the level of abstraction, the more we need to know about the specific implementation details of the algorithm. This is only feasible up to a point because pseudocode will omit most such details. It is also undesirable to some extent because it makes the analysis less general: a different implementation of the same algorithm may end up in a different class of complexity while exhibiting about the same behaviour in practice. On the other hand, the higher the level of abstraction, the higher the chance of obtaining an estimate of complexity that is only loosely connected to reality. The more complex the operations, the more unlikely it will be that they have the same complexity and that their complexity can be taken to be constant.

The estimates of computational complexity produced by algorithm analysis are written using *big-O* and related notations, which define the class of complexity in the limit of the input sizes [183, 184]. (All algorithms are fast with small inputs.) More in detail:

- We describe the *worst-case* scenario using *big-O* notation. Formally, an algorithm with input of size $N \rightarrow \infty$ has a complexity $f(N) = O(g(N))$ if there exists a $c_0 > 0$ such that $f(N) \leqslant c_0 g(N)$. It represents an upper bound in complexity.
- We describe the *best-case* scenario using *big-Ω* notation: $f(N) = \Omega(g(N))$, $f(N) \geqslant c_1 g(N)$ with $c_1 > 0$. It represents a lower bound in complexity.
- We describe the *average case* using *big-Θ* notation: $f(N) = \Theta(g(N))$, $c_2 g(N) \leqslant f(N) \leqslant c_3 g(N)$ with $c_2, c_3 > 0$. It represents the average complexity.

In practice, we often just write things like "it is $O(g(N))$ on average and $O(h(N))$ in the worst case" and use *big-O*

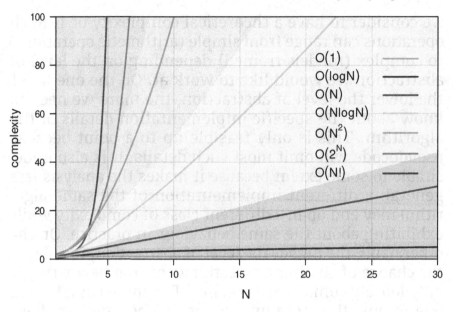

FIGURE 4.1 A graphical comparison of computational complexity classes.

for all three cases. If we are considering inputs that are best described with a combination of different sizes (say, $\{M, N, P\}$), *big-O* will be a multivariate function like $O(g(M, N, P))$.

Different classes of complexity in common use are shown in Figure 4.1. Algorithms that belong to $O(1)$, $O(\log N)$, $O(N)$ and $O(N \log N)$ are considered efficient, while those that belong to $O(N^2)$ or higher classes of complexity are more demanding. In a sense, this classification reflects the economics of running compute systems: it may be feasible to double our hardware requirements every time N doubles, but increasing it by a power of 2 or more is rarely possible!

How can we use *big-O* notation? If we are comparing algorithms in different classes of complexity, we can concentrate only on the leading term: $O(3 \cdot 2^N +$

$3.42N^2) \gg O(2N^3 + 3N^2)$ is functionally equivalent to $O(2^N) \gg O(N^3)$ because the difference in the order of magnitude makes lower-order terms and even the coefficient of the leading term irrelevant. If we are comparing algorithms in the same class of complexity, we only report the leading term and its coefficient: $O(1.2N^2 + 3N) \gg O(0.9N^2 + 2\log N)$ becomes $O(1.2N^2) \gg O(0.9N^2)$. In the former case, we can say algorithms scale in fundamentally different ways as their inputs grow in size. In the latter, we can say that algorithms scale similarly but still rank them.

In most practical settings, however, interpreting big-O notation requires a more nuanced approach because of its intrinsic limitations.

- Big-O notation does not include constant terms, so it may not necessarily map well to real-world performance. Algorithms with complex initialisation phases that do not scale with input sizes may be slower than algorithms with higher complexity for even moderate input sizes. This may be the case of algorithms that cache partial results or sufficient statistics when the caching is more expensive than recomputing those quantities from scratch as needed.
- Similarly, the coefficients in big-O notation are usually not realistic: for instance, a time complexity $O(2N)$ does not guarantee that doubling N will double running time. How the algorithm is implemented, on what hardware, etc. may not affect the class of complexity but they always have a strong effect on the associated coefficients. As a result, we should estimate those coefficients from empirical run-times to obtain realistic performance curves, and use the latter to compare algorithms within the same class of complexity.
- There is a compromise between space and time complexity: we trade off one for the other. Arguably, space complexity is more important than time

complexity. In principle, we can wait a bit longer to get the results, but if our program runs out of memory, it will crash and we will get no results at all.

4.3   Big-O Notation and Benchmarking

Producing empirical performance curves for all relevant dimensions of computational complexity differs from other forms of benchmarking in a few ways. If we know the theoretical class of complexity an algorithm belongs to, a simple linear model will suffice for estimating the coefficients of the terms in its big-O notation: we will show some examples in Section 4.5. However, we should take some care in how performance is measured and in how we interpret the empirical curves.

Firstly, we should plan the collection of the performance measurements following the best practices in the design of physical [225] and computer simulation [308] experiments. If we are measuring complexity along a single dimension, we should collect multiple performance measurements for each input size. The average performance at each input size will provide a more stable estimate than a single measurement, and we can use the distribution of the performance measurements to establish confidence bands around the average. Bands based on empirical quantiles (say, the interval between the [5%, 95%] quantiles) are often preferable to bands based on the quantiles of the normal distribution (say, average performance $\pm$ the standard deviation times the 95% quantile of the standard normal) because the latter is symmetric around the average and fails to account for the fact that performance is skewed. Performance is naturally bounded below by zero (instant execution!) and the average performance may be close enough to zero that the bottom of the confidence band is negative!

If we are measuring complexity along multiple dimensions, it is best to use a single experimental design that involves all of them in order to separate the main effect of each dimension from their interactions. Big-O notation may not include terms that contain more than one dimension, and in that case it is interesting to check whether that is true in practice as well. Or big-O notation may include such terms, and then the only consistent way of estimating their coefficients is to vary all the involved input sizes simultaneously.

If we are comparing two algorithms in the same complexity class, we should do that on performance differences generated on the same sets of inputs to increase the precision of our comparison. If we use different inputs, the performance measures we collect for each input size are independent across algorithms: if those algorithms are $O(f(N))$ and $O(g(N))$ respectively,

$$\text{VAR}(f(N) - g(N)) = \text{VAR}(f(N)) + \text{VAR}(g(N)).$$

However, if we use the same inputs for both algorithms

$$\text{VAR}(f(N) - g(N)) = \text{VAR}(f(N)) + \text{VAR}(g(N)) - \\ 2\,\text{COV}(f(N), g(N))$$

because the performance measures are no longer independent. Since $\text{COV}(f(N), g(N)) > 0$, the empirical differences in performance will have smaller variability and thus greater precision.

Secondly, we should carefully choose the compute system we use. The system should "stand still" while we are taking performance measurements: if other tasks are running at the same time, they may try to access shared resources that are also involved in our performance measures. This has two negative effects: it makes performance measures noisier and it inflates the estimated coefficients by making the average performance worse.

Thirdly, we should be careful in using performance curves to predict performance outside the range of the input sizes (or the combinations of input sizes) we actually measured. In any compute system with finite resources, resource contention will increase as the system reaches saturation. Hence we should use a compute system with enough resources to handle all the input sizes we consider without going anywhere near capacity. We are interested in measuring the performance of the algorithm, not of the compute system, so we should put stress on the former and not on the latter.

Finally, note that most experimental design approaches assume that performance measures are independent. Hence we should strive to make our empirical measures as independent as possible by resetting the state of the compute system before each run: for instance, we should remove all temporary objects.

4.4 Algorithm Analysis for Machine Learning

Algorithm analysis presents some additional complications in the context of machine learning software.

The first set of complications is related to defining the size of the input. Machine learning algorithms typically have a large number of different inputs, and the size of each input has several dimensions (such as the sample size and the number of variables). Hence algorithms will belong to different classes of complexity for different dimensions, and it will be unlikely that any will dominate the others in all dimensions. Sometimes we can reduce the number of dimensions we are considering by assuming some are bounded because of the intrinsic nature of the inputs or by expressing one dimension as a function of another (say, the number of variables is $p \approx \sqrt{n}$ where n is the sample size).

Furthermore, computational complexity depends strongly on the assumptions we make on the distributions of the inputs and not just on their sizes. More assumptions usually allow us to access algorithms with better performance, and make it possible to use closed-form results: the more knowledge we put in the form of assumptions, the less we have to learn empirical measures. Assuming some form of sparsity or regularity, or actively enforcing it in the learning process, will reduce the complexity of machine learning models to the point they become tractable. In most settings, not making any such assumption will mean exponential or combinatorial worst-case complexity. It is another trade-off: assumptions versus complexity.

For stochastic algorithms, we can only meaningfully reason on the average case. Consider Markov chain Monte Carlo (MCMC) posterior inference in Bayesian models, or stochastic gradient descent (SGD) for deep neural networks. Each time we run them, they go through a different sequence of steps and they may produce a different posterior distribution or model. As a consequence, each run will take a different amount of time and it will use a different amount of memory. The construction of such algorithms gives convergence guarantees and convergence rates, so we have some expectations about average complexity, but there is always some degree of uncertainty.

4.5 Some Examples of Algorithm Analysis

We will now apply the concepts we just introduced by investigating the time complexity of estimating the coefficients of linear regression models (Section 4.5.1); the trade-off between time and space complexity in sparse matrices (Section 4.5.2); and the time and space complexity of an MCMC algorithm to generate random directed acyclic graphs from a uniform distribution (Section 4.5.3).

4.5.1 Estimating Linear Regression Models

Linear models are the foundation upon which most of statistics and machine learning are built: we often use them either as standalone models or as part of more complex ones. Generally speaking, a linear model takes a vector **y** and a matrix **X** of real numbers and tries to explain **y** as a function of **X** that is linear in the parameters $\boldsymbol{\beta}$. We can famously [398] estimate $\boldsymbol{\beta}$ with the closed-form expression

$$\underset{p\times 1}{\widehat{\boldsymbol{\beta}}_{\text{EX}}} = (\underset{p\times n}{\mathbf{X}^{\text{T}}} \underset{n\times p}{\mathbf{X}})^{-1} \underset{p\times n}{\mathbf{X}^{\text{T}}} \underset{n\times 1}{\mathbf{y}}$$

which is, at the same time, the ordinary least squares estimate (from the orthogonal projection of **y** onto the space spanned by the **X**) and the maximum likelihood estimate of $\boldsymbol{\beta}$ (under the assumption residuals are independent and normally distributed with a common variance). Note how we have annotated the formula above with the dimensions of both **X** and **y**. Those are our inputs: their dimensions depend on the sample size n and on the number of variables p.[1] The algorithmic complexity of estimating $\boldsymbol{\beta}$ will be a function of both.

Another option to estimate $\boldsymbol{\beta}$ is to use the QR decomposition of **X** [398, Appendix A.9]. Starting from

---

[1]This assumes that each row of **X** corresponds to a data point and that each column corresponds to a variable. Sometimes these dimensions are inverted (variables on the rows, data points on the columns) in the literature.

the $\mathbf{X}\boldsymbol{\beta} = \mathbf{y}$ formulation of the linear regression model, we perform the following steps:

1. compute the QR decomposition of $\mathbf{X}$ ($\mathbf{Q}$ is $n \times p$, $\mathbf{R}$ is $p \times p$);
2. rewrite the problem as $\mathbf{R}\boldsymbol{\beta} = \mathbf{Q}^{\mathrm{T}}\mathbf{y}$;
3. compute $\mathbf{Q}^{\mathrm{T}}\mathbf{y}$;
4. solve the resulting (triangular) linear system for $\boldsymbol{\beta}$.

Let's call this estimator $\widehat{\boldsymbol{\beta}}_{\mathrm{QR}}$. If we discount numerical issues with pathological $\mathbf{X}$s, $\widehat{\boldsymbol{\beta}}_{\mathrm{QR}}$ and $\widehat{\boldsymbol{\beta}}_{\mathrm{EX}}$ give identical estimates of $\boldsymbol{\beta}$: they are identical in terms of statistical properties, and neither makes any assumption of the distribution of $\mathbf{X}$. However, we may still prefer one to the other because of their time complexity.

Firstly, what is the time complexity of computing $\widehat{\boldsymbol{\beta}}_{\mathrm{EX}}$? The steps we would perform if we were estimating it by hand are:

1. compute $\mathbf{X}^{\mathrm{T}}\mathbf{X}$;
2. invert it and compute $(\mathbf{X}^{\mathrm{T}}\mathbf{X})^{-1}$;
3. compute $\mathbf{X}^{\mathrm{T}}\mathbf{y}$;
4. multiply the results from steps 2 and 3.

Given the simplicity of $\widehat{\boldsymbol{\beta}}_{\mathrm{EX}}$, this description will suffice as the pseudocode for our analysis. From easily available sources (say, Wikipedia), we can find the time complexity of the operation in each step:

- multiplying an $r \times s$ matrix and an $s \times t$ matrix takes $O(rst)$ operations [408];
- computing the inverse of an $r \times r$ matrix is $O(r^3)$ using a Cholesky decomposition [407] or Gram–Schmidt [409].

These time complexities use arithmetic operations as the elementary operations, which is natural because matrices are just sets of numbers that are combined and transformed using those operations. The actual contents of $\mathbf{X}$ and $\mathbf{y}$ are irrelevant: both matrices appear in the big-O notation just with their dimensions.

Therefore, step 1 is $O(pnp) = O(np^2)$, step 2 is $O(p^3)$, step 3 is $O(np)$ and step 4 is $O(p^2)$. The overall time complexity is

$$O(np^2 + p^3 + np + p^2) = O(p^3 + (n+1)p^2 + np) \quad (4.1)$$

and it can be interpreted as follows:

· Estimating $\widehat{\boldsymbol{\beta}}_{\mathrm{EX}}$ is $O(p^3)$ in the number of parameters p: if p doubles, it takes eight times as long.
· Estimating $\widehat{\boldsymbol{\beta}}_{\mathrm{EX}}$ is $O(n)$ in the sample size n: if n doubles, it takes twice as long.

Let's look now at $\widehat{\boldsymbol{\beta}}_{\mathrm{QR}}$. For time complexity we have that:

· solving an $r \times s$ linear system with Gram–Schmidt is $O(rs^2)$;[2]
· back-substitution to solve the triangular linear system in step 4 is $O(s^2)$.

Therefore, step 1 is $O(np^2)$, step 3 is $O(np)$ and step 4 is $O(p^2)$. (Step 2 is merely for notation.) The overall time complexity is then

$$O(np^2 + np + p^2) = O((n+1)p^2 + np), \quad (4.2)$$

making $\widehat{\boldsymbol{\beta}}_{\mathrm{QR}}$ quadratic in the number of parameters and linear in the sample size. We can expect it to be faster than the closed-form estimator as p grows ($O(p^2)$ instead of $O(p^3)$), but we cannot say which approach is faster as n grows because they are both $O(n)$.

---

[2]We can do better, but not much: combining Gram–Schmidt and Householder transformations gives $O(rs^2 - s^3/3)$.

Therefore, which algorithm is best depends on the data we expect to work on:

- if $n \to \infty$ but p is bounded, $\widehat{\boldsymbol{\beta}}_{EX}$ and $\widehat{\boldsymbol{\beta}}_{QR}$ perform similarly well;
- if $p \to \infty$, $\widehat{\boldsymbol{\beta}}_{QR}$ will be faster.

How well do the time complexities in (4.1) and (4.2) map to real-world running times? We can answer this question by benchmarking $\widehat{\boldsymbol{\beta}}_{EX}$ and $\widehat{\boldsymbol{\beta}}_{QR}$ as we discussed in Section 4.3.

```r
library(microbenchmark)
library(doBy)

# define the estimators.
betaEX = function(y, X) solve(crossprod(X)) %*% t(X) %*% y
betaQR = function(y, X) qr.solve(X, y)
# define the grid of input sizes to examine.
nn = c(1, 2, 5, 10, 20, 50, 100) * 1000
pp = c(10, 20, 50, 100, 200, 500)
# a data frame to store the running times.
time = data.frame(
  expand.grid(n = nn, p = pp, betahat = c("EX", "QR")),
  lq = NA, mean = NA, uq = NA
)
# quantiles defining a 90% confidence band.
lq = function(x) quantile(x, 0.05)
uq = function(x) quantile(x, 0.95)
# for all combinations of input sizes...
for (n in nn) {
  for (p in pp) {
    # ... measure the running time averaging over 100 runs...
    bench = microbenchmark(betaEX(y, X), betaQR(y, X),
            times = 100,
            control = list(warmup = 10),
            setup = {
              X = matrix(rnorm(n * p), nrow = n, ncol = p)
```

```
            y = X %*% rnorm(ncol(X))
          })
  # ... and save the results for later analyses.
    time[time$n == n & time$p == p, c("lq", "mean", "uq")] =
      summaryBy(time ~ expr, data = bench,
              FUN = c(lq, mean, uq))[, -1]
  }#FOR
}#FOR
```

We plotted the results in Figure 4.2. The top panels confirm the conclusions we reached earlier: both $\widehat{\boldsymbol{\beta}}_{EX}$ and $\widehat{\boldsymbol{\beta}}_{QR}$ have a time complexity that is linear in n, hence they scale similarly; but $\widehat{\boldsymbol{\beta}}_{EX}$ has a cubic time complexity in p, which makes it much slower than $\widehat{\boldsymbol{\beta}}_{QR}$ as p increases. The level plots in the bottom panels show that n and p jointly influence running times, which we should expect since both (4.1) and (4.2) contain mixed terms in which both n and p appear.

Considering how little noise is in the running times we measured, we can reliably estimate the coefficients of the terms in (4.1) and (4.2) using a simple linear regression.

```
# rescale to make the coefficients easier to interpret.                    R
time$mean = time$mean * 10^(-9)
time$n = time$n / 1000
bigO.EX = lm(mean ~ I(p^3) + I((n + 1) * p^2) + I(n * p),
            data = subset(time, betahat == "EX"))
coefficients(bigO.EX)
##      (Intercept)               I(p^3) I((n + 1) * p^2)
##    -0.0120329302    -0.0000000025      0.0000017156
##        I(n * p)
##     0.0000244271

bigO.QR = lm(mean ~ I((n + 1) * p^2) + I(n * p),
            data = subset(time, betahat == "QR"))
coefficients(bigO.QR)
##      (Intercept) I((n + 1) * p^2)          I(n * p)
```

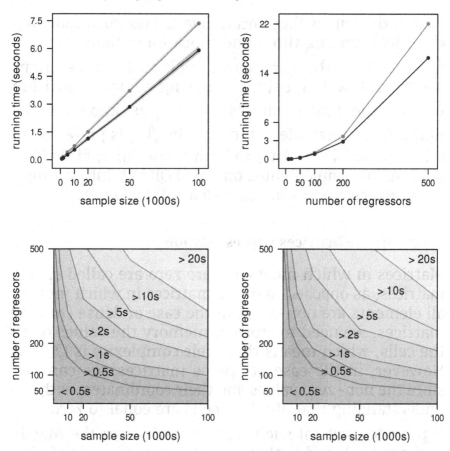

FIGURE 4.2 Marginal running times as a function of n (with $p = 200$, top left) and of p (with $n = 50000$, top right); the closed-form formula is shown in orange and the QR estimator in blue, each with 90% confidence bands. Joint running times in (n, p) are shown in the bottom left and right panels for the closed-form formula and the QR estimator, respectively.

| ## | -0. 110 33 15 | 0. 000 001 3 | 0. 000 050 2 |

The models in bigO.EX and bigO.QR allow us to predict the running times for any combinations of n and p. We can also use them to check how much the empirical complexity curves they encode overlap the corresponding empirical running times and check for outliers.

As a final note, there are several additional considerations we should weigh before choosing which algorithm to use: the matrix inverse in $\widehat{\beta}_{EX}$ is known to be numerically unstable, which is why $\widehat{\beta}_{QR}$ is preferred in scientific software. lm() in both R and Julia, fitlm() in MATLAB are implemented on top of QR but, interestingly, LinearRegression() in Scikit-learn [311] is not.

4.5.2   Sparse Matrices Representation

Matrices in which most cells are zero are called sparse matrices, as opposed to dense matrices in which most or all elements are non-zero. In the case of dense $(m \times n)$ matrices, we need to store in memory the values of all the cells, which means that their complexity is $O(mn)$. However, in the case of sparse matrices, we can just store the non-zero values and their coordinates, with the understanding that all other cells are equal to zero.

R provides several such representations in the Matrix package [30], and Python does the same in scipy [388]: the default is the column-oriented, compressed format described in Section 3.2.3. Consider the matrix originally shown in Figure 3.4, in which 9 cells out of 15 are zeroes.

```
library(Matrix)                                                        R
m = Matrix(c(0, 0, 2:0), 3, 5)
m
## 3 x 5 sparse Matrix of class "dgCMatrix"
##
## [1,] . 1 . . 2
## [2,] . . 2 . 1
## [3,] 2 . 1 . .
```

How are the elements of m stored in memory?

```
str(m)                                                          R
## Formal class 'dgCMatrix' [package "Matrix"] with 6 slots
##   ..@ i        : int [1:6] 2 0 1 2 0 1
##   ..@ p        : int [1:6] 0 1 2 4 4 6
##   ..@ Dim      : int [1:2] 3 5
##   ..@ Dimnames:List of 2
##   .. ..$ : NULL
##   .. ..$ : NULL
##   ..@ x        : num [1:6] 2 1 2 1 2 1
##   ..@ factors : list()
```

Comparing the notation in Section 3.2.3 and the documentation of Matrix, we can see that:

- i contains the vector R, row coordinates of the non-zero cells in the matrix;
- p contains the vector C, the start and end indexes of the columns; and
- x contains the vector V of the values of the non-zero cells.

Note that both i and p are 0-based indexes to facilitate the use of the dgCMatrix class in the C++ code inside the Matrix package, while R uses 1-based indexing.

The overall space complexity of such a sparse matrix is then $O(3z)$, where z is the number of non-zero cells. R stores real numbers in double precision (64 bits each) and indexes as 32-bits integers, which means m needs 128 bits (16 bytes) of memory for each non-zero cell. So dense matrices use $8mn$ bytes of memory while sparse matrices use $16z$ bytes; if $z \ll mn$ we can save most of the memory we would have allocated for a dense matrix.

The catch is that operations may have a higher time complexity for sparse matrices than for dense matrices. Even the most simple: looking up the value of a cell (i, j) has time complexity $O(1)$ in a dense matrix, but for a sparse matrix such as m we need to:

- Look up what are the first and the last values in x for the column j by reading the jth element of p.
- Position ourselves on the row number for that first value in i, and read every successive number until we find the row number j or we reach the end of the column.
- Read the value of the cell from x, which has the same position in x as the row number in i; or return zero if we reach the end of the column.

These three steps have an overall time complexity of $O(1) + O(z/n) + O(1) = O(2 + z/n)$ assuming z/n non-zero elements per column on average. Hence reading a cell from a sparse matrix appears to be more expensive than reading the same cell from a dense matrix.

Assigning a non-zero value to a cell in a sparse matrix is more expensive as well. For each of i and x we need to:

- allocate a new array of length $z + 1$;
- copy the z values from the old array;
- add the values corresponding to the new cell;
- replace the old array with the new one.

Therefore, time and space complexity both are $O(z)$. Handling p is also $O(z)$, and it is more complex since we will need to recompute half of the values on average.

This is troubling because we cannot predict the average time and space complexity just by looking at the input size: we can only do that by making assumptions on the distribution of the values in the cells. Furthermore, this distribution may change during the execution of our software as we assign new non-zero values to the sparse matrix. We can, however, compare the empirical running times of read and write operations on dense and sparse matrices to get a practical understanding of how they differ, as we did in the previous section with $\widehat{\beta}_{EX}$ and $\widehat{\beta}_{QR}$.

Consider a square matrix allocated as either a sparse or a dense matrix with $n = 1000$ and the proportions of non-zero cells of $z/n = \{0.01, 0.02, 0.05, 0.10, 0.20, 0.50, 1\}$. We can measure the time it takes to read (with the `read10()` function) or write (with the `write10()` function) the values of 10 random cells for either type of matrix as z (zz in the code below) increases.

```
read10 = function(m) m[sample(length(m), 10)]                    R
write10 = function(m) m[sample(length(m), 10)] = 1
[...]
for (z in zz) {
  bench = microbenchmark(
            read10(sparse), read10(dense),
            write10(sparse), write10(dense),
            times = 200,
            control = list(warmup = 10),
            setup = {
                sparse = Matrix(0, n, n)
                sparse[sample(length(sparse), round(z))] = 1
                dense = matrix(0, n, n)
            })
  [...]
}#FOR
```

The resulting running times are shown in Figure 4.3. As we expected, both reading from and writing to a dense matrix is $O(1)$: running times do not change as z increases. This is not true in the case of a sparse matrix. The running time of `write10()` increases linearly in z/n, and so does that of `read10()` until $z/n = 0.5$. Reading times do not increase further for $z/n = 1$: in fact, they decrease slightly. We can interpret this as $O(2 + z/n)$ converging to a constant $O(3)$ as $z/n \rightarrow 1$, making a (no longer) sparse matrix just an inefficient dense matrix that requires extra coordinate look-ups.

Finally, we can regress the running times (in seconds) on $O(z/n)$ to determine the slope of the linear trends we see for sparse matrices, that is, the orange lines in the two panels of Figure 4.3. For writing performance, the slope

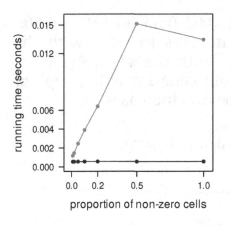
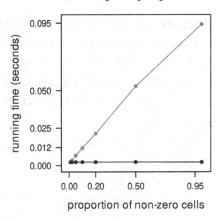

proportion of non-zero cells　　　　　　proportion of non-zero cells

FIGURE 4.3 Read (left) and write (right panel) performance for sparse (orange) and dense (blue) square matrices of size 1000. 90% confidence bars are so thin as to not be visible.

is 0.09; while for reading performance it is 0.03 if we consider only $z/n \leqslant 0.5$. Hence writing times increase by approximately 10% for every million cells in the matrix, and read times by 3%. This, of course, is true for large matrices with millions of elements; performance may very well be different for smaller matrices with just a few tens of elements.

4.5.3　Uniform Simulations of Directed Acyclic Graphs

Many complex probabilistic models can be represented graphically as *directed acyclic graphs* (DAGs), in which each node is associated with a random variable and arcs represent dependence relationships between those variables: notable examples are Bayesian networks [314], neural networks [122], Bayesian hierarchical models [109] and vector auto-regressive (VAR) time series [375]. The DAGs make it possible to divide and conquer large multivariate distributions into smaller ones in which each variable only depends on its parents.

When evaluating various aspects of these models, it may be useful to be able to generate random DAGs to use in simulation studies. In particular, we may want to generate DAGs with uniform probability since this is considered a non–informative prior distribution on the space of the possible model structures. A simple MCMC algorithm to do this is illustrated in [209]. We wrote it down as pseudocode in Algorithm 1. For simplicity, we omit both *burn-in* (dropping the DAGs generated in the initial iterations to give time to the algorithm to converge to the uniform distributions over DAGs) and *thinning* (returning only one DAG every several generated DAGs to return a set of DAGs that are more nearly independent) even though both are standard practice in the literature.

Algorithm 1 Random DAG Generation

Input: a set of nodes **V** (possibly with associated labels), the number N of graphs to generate.
Output: a set **G** of N directed acyclic graphs.

1. Initialise an empty graph with nodes **V** and arcs $A_0 = \{\emptyset\}$.
2. Initialise an empty set of graphs **G**.
3. For a large number of iterations $n = 1, \ldots, N$:
   (a) Sample two random nodes v_i and $v_j \in$ **V** with $v_i \neq v_j$.
   (b) If $\{v_i \rightarrow v_j\} \in A_{n-1}$, then $A_n \leftarrow A_{n-1} \setminus \{v_i \rightarrow v_j\}$.
   (c) If $\{v_i \rightarrow v_j\} \notin A_{n-1}$, check whether the graph is still acyclic after adding $\{v_i \rightarrow v_j\}$.
       i. If the graph is still acyclic, $A_n \leftarrow A_{n-1} \cup \{v_i \rightarrow v_j\}$.
       ii. If the graph is no longer acyclic, nothing is done.
   (d) **G** $\leftarrow$ **G** $\cup A_n$.

How can we represent DAGs in this algorithm? Any graph is uniquely identified by its nodes $\mathbf{V}$ and its arc set A. As an example, consider a graph with nodes $\mathbf{V} = \{v_1, v_2, v_3, v_4\}$ and arcs $\{\{v_1 \rightarrow v_3\}, \{v_2 \rightarrow v_3\}, \{v_3 \rightarrow v_4\}\}$. Its *adjacency matrix* is a square matrix in which the cell (i, j) is equal to 1 if the arc $v_i \rightarrow v_j$ is present in the DAG, and to 0 if it is not:

$$\begin{array}{c c c c c} & v_1 & v_2 & v_3 & v_4 \\ \begin{array}{c} v_1 \\ v_2 \\ v_3 \\ v_4 \end{array} & \left(\begin{array}{c c c c} 0 & 0 & 1 & 0 \\ 0 & 0 & 1 & 0 \\ 0 & 0 & 0 & 1 \\ 0 & 0 & 0 & 0 \end{array}\right. & & & \left.\begin{array}{c} \\ \\ \\ \end{array}\right). \end{array}$$

We can store an adjacency matrix in a dense or a sparse matrix of size $|\mathbf{V}|$: depending on how many arcs we expect to see in the DAG, the trade-off between space and time complexity may be acceptable as discussed in Section 4.5.2. The *adjacency list* of a graph is a set containing the children sets of each node:

$$\{v_1 = \{v_3\}, v_2 = \{v_3\}, v_3 = \{v_4\}, v_4 = \varnothing\}.$$

This representation is competitive with a sparse adjacency matrix in terms of space complexity: both are $O(|A|)$, where $|A|$ is the size of the arc set of the DAG (that is, the number of arcs it contains). If we assume that the DAGs contain few arcs so that $O(|A|) = O(|\mathbf{V}|)$, then space complexity is better than the $O(|\mathbf{V}|^2)$ of adjacency matrices. As for time complexity, path finding is $O(|\mathbf{V}| + |A|)$ in adjacency lists but $O(|\mathbf{V}|^2)$ for adjacency matrices. Adjacency matrices, on the other hand, allow for $O(1)$ arc insertion, arc deletion, and finding whether an arc is present or not in the DAG. All these operations are either $O(|\mathbf{V}|)$ or $O(|A|)$ in adjacency lists.

For the moment, let's represent DAGs with dense adjacency matrices. We can determine the time complexity of an MCMC step in Algorithm 1 as follows:

- For each iteration, adding and removing arcs is $O(1)$ since we just read or write a value in a specific cell of the adjacency matrix.
- Choosing a pair of nodes at random can also be considered $O(1)$, since we choose two nodes regardless of $|\mathbf{V}|$ or $|A_n|$.
- Both depth-first and breadth-first search have time complexity $O(|\mathbf{V}|^2)$ since we have to scan the whole adjacency matrix to look for each node's children. We only perform such a search if we sample a candidate arc that is not already present, because in order to include an arc $v_i \rightarrow v_j$ we must make sure that there is no path from v_j to v_i in order to keep the DAG acyclic. That in turn happens with probability $O(|A_n|/|\mathbf{V}|^2)$.

The overall time complexity of Algorithm 1 for N MCMC iterations then is:

$$
O\left(N\left(1 + 1 + |\mathbf{V}|^2 \frac{|A_n|}{|\mathbf{V}|^2}\right)\right) \approx O(N|A_n|).
$$

However, we are assuming a uniform probability distribution over all possible DAGs: under this assumption [209] reports that $O(|A_n|) \approx O(|\mathbf{V}|^2/4)$, making Algorithm 1 $O(N|\mathbf{V}|^2/4)$. If we assumed a different probability distribution for the DAGs, the time complexity of the algorithm would change even if $\mathbf{V}$ and N stayed the same because the average $|A_n|$ would be different. Furthermore, note that computing the overall time complexity of Algorithm 1 as N times the complexity of an individual step implies that we are assuming that all MCMC steps have the same time complexity. This is not exactly true because of the $O(|A_n|/|\mathbf{V}|^2)$ term, which may be lower for early MCMC steps (when $|A_n|$ is bound by the number of steps n) that for later steps (when $|A_n| \approx |\mathbf{V}|^2/4$ because Algorithm 1 has converged to the uniform distribution). It is, however, a reasonable working assumption if N is large enough and if most MCMC steps will be performed after reaching the stationary distribution.

For each DAG we generate, we also have to consider the cost of saving it in a different data structure for later use. Transforming the adjacency matrix into another data structure is necessarily $O(|V|^2)$ since we need to read every cell in the adjacency matrix to find out which arcs are in the DAG. We do not always perform that transformation because we may reject a new DAG instead of returning it, but it is difficult to evaluate how often that happens. A reasonable guess is that we almost always save sparse graphs, since there will typically be no path between v_j and v_i (that is the only case in which we do reject the current DAG proposal, and we do not need the transformation). As $|A_n| \rightarrow |V|$ that condition will become easier to meet, so we can say that for a large number of iterations $\approx O(|V|^2 \cdot 0) = O(1)$ for most iterations.

As for space complexity, the adjacency matrix uses $O(|V|^2)$ space: it is the most wasteful way of representing a graph. Any other data structure we may save DAGs into will likely use less space.

We can investigate all the statements above as in Sections 4.5.1 and 4.5.2.

```
library(bnlearn)                                                    R

melancon = function(nodes, n) {
  # step (1)
  dag = empty.graph(nodes)
  adjmat = matrix(0, nrow = length(nodes), ncol = length(nodes),
            dimnames = list(nodes, nodes))
  # step (2)
  ret = vector(n, mode = "list")
  for (i in seq(n)) {
    # step (3a)
```

```
    candidate.arc = sample(nodes, 2, replace = FALSE)
    # step (3b)
    if (adjmat[candidate.arc[1], candidate.arc[2]] == 1) {
      adjmat[candidate.arc[1], candidate.arc[2]] = 0
      amat(dag) = adjmat
    }#THEN
    else {
      # step (3c)
      if (!path.exists(dag, from = candidate.arc[2],
          to = candidate.arc[1])) {
        adjmat[candidate.arc[1], candidate.arc[2]] = 1
        amat(dag) = adjmat
      }#THEN
    }#ELSE
    # step (3d)
    ret[[i]] = dag
  }#FOR
  return(ret)
}#MELANCON
```

How do time and space complexity change if we represent DAGs with adjacency lists instead? Both path finding (say, by depth–first search) and saving DAGs in a different data structure have a time complexity of $O(|V| + |A_n|)$ for adjacency lists. However, the overall time complexity of each MCMC iteration is still quadratic:

$$O\left(N\left(1 + 1 + (|V| + |A_n|)\frac{|A_n|}{|V|^2}\right)\right) \approx$$

$$O\left(N\left(1 + 1 + (|V| + |V|^2)\frac{|V|^2}{|V|^2}\right)\right) \approx O(N|V|^2),$$

again assuming that $O(|A_n|) \approx O(|V|^2/4)$. The space complexity of an adjacency list is $O(|V| + |A_n|)$. On average, this becomes $O(|V|^2)$ under the same assumption.

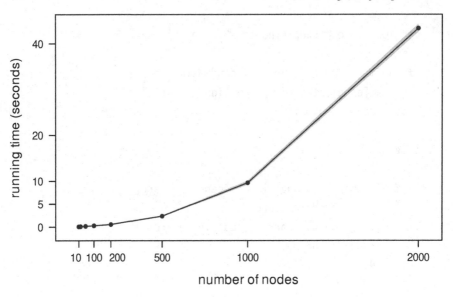

FIGURE 4.4 Running times for Algorithm 1 as a function of the number of nodes, generating 200 DAGs.

4.6 Big-O Notation and Real-World Performance

Big-O notation is a useful measure to assess scalability, and it can often be related to the practical performance of real machine learning software. However, this becomes increasingly difficult as such software becomes more complex, for several reasons. For instance:

• Software in a machine learning pipeline is heterogeneous: various parts are typically written in different programming languages and are built on different libraries. Each part may be faster or slower than another because of that, even when they belong to the same class of complexity. More on that in Section 6.1. Software upgrades may also change the relative speeds of different parts of the pipeline and introduce new bottlenecks.

- Both these things being equal, the same algorithm may be faster or slower depending on the data structures used to store its inputs and outputs. We saw that to be the case in Section 4.5.2, and we touched on this point in Section 3.4 as well. The same is true for variable types, as discussed in Section 3.3. High–level languages abstract these details to a large extent, which may lead to surprises when benchmarking software.
- Differences in hardware can be impactful enough to completely hide differences in the class of complexity of different algorithms for practical ranges of input sizes. Conversely, they can also introduce apparent discrepancies in performance. This can realistically happen when the input sizes are small enough to make adjacent classes of complexity comparable: an $O(N^2)$ algorithm on a CPU core will be slower than an $O(N^3)$ algorithm on a GPU with a hundred of free units for $N \leqslant 100$. Fixed costs that are ignored when deriving computational complexity may also be relevant due to the relative difference, for instance, in the latency of different types of memory (Section 2.1.2).
- If we use any remote systems (Section 2.3), the hardware we are running a machine learning pipeline on may vary without our knowledge, either in its configuration or in its overall load. Furthermore, benchmarking remote systems accurately is inherently more difficult, as is troubleshooting them.
- The performance of some parts of the pipeline may be artificially limited by that of the external systems that provide the inputs to the machine learning models or that consume their outputs. Individual parts of the same system may also slow down each other as they consume each other's outputs.

To summarise, we may be able to map computational complexity to real–world performance for the individual components of a machine learning pipeline running on simple hardware configurations. It is unlikely that we can do that with any degree of accuracy when systems become larger and contain a larger number of software and hardware components. The resulting complexity can easily make our expectations and intuitions about performance unreliable. In such a situation, identifying performance issues requires measuring the current performance of each component as a baseline, identifying which components are executed most often (which are sometimes said to be in the "critical path" or in the "hot path") and trying to redesign them to make them more efficient.

Part II

Best Practices for Machine Learning Pipelines

5

Designing and Structuring Pipelines

When we start writing a new piece of software, one of our first challenges is to identify its logical components and how they interact with each other. We can then *structure* our software into a series of modules, be they classes, libraries or completely separate programs, that implement those logical components in such a way as to make reasoning about the software as easy as possible. In other words, we *design* software to divide and conquer complexity into manageable chunks so that we only need to face a small fraction of it at any given time [252]. Failure to do so quickly leads to software that is impossible to understand and to work on (Chapter 6), which in turn makes it difficult to deploy (Chapter 7), document (Chapter 8), test or troubleshoot (Chapter 9), and in general to keep running.

In this chapter we discuss the unique challenges that define machine learning software design: the role of data (Section 5.1), the nature of technical debt (Section 5.2) and the anatomy of a machine learning pipeline (Section 5.3).

5.1 Data as Code

Machine learning software is fundamentally different from most other software in one important respect: *it is tightly linked with data* [25]. The structure and the

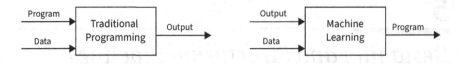

FIGURE 5.1 The inversion of roles in machine learning software (right) compared to other software (left).

behaviour of a piece of traditional software[1] arise from some combination of processes gleaned from experts in the field, a specification of the desired output, and the set of technologies we can use to support its operations (Figure 5.1, left). We are in charge of designing a software architecture that produces the desired behaviour. For instance, we structure web services to direct user navigation patterns through established procedures for different tasks, taking information retrieved from some database or from various vendor APIs and producing outputs to be consumed through some dashboard (by humans) or API (from other computer systems). Desktop applications do the same through windows and dialogs. Obviously, our freedom in designing software architectures is limited for good reasons (performance requirements, good practices and maintainability among them) as well as bad reasons (like less-than-ideal requirements, limitations in the chosen technological stack and unclear requirements) but this still leaves us a substantial amount of control.

On the other hand, the behaviour of machine learning software is dictated as much by the data we train our models on as it is by our design choices. We may decide how to measure model performance but the best performer will then be determined by the data: the distribution of the variables in the data and their probabilistic structure will be better captured by some

---

[1]By "traditional software", we mean any software that is not related to analytics, data science or machine learning.

models than others. So we may choose to try, say, random forests, deep neural networks and some hierarchical Bayesian model but, in the end, we will end up using the model that the data say is best regardless of our personal preferences. *The information in the data is compiled into the software* through the models, which program the software automatically: developers do not completely encode its behaviour in the code (Figure 5.1, right).

This realisation leads to a paradigm shift: *we should treat data as code* because data functionally replaces parts of our source code and because changes in the data may change the behaviour of the software. Hence we should *test the data* to ensure that their characteristics do not change over time (Section 5.2.1). After all, if the data change, our models may no longer be fit for purpose and we may have to retrain them to retain suitable levels of performance. In the case of offline data, this means that *data should be versioned along with the code* and that changes in either of them should trigger testing by continuous integration tools. In the case of online data, we should also implement a *real-time monitoring and logging* of the characteristics of new data and of the performance of the deployed models (Section 5.3.6). Once we are confident that the data are as we expect them to be, we can use them to test that our software (the implementation) is behaving correctly and ensure that the models themselves are correctly specified (in their mathematical and probabilistic formulation). We will discuss the troubleshooting and testing of both data and machine learning models in more detail in the next section and in Chapter 9.

Ideally, we should have a configuration management platform (often called an "experiment tracking" or "experiment management" platform in this context) using version control (Section 6.5) to track the hardware, the source code, the environment configurations, the parameters, the hyperparameters, the model characteristics, the input data and the outputs of all instances of model training and inference. (Including those we use to explore the data.) We can then tag the exact version of all the components used in each development and production environment, as we would do in a traditional software engineering setting. In turn, this means that we can (re)create any of those environments as needed, which makes automated deployments possible (Chapter 7) and greatly facilitates troubleshooting. Given the limited interpretability and explainability of most machine learning models, which are essentially black boxes, only a solution approaching a reproducible build setup [153] can hope to make in-depth debugging and root cause analyses possible.

5.2 Technical Debt

Treating data as code means we should *consider data a potential source of technical debt*. Models can also be sources of technical debt because of their dependence on data and in their own right. In practice, the data and the models are dependencies of our machine learning code: like all dependencies, they are a potential liability and should be handled as such.

The term "technical debt" has commonly had a negative connotation since it was first introduced [73, 74]: it highlights how hasty design choices can lead to unexpected costs, not only in purely economic terms, but by introducing latent complexity that makes the software more difficult to evolve over time. Technical debt allows us to produce results faster by trading quality for speed but, as with borrowed money, we must eventually pay it off with (compound) interest. It is unavoidable when tight deadlines reduce the time spent on analysis and design [96], leading to solutions that are suboptimal in terms of functionality, code quality or technical implementation. Establishing and following the practices we advocate in Part II of this book is a good way of keeping it in check and of paying it off quickly enough to reduce it over time.

Machine learning models and the underlying training, testing and serving software infrastructure, which we will introduce in Section 5.3 as a *machine learning pipeline*, combine all the complexities of traditional software development with the issues arising from the experimental nature of data analysis. (More about this in Chapter 6.) Therefore, we find it useful to rethink the nature of technical debt in machine learning software in a unified, comprehensive way. We classify it into four broad areas: *data*, *model*, *architecture* (*design*) and *code* debt. These areas span issues both in various parts of the machine learning practice, such as data collection, data validation, feature extraction, data visualisation and observability; and in the software that we use to interact with machine learning models, such as monitoring, configurations, training and serving infrastructure. The libraries that power the models themselves, like PyTorch [259] or Scikit-learn [311], are typically very stable and we rarely find them to be a source of technical debt.

5.2.1   At the Data Level

Section 5.1 suggests that data can be a liability for three reasons. Firstly, they may originate from *untrusted sources*, either from in-house or from third-party systems. Data sources that are outside of our control or that do not have strict quality standards should be treated as an unknown quantity: data may unexpectedly change over time in shape (raw data structure or type change), in general quality (data duplication, missing data, null data or incorrectly normalised data) or in relevance and statistical properties (*data* or *concept drift*). This is particularly the case for online data that come in the form of event streams or that are generated by aggregating data from multiple sources. (More on that in Sections 9.1 and 9.4.3.) In order to prevent such anomalies from affecting both the training of models and their subsequent use, we should only allow data that have been versioned and validated by our suite of software tests (Section 9.4) to enter the machine learning pipeline. Systematic testing acts as a *quality gate* that the data must pass before entering later processing stages. Data drift will make models become *stale*: their accuracy will decrease as the data they will perform inference on become increasingly different from those that were used to train them [107, is an extensive review of this topic]. The same may happen if the general quality of the data degrades over time. Unless such changes are sudden enough and sharp enough, their effects will be difficult to detect without a test suite. This is what appears to have happened to Zillow [319], the online real-estate company: the machine learning model they used to price properties to buy was trained on self-reported data, which were untrusted and difficult to validate, and it was left to overestimate prices for too long as the market cooled down. By the time the model was retired in 2021, Zillow had to sell between 60% and 85% of the properties it bought at a loss and fire 25% of its staff just to remain afloat.

Secondly, data may originate from *untracked sources*: we should always take into account that third-party sources can be volatile and can also suddenly become unavailable. If that happens to a data source we are not aware we depend on, troubleshooting the resulting issues may be challenging. Furthermore, untracked sources are often untrusted as well, but unlike tracked sources they are not systematically versioned and validated: any issue they may have can potentially go unnoticed for long periods of time. In this context, where a piece of data comes from and how it was produced is called *data provenance* or *data lineage* [63].

Finally, we may introduce in the data when we prepare them for use in the pipeline. In many applications, we can only collect *unlabelled data* that we have to annotate manually: this is an expensive, time-consuming and error-prone process that requires a team of domain experts. Automated labelling using machine learning models is a poor substitute as it is known to have 0.15–0.20 lower accuracy for both natural language processing and computer vision tasks [413]. The lack of ground truth labels makes it very difficult to spot these errors, which in turn impacts both other data quality controls and model training. Furthermore, manual labelling is too slow to allow us to monitor the outputs of the pipeline in real time, limiting our ability to detect data drift and model staleness. Hence this issue can produce technical debt at different levels in ways that are difficult to detect.

5.2.2 At the Model Level

Issues with model performance, caused by data or otherwise, are unlikely to be limited to a single model. Consider data drift again: if any output of machine learning model A is used as an input to another machine learning model B, any degradation in accuracy in model A will propagate to model B and possibly be amplified in the process. As was the case with the data, we can detect such issues by using integration tests as quality gates to ensure that the inputs and the outputs of each model behave as expected. This is only possible if we track the dependencies between the models, for instance, by recording them as-code in the orchestrator configuration (Section 7.1.4) or by putting in place authentication and authorisation mechanisms to access models (say, with OAuth2 [95]).

Therefore, we can say that technical debt at the model level arises mainly from *feature and model entanglement*: any issue that impacts one model's inference capabilities will propagate to all the downstream models that depend on it, directly or indirectly, in what is called a *correction cascade* (Section 9.1.2). Entanglement between features, between models, and between features and models is unavoidable in practical applications: "changing anything changes everything" [312]. Features are rarely completely independent of each other, and black-box models (Section 9.2.2) like deep neural networks deliberately "entangle them" in ways that are difficult to understand. Models are also entangled with each other because they consume each other's outputs (Section 9.1.2). This complex interplay unfortunately means that it can be difficult to find the root causes of the issues we are troubleshooting even when we observe tell-tale signs that something is wrong (Section 9.3).

On top of that, models are entangled with the real world: for instance, if the suggestions made by the model that drives a recommender system change, the behaviour of the system's users will change in response. This creates a *feedback loop* because the users consume the model's outputs and at the same time provide the data the model is trained on. Whether this is desirable or not depends on the specific application and on whether this feedback loop has a positive or negative effect: uncontrolled *direct feedback loops* can lead to an amplification of bias while artificially improving the model's accuracy. Microsoft's Tay chatbot [154] is a good case in point. Launched on Twitter in 2016 to "engage and entertain people through casual and playful conversation" while self-training from those conversations, it was shut down a few days later because every tweet it posted contained conspiracy theories or racist, inflammatory statements. (Maybe it maximised some abstract engagement metric in doing so?) *Hidden feedback loops* where machine learning models directly affect each other through exogenous events are also possible and harder to spot. Techniques such as reject inference [71] and contextual bandits [79, 80], collecting feedback from users and domain experts (Sections 5.3.4 and 5.3.5) and including additional features can help to break such loops by exploring new models and by suggesting whether the current ones should be retrained.

Finally, models may be entangled with each other when we take a pre-trained model and we fine-tune it for different tasks. This practice reduces computational requirements and speeds up model development: we buy a pre-trained model A for a general task (say, object detection) and then use tightly-focused data sets to specialise it into models B, C, etc. for specific tasks (say, detecting impurities in the semi-finished products of an industrial process). However, models B, C, etc. are likely to inherit similar failure modes from A, thus introducing coupling between models with no tracked dependencies and producing unexpected correction cascades in the machine learning pipeline. Furthermore, models B, C, etc. become more difficult to evolve independently because any bug we fix in model B should also be fixed in models A, C, etc. (or confirmed not to affect them) and the software tests for all models should be updated at the same time. Similarly, any enhancement that is meaningful for model B is likely to be meaningful for models A, C, etc. as well. We can manage these issues by using a configuration management platform, as we pointed out in Section 5.1, to track dependencies between models and between models and data, to version them and to enable systematic testing (Section 9.4.2).

5.2.3   At the Architecture (Design) Level

The architecture of a machine learning pipeline directs how data and models interact to achieve its goals: it is implemented as an *orchestration system* that schedules and coordinates various tasks such as data ingestion, data validation, feature engineering, model training and validation, model deployment on production systems, and serving. We will discuss them in detail in Section 5.3.

Machine learning pipelines are inherently complex systems with many moving parts, and they can easily hide *architecture (design) debt*. The key to keeping this type of technical debt in check is to *give visibility into all aspects of their configuration as code* using files in a human-readable data serialisation language like XML, YAML or JSON.[2] These files should be under version control in a configuration management solution along with the data (Section 5.1) and the models (Section 5.2.2), and for similar reasons. Each change in design can then be expressed in those configuration files or using environment variables. Configuration files should be used for parameters, options and settings for which we need complete versioning across iterations, such as data set locations, training hyperparameters and model parameters. These files can also be linked to and supplement architecture documentation, which describes the pipeline using the more accessible ubiquitous language (Section 8.3). Environment variables should be used to store runtime configurations such as log-levels (Section 5.3.6), feature flags (Section 6.5) and the labels of target testing or production environments. Environment variables are also commonly used for secrets management, that is, to store credentials, certificates and other sensitive information. All modern

---

[2]The choice of the language is often dictated by the orchestration software. However, YAML is becoming a de facto standard because of its readability, portability and maturity.

software solutions to build machine learning pipelines provide mechanisms for configuring, overriding and exposing environment variables, including secrets. Only with a comprehensive formal description of the pipeline and of all its components we may be able to evolve and extend both over time without accidentally accruing architecture debt. Tracking and versioning the architecture along with the data and the models reduces the time spent on troubleshooting and debugging, and makes it possible to implement efficient deployment strategies (Section 7.2) and to roll back problematic models (Section 7.6). The alternative is to perform these operations manually, which is time-consuming and error prone: Knight Capital [317] proved that clearly to the world by burning $460 million in 45 minutes due to a botched manual deployment of their algorithmic trading software.

Unfortunately, we cannot control and version models from third-party libraries or remote systems as easily as those we train ourselves. Hence we are left to integrate them by wrapping their APIs with *glue code* to interface them with the rest of the machine learning pipeline. Glue code is a piece of ad hoc code, often in the form of a one-off script, that has no function other than to adapt software that would otherwise be incompatible. It is a common source of technical debt both at the model level (if shipped in the model) and at the architecture level (if used to bind together different modules in non-standard ways) where it creates what is known as the "pipeline jungle" anti-pattern [45].

Glue code is also commonly used to wrap libraries and remote APIs because it allows us to quickly expose them with new domain-specific names, interfaces and data structures (Section 8.2). While this practice may seem expedient, it can couple glue code tightly with what it is wrapping, causing it to break when the library or the remote API changes its public interface. We should only use glue code wrappers when we strictly need them, for example: to instrument a function for debugging purposes; to expose different versions or different features of the same library to different modules in the pipeline; or to integrate a legacy library or API that we would be otherwise unable to use.

5.2.4 At the Code Level

As for *code debt*, we should avoid mixing different versions of interpreters, programming languages and frameworks in the same machine learning pipeline. Unfortunately, this is a common issue for two reasons. Firstly, machine learning experts and data scientists often work in isolation, without a shared development environment. Secondly, microservices and similar architectures favour the use of multiple programming languages inside the same application in what they call *polyglot programming*. While it is often the case that different programming languages are better suited to different parts of a pipeline (Section 6.1), having too much variety can lead to *organisational anti-patterns* like an unbalanced distribution of skills and skill levels (say, there is only one developer with expertise in a key framework) and inadequate knowledge transfer (because there are too many technologies to keep track of). From a practical standpoint, a good compromise is to build any new machine learning pipeline from a small, up-to-date set of technologies and to involve all developers when incorporating new ones. The latter should be done sparingly: resume-driven development rarely ends well.

A related problem is that of *vendoring software libraries*, that is, including the source code of a specific version of a third-party software in our codebase instead of managing it as an external library through a package manager. Vendored libraries become untracked dependencies (Section 6.3), are often integrated using glue code, and are problematic to update because package managers and other automated tooling are unaware of their existence.

Another source of code debt is the amount of exploration and experimentation involved in creating machine learning models. It can easily produce dead experimental code paths, which are usually badly documented by comments (Section 8.1) and can lead to wasted effort as we try to achieve code coverage (Section 9.4.6). It can also limit the time we can spend on improving the quality of the code we produce from prototype to production level. Practices such as code review (Section 6.6) and constant refactoring (Section 6.7) can address both these issues, as we will discuss in the next chapter. They will also help in tackling low-quality code which, as a source of technical debt, significantly increases the number of bugs and the time required to fix them, slowing down development [371].

5.3 Machine Learning Pipeline

Modern software development schools like Agile [36] and DevOps [153] have pushed for the automation of testing, release management and deployment processes since the early 2000s, leading to the adoption of *continuous integration / continuous delivery* and *deployment* (CI/CD) solutions [86] to manage the software development life cycle. Continuous integration is the practice of developing code by committing small changes frequently to a version control repository. Each change is validated by an automated software testing solution, manually reviewed, and then integrated into the mainline branch the production builds are created from. As a result, the mainline branch is always in a working state and changes to the code are immediately visible to all developers. (More on that in Chapter 6.) Continuous delivery and continuous deployment focus on being able to release a working version of the software at any time and to deploy

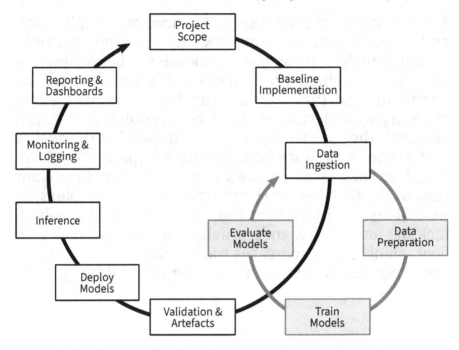

FIGURE 5.2 Life cycle of a machine learning pipeline.

it on production systems. (More on that in Chapter 7.) In both cases, the emphasis is on using automated processes, versioning, configuration management, software testing and code review to enable an effortless, fast and reliable software development life cycle.

Nowadays, we have many integrated CI/CD solutions to build machine learning pipelines (called "MLOps"). However, a complete understanding of how a pipeline works becomes crucial when its development evolves from a simple proof of concept running on some developer's local environment into a larger piece of software managed by a team and running on multiple systems. (Most real-world pipelines are complex enough to require a team to manage them.) At first, we explore some sample data and we try different models to gauge their performance, spending little to no time on software tests. Developing a pipeline then becomes the iterative and increasingly complex process shown in Figure 5.2:

feeding new data from the ingestion phase to existing models for validating, monitoring and troubleshooting them; generating new models as the data change; deploying models and serving them continuously to downstream models or to the application or service that users will access. This is what we call a *machine learning pipeline*: the codification of these steps into independent, reusable, modular parts that can be pipelined together to orchestrate the flow of data into, and outputs from, machine learning models.[3] MLOps practices standardise and automate how a pipeline is developed, giving us all the advantages that CI/CD brought to traditional software engineering, and builds on the same foundations: effective use of versioning, configuration management, automated testing, code review and automated deployments. Continuous integration, in addition to the testing and validation of code, now covers the testing and validation of the data and the models. Continuous delivery and continuous deployment expand to the production and deployment of the entire machine learning pipeline, again including the models. This extended definition of CI/CD allows us to focus on the development, testing and validation of the machine learning models, replacing homegrown solutions based on glue code with systematic solutions based on industry standards.

Figure 5.2 takes the software development life–cycle representation from Figure 1.2 and puts it into context. It shows the key logical steps of reproducible machine learning: what we should take care of to build a solid and maintainable pipeline. Some boxes represent development stages, some are actual pieces of software

---

[3]In software engineering, "pipeline" is used to mean the process of developing and delivering software: CI/CD is a pipeline. In this book, we use it to mean the software infrastructure to develop and put to use the machine learning models and, by extension, the process of building and operating it.

that will become modules in our pipeline, others are both. Broadly speaking, we can group the modules in a pipeline into four stages: *data ingestion* and *preparation*; *model training, evaluation* and *validation*; *model deployment* and *serving*; and *monitoring, logging* and *reporting*. How the functionality provided by each stage is split into modules is something that we can decide when we define the scope of the pipeline; we can then produce a baseline implementation to develop an understanding of its size and structure. However, well-established design principles from software engineering apply [252, 369]. Each module should do one thing and do it completely (the "Single Responsibility Principle"), encapsulating as much complexity as possible and abstracting it behind a simple interface (a "deep module"). Thus, we can keep the complexity of the pipeline in check by avoiding *change amplification* (making a simple change requires modifying code many different locations) and by reducing *cognitive load* (how much does a developer need to know in order to successfully make the change) as well as *unknown unknowns* (which parts of the code should be touched is not obvious). Simple interfaces are less likely to change: they also reduce coupling between the modules if we limit the number of dependencies and avoid common anti-patterns such as implicit constraints (say, functions should be called in a specific order) and pass-through variables containing all kinds of unrelated information (say, the whole global state in a context object). Simple interfaces should also reflect domain knowledge by exposing methods and data structures with domain meaning, with names taken from the ubiquitous language (Chapter 8) and with default settings that make common cases simple to implement. This approach is likely to result in a pipeline architecture patterned after the workflow of domain experts, which allows them to help validate models and inference outputs in a "human-in-the-loop" setup [413, 416]. Furthermore, a modular pipeline can be easily managed by an *orchestrator* which can deploy the modules (Chapter 7), allocate them to systems with the appropriate hardware resources (Chapter 2) and control their execution.

5.3.1 Project Scoping

Starting from the top of Figure 5.2, the first step in building a machine learning pipeline is to understand the problem it should solve, what data it can use to do so, what outputs it should produce, and who its end users will be. To clarify these points, we should first identify who will be involved in developing the pipeline or will interact with it (the "stakeholders"): a combination of software developers, machine learning experts, domain experts and users. Together they will have all the information necessary to define the scope of the pipeline.

The process of scoping a machine learning pipeline and the underlying systems (Chapter 2) involves the following steps:

1. *Identifying the problem we want to solve:* the stakeholders should work together to explicitly define the problem that the pipeline should solve and to evaluate its impact. Domain experts should have a concrete business or academic need to address and, together with the other stakeholders, they should decide whether the problem is worth solving and whether solving it will be valuable to enough people. This process is much smoother if the domain experts have some familiarity with the classes of problems that can be effectively tackled with machine learning.

2. *Identifying the targets we want to optimise for:* the stakeholders should decide what it means to have solved the problem successfully. To this end, the domain experts should set measurable domain

metrics with achievable threshold values to define "success". These metrics should be:

- ·comparable across different data, models and technical solutions to make it possible to contrast different pipeline implementations;
- ·easy to understand and to interpret;
- ·simple enough that they can be collected in real-time for logging and monitoring (Section 5.3.6);
- ·actionable.

3. *Identifying what data we need*: data are a critical component of a machine learning pipeline because they determine its performance (Section 5.1). Therefore, it is essential to identify all the data sources we want to use, who owns them, and the technical details of how the data are stored (files, databases or data lakes) and structured (data schema). This allows us to track data provenance and reduce technical debt (Section 5.2.1). In particular, we should be wary about data sources that provide overlapping information because they introduce hidden dependencies in the pipeline. They can easily be inconsistent because of differences in their schemas (say, the same variable is scaled or discretised in different ways) and, even if they are consistent, they can diverge over time (say, one data source changes schema and the others do not). A common case is that of partially pre-processed data, which should always be reconciled with the raw data they originate from and stored in the same versioned repository. In addition, we should collect data following the best practices accumulated in decades of survey sampling [137, 198] and experimental design [225] to make sure that the data we collect to train the machine

learning models (Section 5.3.4) are representative of the data the models will perform inference on (Section 5.3.5). Sampling bias can have unpredictable effects on the performance of the pipeline.

4. *Analysis:* we should assess how much data we can collect and what variable types they will contain. With this information, we can start evaluating different models based on their sample size requirements, their probabilistic assumptions and the inference types they support (prediction, classification, etc.). As a general rule, it is always preferable to start with simpler models because they enable a fast feedback loop: if simple models cannot achieve our targets, we can move to more complex models and use the simpler ones as baselines. In addition, we should take into consideration:

    •The *robustness* of the model against the noise in the data, against model misspecification and adversarial attacks.

    •*Interpretability* and *explainability*, that is, how well we can understand the behaviour and the outputs of the models. Some models are inherently interpretable either because of their simple structure (say, regression models) or because of their construction (say, Bayesian networks [314]). For others (say, deep neural networks), we can introduce auxiliary models to provide post hoc explanations: some of them are application–agnostic [193] while others are specific to natural language processing [191] or computer vision [325].

    •The *fairness* of model outputs, which should not induce the machine learning pipeline to discriminate against individuals or groups based on sensitive attributes such as gender, race or age. While there is much literature on this topic [208], there is no consensus on how fairness should be measured. What there is consensus on is that machine learning models can easily incorporate the biases present in the data they are trained from. Therefore, we should consider carefully how the data are collected and we should constrain models to limit or disregard the discriminating effect of known sensitive attributes. Failures to do so have often ended in the news: Amazon's sexist recruitment tool [31], Facebook image recognition labelling black men as primates [32] and Twitter's racist preview cropping [33] are just a few examples.

• *Privacy* and *security* concerns for sensitive data [258]. Machine learning models excel at extracting useful information from data, but at the same time, they should protect privacy by not disclosing personally identifiable information. How to achieve that is an open problem, with research investigating approaches like differential privacy [121], defences against adversarial attacks and data re–identification [232], and distributed learning implementations such as federated learning [192] and edge computing [181] (Section 2.3).

A machine learning pipeline typically spans several data sources and several models: as a result, we will iterate over these steps a few times depending on the nature of the project and of the organisation undertaking it. In the end, we will have the information we need to compile a mission statement document (Section 8.4) and to sketch the layout of the architecture (Section 8.3) and of our software test suite (Section 9.4.1). The architecture is typically represented with a directed acyclic graph (DAG): see Figure 8.2 for an illustrative example. Each node will correspond to one of the modules in the pipeline, with incoming and outgoing arcs showing its inputs and outputs, respectively. The DAG therefore maps the paths of execution of the pipeline and the flow of data and information from data ingestion to training, inference and reporting. The DAG may be quite large for particularly complex pipelines: splitting it into smaller DAGs corresponding to different sections of the pipeline and working with them independently may be more convenient.

5.3.2 Producing a Baseline Implementation

Data validation, model development, tuning, training and validation are initially explored by individual developers and machine learning experts on local hardware, if suitable hardware is available. After experimentation, they will eventually produce a minimal, working prototype of some part of the pipeline. This is often called a *baseline implementation* or *proof of concept*, and it will only involve the smallest amount of code that allows us to check whether we can achieve our targets.

This initial exploration of the problem does not typically involve all the CI/CD development workflows discussed above and in Chapter 6: at this stage, the code and the models are too volatile. However, developers and machine learning experts should at least agree on a common, unified development environment (software dependencies management, build processes and configurations). This environment should be buildable in a reproducible and reliable way, which requires configuration management, and it should be as close as possible to our target production environment.

For convenience, the development environment should be modular in the same way as the pipeline, so that we can run only the modules we are working on: it is typically impossible to run the whole pipeline on a developer workstation.

After checking that our proof of concept achieves all its targets, we then:

1. Construct a suite of software tests (Section 9.4.2) and push both to our version control repository to start taking advantage of continuous integration. We can then transform the proof of concept into production-quality code by gradually refactoring (Section 6.7) and documenting it (Chapter 8) with the help of code review (Section 6.6).

2. Improve scalability. A proof of concept is typically built using a small fraction of the available data, so we must ensure that its computational complexity (Chapter 4) is small enough to make learning and inference feasible in production when all data are used. Time complexity is important to allow for timely model retraining and for inference under latency constraints; space complexity must fit the machine learning systems (Chapter 2) we have available. If our development system is similar to the production systems, we can expect computational complexity to translate into practical performance in similar ways and predict the latter reliably.

5.3.3 Data Ingestion and Preparation

After scoping the pipeline and producing a baseline implementation of its parts, we can start designing and implementing its modules in a more structured way. A machine learning pipeline is the formalisation of a data processing workflow. Therefore, the first part of the pipeline will comprise one or more *data ingestion* modules where we collect data from various sources such as relational databases, legacy OLTP/OLAP systems and modern in-house or cloud data lakes. These modules vary in nature depending on the machine learning systems the pipeline will run on: their design will be heavily influenced by factors such as data locality (Sections 2.2 and 2.3), data provenance (Section 5.2.1), the availability of different types of storage (Section 2.1.2) and compliance with privacy frameworks like HIPAA and FCRA in the United Stated or GDPR in Europe (Section 5.3.1).

Data ingestion is followed by *data preparation*. Preparing and cleaning the data is a hard but crucial step involving data scientists, domain experts and machine learning experts [179]. Modules for data preparation build on the exploratory analysis of the data used to produce the baseline implementation of the models, which is often limited to a high-level analysis of summary statistics, graphical visualisations and some basic feature selection. Their purpose is to clean and improve the quality of the data in the most automatic and reproducible way possible, making subsequent stages of the pipeline more reliable. In addition to validating the types, the acceptable values and the statistical distribution of each feature, data preparation modules should address the issues discussed in Section 9.1. They can also automate both feature selection and *feature engineering* (that is, the transformation of existing features into new ones that are better suited to model training or that are more meaningful in domain terms). Current software solutions for data and machine learning pipelines handle these tasks in a flexible way by taking as configuration arguments a processing function and a validation function that checks the properties of the now-clean data. The former may, for example, remove outliers, impute missing data and sort labels and features; the latter serves as a quality gate (Section 5.2.1) and as the kernel of a property-based software test (Section 9.4.2).

Finally, the data are split into multiple sets for later use as training, validation and test sets. (Making sure to avoid data leakage, see Section 9.3.) Each data set is tagged with information about its origin and with the version of the code that was used to extract and clean it, to track data provenance. These tags become part of our configuration management, and the data is stored as an artefact under versioning for later use.

5.3.4 Model Training, Evaluation and Validation

After ingestion and preparation, a machine learning pipeline passes the data either to *model training* modules or to *inference* modules (which we will discuss in Section 5.3.5). The trained models are then *evaluated* (on their statistical performance) and *validated* (in domain terms) using software tests and human expert judgement to ensure they are efficient, reproducible and scalable. Only models that perform sufficiently well in both statistical and domain terms will be considered suitable for deployment and serving.

Training a machine learning model consists in identifying an optimal instance in some model class (neural networks, random forests, etc.) by iteratively applying a combination of feature engineering, hyperparameter tuning and parameter optimisation. This is what the "learning" in "machine learning" refers to: a computer system is trained to learn a working model of some piece of the real world from the information contained in the data. The probabilistic techniques used for this purpose are specific to each model class and are beyond the scope of this book: see Kuhn and Johnson [188] for an approachable treatment of this topic. Training is a computationally demanding task, especially in the case of deep learning. The role of the pipeline is to schedule the training workload on compute systems with the appropriate hardware capabilities (as discussed in Section 2.4) and to monitor its progress. It should also simplify the parallel training of models with predefined, regular patterns of hyperparameters; and it should automate software tests implementing property-based testing of the model's probabilistic properties (Section 9.4.2).

Training can take quite different forms depending on the nature of the data (Section 9.4.3). In *static learning*, the model is trained from scratch on *cold* (offline) data selected to be representative of the data currently observed in production. Its statistical performance is then evaluated against either a separate set of cold data or a small stream of production data. In either case, the data should be labelled or validated by domain experts to address the issues discussed in Section 5.2.1 and to maximise model quality. In *dynamic learning*, the model is continuously trained and evaluated on a live *stream* of (online) production data collected in real time. This requires fine-grained monitoring to be in place (Section 5.3.6). If data drift is gradual, we may prevent the model from going stale by fine-tuning it [107]. If, on the other hand, data drift is sudden, it may be preferable to retrain the model from scratch with a batch of recent data.

Model evaluation modules check whether the predictive accuracy of the model the pipeline just trained is better in statistical terms than that of the corresponding model currently in production. To assess both simultaneously, we can perform a *canary deployment*: running the current and the new model in parallel on the same data to compare them directly. (More on this in Chapter 7.) In the case of streaming data, it is standard practice to use A/B testing [7, 425] for this purpose, assigning new data points at random to either model. At the same time, we can check whether the new model is preferable to the current one in domain terms using the metrics we decided to optimise for (Section 5.3.1). We call this *model validation*, in contrast with the evaluation of the model in purely statistical terms. The two may be related because models with poor statistical properties will typically not encode the domain well enough for practical use. However, models with good statistical properties are not always of practical use either: in particular when the loss function the model is trained to minimise is too different from that implied by how costly prediction errors are in business or domain terms. In general, it is better to choose well-matched domain metrics and statistical accuracy measures for consistency. Unlike model evaluation, which can be automated to a large extent using software tests and continuous integration, model validation should involve domain experts. Even if we practise domain-driven development [96] and involve them in the design of the pipeline, in implementing it (Chapter 6) and in documenting it (Chapter 8), there will always be some domain knowledge or intuition that they were not able to convey to developers and machine learning experts. As unscientific as it may sound, there is knowledge that is essentially impossible to put into numbers. Therefore, there will be issues we cannot write tests for, but that experts can "eyeball" and flag in model outputs because "they look wrong" and "do not quite make sense." This approach is known as "human-in-the-loop" in the literature, and it is known to improve the quality of machine learning across tasks and application fields [413, 416].

When a model is finally found to perform well in both statistical and domain terms, the pipeline should trigger a CI/CD process to generate an *artefact* containing the model and all the relevant information from the training process. An artefact can be, from simple to complex:

1. A (usually binary) file in a standardised format that will be stored and versioned in a

general-purpose *artefact registry*. The format can be either model-independent, like ONNX [247], or specific to the machine learning framework used for training.

2. A (usually Docker [82]) container that embeds the model and wraps it with application code that provides APIs for inference, health checking and monitoring. The container is then stored and versioned in a *container registry*.

3. An annotated file uploaded to a *model registry* that provides experiment tracking, model serving, monitoring and comparison between models in addition to versioning.

Platforms like GitHub and GitLab integrate both a general-purpose artefact registry [112, 114] and a container registry [113, 115], as does Nexus [328]. MLOps platforms like TensorFlow Extended (TFX) [342] implement experiment tracking and other machine-learning-specific features. We will return to this topic in Section 7.1.

Regardless of their form, artefacts should be *immutable*: they cannot be altered once generated so they can be used as the single source of truth for the model. Data artefacts (Section 5.3.3), code (Section 6.5) and often other software artefacts are also stored as immutable artefacts and versioned. When their versions are linked, we have a complete configuration management solution that allows for reproducible builds of any development, testing or production environment that has ever been used in the pipeline.

5.3.5 Deployment, Serving and Inference

Not all the artefacts we produce will be *deployed* immediately, or at all: continuous delivery only ensures that we are always ready to deploy our latest models.

In academia, we cannot make any change to a pipeline halfway through a set of experiments without potentially introducing confounding in the results. In business, we may have service-level agreements with our customers that make it risky to deploy new models without a compelling reason to do so. Artefacts may also be found to be unsuitable for deployment for security reasons: for instance, we may find out that a container contains vulnerable dependencies or is misconfigured (Section 7.1.4).

Model deployment is not implemented as a module: rather, it is the part of the pipeline orchestration that enables models to be deployed to a target environment. Models deployed in production will be *served* so that users, applications or other models can access their inference capabilities. Models deployed to test environments will be evaluated by software tests and expert judgement, and those deployed to development environments can be used for troubleshooting bugs or further investigation of the data.

How a machine learning model is deployed depends on how it has been packaged into an artefact and on how it will be used. File artefacts can be either embedded in a software library that exposes inference methods locally or served "as-a-service" from a model registry using suitable remote APIs and protocols (such as RESTful or, when we need low latency, gRPC [108]). Container artefacts can be deployed by all orchestration platforms in common use, which provide built-in monitoring and logging of hardware and software metrics (load, memory and I/O use) as well as troubleshooting facilities. Despite being intrinsically more complex, container artefacts are easier to deploy because they are ephemeral and highly portable, and because we can manage as-a-code both their runtime dependencies and configuration. We will develop this topic in detail in Sections 7.1.4 and 7.2 using Dockerfiles as a reference.

5.3.6 Monitoring, Logging and Reporting

Monitoring modules collect the metrics we identified in the scoping phase (Section 5.3.1) to track at all times whether the pipeline achieves the required statistical and domain performance levels. The metrics should describe both the pipeline as a whole and individual modules to allow us to pinpoint the source of any issue we may have to troubleshoot. In particular:

- Data ingestion and preparation modules (Section 5.3.3): we should monitor the same data metrics we check with property-based software tests to guard against data drift and data degradation.
- Training modules (Section 5.3.4): we should monitor the same metrics we use for model validation and evaluation consistently across all models in the pipeline to separate issues with individual models from issues arising from the data. Especially when using online data.
- Serving and inference modules (Section 5.3.5): we should monitor the same metrics we monitor during training to ensure that performance has not degraded over time (the so-called "training-serving skew"). And we should do that for all inference requests (possibly in small batches) so that we can guarantee that outputs are always in line with our targets. This is crucial to enable human-in-the-loop validation by domain experts for black-box models whose failure modes are mostly unknown and difficult to test.

The coverage of monitoring facilities is important for the same reason why test coverage is important: both are tasked to identify a broad range of issues with the data (Section 9.1), with the models (Section 9.2) and with the pipeline (Section 9.2.4) with enough precision to allow for root-cause analyses. Software tests perform this function at development and deployment time; monitoring does it at runtime.

In practice, we can implement monitoring with a client–server software such as Prometheus [275]. Each module in the pipeline produces all relevant metrics internally, tags them to track provenance (which module, and which instance of the module if we have multiple copies running in parallel) and makes them available in a structured format through the client interface. Monitoring modules then provide the corresponding server that pulls the metrics from all clients and saves them into an *event store* database. They will also filter the metrics, sanitise them, and run frequent checks for anomalies. If any is found, the monitoring modules can then trigger alerts and send failure reports to the appropriate people using, for instance, Alertmanager (which is part of Prometheus) or PagerDuty [255]. If our pipeline is sufficiently automated, we may also trigger model retraining automatically at the same time. This is the only way to address anomalies in a timely manner and to provide guarantees on the quality of the outputs of the pipeline. Cross–referencing the information in the event store to that in our configuration management system is invaluable in comparing the performance of our current production environment against that of past (now unavailable) environments. The same metrics may also be useful for troubleshooting infrastructure issues, like excessive consumption of computing resources, memory and I/O, as well service issues that impact downstream services and models, like readiness (whether a specific API is ready to accept requests) and excessive inference latency (how long it takes for the API to respond).

Logging modules complement monitoring by recording relevant information about events that occur inside individual modules or within the pipeline orchestration, capturing exceptions and errors. Typically, at least part of a machine learning pipeline runs on remote systems: since we cannot access them directly, especially in the case of cloud instances (Section 2.3), we are limited in our ability to debug and troubleshoot issues. Logging makes this problem less severe by recording what each module is doing in a sequence of timestamped *log messages*, ranging from simple plain-text messages (as we may produce ourselves) to more structured JSON or binary objects (from frameworks or language interpreters). Each log message has a "level" that determines its severity and that allows us to control how much we want to log for each module: for instance, a set of labels like DEBUG, INFO, WARNING, ERROR, and CRITICAL. Each log message is also tagged with its provenance, which allows us to distinguish between:

- system logs, which provide information on the load of the machine learning systems, the runtime environment and the versions of relevant dependencies;
- training logs, which describe the model structure, how well it fits the data and the values of its parameters and hyperparameters for each training iteration;
- inference logs, which describe inputs, outputs, accuracy and latency for each request and each API.

Therefore, logs provide a measure of observability when we otherwise would have none: all modules should implement logging as much as monitoring. However, the more messages we generate, the more resources logging requires: which poses practical limits on how much we can afford to log, especially on production systems. In development environments, we may just append log messages to a file. In production environments, we should aggregate log messages from the whole pipeline to a remote log collector instead of locally. Log collectors can normalise log messages, make them easy to browse and make it possible to correlate events happening in different modules.

Similar to monitoring modules, logging modules are implemented with a client–server software such as Fluentd [359] complemented by a search engine like

Elasticsearch and a web frontend like Kibana [91]. The two software stacks have some apparent similarities: both have a remote server aggregating information from clients inside the modules. The underlying reason for this architecture is that we should locate the server on a system that is completely separate from those the machine learning pipeline runs on: when the latter crashes and burns, we need to be able to access the information stored by monitoring and logging servers to investigate what its last known status was and decide how to best restore it.

However, monitoring and logging have two key technical differences. Firstly, logging should support unstructured data, whereas monitoring only handles data in the form of {key, type, value} triplets. Logging gives observability from outside the code we wrote to implement a module, reporting information that we do not produce directly and whose format we cannot necessarily control. Monitoring gives observability from the inside: we incorporate the client component into our code and we give it access to its internal state. Hence the information we expose to the monitoring server is necessarily structured in various data types and data structures (Chapter 3). Secondly, logs are pushed from the clients to the servers as they are generated, whereas monitoring servers pull the metrics from the clients in the modules at regular intervals. Therefore, the databases used by the logging servers are general-purpose event stores, whereas those used for monitoring are optimised for time series data. The ability to access the internal state of all modules at regular intervals makes monitoring servers ideal for observing any gradual degradation in the machine learning pipeline.

Reporting modules implement graphical interfaces that display the information collected by the monitoring and logging modules. Building on best practices from data science [179], they provide web interfaces with intuitive, interactive *dashboards* that can be used by developers, machine learning experts and domain experts alike. Graphical displays in common use are:

- Data ingestion and preparation modules (Section 5.3.3):
  - Plots of the empirical distribution both of individual features and of pairs of features against each other such as histograms, boxplots, heatmaps and pairwise scatterplots (for continuous features) or barplots and tileplots (for discrete features).
  - Plots of key summaries from minimal statistical models such as simple linear regressions to assess the magnitude and the sign of the relationships between features and to explore potential fairness issues.
- Training modules (Section 5.3.4):
  - Plots of model performance over the course and at the end of the training process, like profile plots of the loss function against epochs for deep neural networks and heatmaps for confusion matrices produced by classification models.
  - Plots that help interpret the model behaviour, showing either its parameters or the outputs of explainability approaches like LIME [296] and SHAP [201].
  - For less computationally-intensive models, interactive dashboards that can trigger model training, with sliders to pick hyperparameters on the fly.
- Serving and inference modules (Section 5.3.5):
  - Plots of the empirical distribution of input data against historical data, to detect data drift.
  - Time series plots of the accuracy measures used in model validation and the metrics used for model evaluation, to detect when models become stale.
  - Time series plots of latency and readiness.

All plots should also include confidence intervals to convey the likely range of values for each of the quantities they display, wherever it makes sense.

Domains like natural language processing and computer vision may require specialised graphical interfaces in addition to the above: for instance, visualising word relevance in natural language processing [191] and pixel relevance in computer vision [325] or splitting images into layers with semantic meaning [296]. Such interfaces can be very useful to involve domain experts in validating model training and the outputs from the inference modules. Instances that were not classified or predicted correctly can then be visually inspected, labelled and used to retrain the machine learning models.

6

Writing Machine Learning Code

Programming is, in many ways, a conversation with a computer, but it is also conversation with other developers [105]. As vague as it sounds, we should strive to write code that is simple to read and whose meaning is obvious [252]. Code is read much more often than it is written: most of the cost of a piece of software is in its maintenance, which is typically performed by people other than those who first wrote the code.

Achieving clarity involves effort on several fronts. Different trade-offs between clarity, consistency, development speed and the existence of useful libraries may motivate the use of particular programming languages for different modules (Section 6.1). Things should be named appropriately (Section 6.2), code should be formatted and laid out consistently (Section 6.3), functions and modules should be organised tidily in files and directories (Section 6.4).

Finally, having multiple people go through the code and *review* it (Section 6.6) helps in identifying how to improve it. We can then change it gradually by *refactoring* it (Section 6.7), which is the safest way to make sure we do not introduce any new bugs. Both activities require an efficient use of source *version control* (Section 6.5), which will also be key for deploying (Chapter 7), documenting (Chapter 8) and testing (Chapter 9) our machine learning pipeline. As an example, we will refactor a sample of code used for teaching in academia (Section 6.8).

6.1 Choosing Languages and Libraries

The choice of what programming languages to use to write machine learning software is mainly determined by their performance, their observability, the availability of libraries whose functionality we can use and ease of programming.

The performance of a programming language depends mainly on whether it is *compiled* (like C, C++ and Rust) or *interpreted* (like R and Python). Compilation takes a program and generates machine instructions that are stored in binary executable files or libraries, which can then be run repeatedly. Compiled code is generally high-performance because it does not require further processing when run: all the work of finding the most efficient sequence of machine instructions is done ahead of runtime. This includes deciding what instructions are appropriate to use for taking advantage of the CPUs, GPUs and TPUs on the system the program will run on. In contrast, interpreted languages execute a program by translating it into machine instruction during runtime. Interpreted code, therefore, does not necessarily exhibit high performance but is typically higher level (in the sense that it is more abstracted from hardware specifics, such as managing memory) and is easier to program because we can work with it interactively in REPLs.[1] In practice, programming languages used for machine learning exist on a spectrum between these two extremes. Both R and Python, despite being interpreted languages, have packages that are just thin wrappers around

---

[1]A REPL ("Read-Eval-Print Loop") is an interactive programming environment where the user can write code statements that are instantly evaluated and whose outputs are returned to the user. They are invaluable to run software piecewise and understand the behaviour of its components.

high-performance libraries like BLAS, LAPACK, Tensor-Flow or Torch that are written in compiled code. Depending on what packages we use in our machine learning code, we may achieve performance comparable to that of compiled code without sacrificing ease of programming for those parts of our code that are not computationally intensive. Julia, on the other hand, uses *just-in-time compilation* to compile and optimise code just before each module or function is called at runtime. As a result, the time it takes to start executing Julia code is fairly slow but has little overhead once running.

Compiled and interpreted languages are very different in terms of observability as well. We can observe the behaviour of compiled code easily by profiling it (recording relevant metrics at regular intervals) or by tracing it (recording the program and the compute system status when particular events are recorded) at the system level because it runs exactly the same sequence of instructions every time it is executed. On the other hand, interpreted code is mapped to machine instructions dynamically by the interpreter as the software is run. Mapping performance to specific blocks of code is more difficult unless the interpreter can expose its internal state to a profiler while running the program. As a result, interpreted code is often studied by simply adding print statements and timestamps. A more rigorous alternative is to *instrument* the code itself, that is, to ask the interpreter to record its state at predetermined intervals or events. However, most types of instrumentation dramatically increase execution time and are unwieldy to use even for debugging. This is well known to be the case for R's Rprof() and Rprofmem(), for instance.

In terms of ease of programming, all compiled languages in common use are *low-level languages*: the code we write in them is not abstracted away from the compute system it will run on. Manual memory management, dependency management, heavy focus on the implementation details of data structures (Chapter 3), structuring code to take advantage of specific hardware capabilities (Chapter 2) are everyday concerns when working with languages like C or C++. In contrast, interpreted languages in common use are *high-level languages*. They allow us to write code that is in many respects like pseudocode and to concentrate to a greater extent on the models and the algorithms we are implementing. As a result, they make it easier to keep track of the overall design and of the structure of the machine learning pipeline. High-level languages such as R, Python and Julia also come with package repositories and dependency management [70, 171, 280]. Once more, this suggests that the best trade-off is to use low-level, compiled languages for the few parts of the machine learning pipeline that are performance-critical and to use high-level languages for everything else. The former will include model training and inference; the latter may include data cleaning, visualisation and performance monitoring. Orchestrating the different parts of the pipeline may or may not be performance-critical, depending on its scale and complexity.

Finally, the availability of libraries that we can build on is important as well. Ideally, we want to focus our efforts on implementing, optimising and running our machine learning systems and pipelines instead of reimplementing functionality that is already available elsewhere. And even if we were fine with reinventing the wheel, we are unlikely to match the design quality and performance optimisations of most popular software libraries. There is a significant overlap in the machine learning models available in various languages, but some have better implementations than others in particular cases. Python is probably the best choice for neural networks, for probabilistic programming and for applications in computer vision and natural language processing. R has the widest selection of models from classical and modern statistics, including the reference implementation of popular ones such as mixed-effects models and the elastic net penalised regression. Behind the scenes, both languages (and Julia as well) use the same standard numerical libraries so they often have similar levels of performance.

Last but not least, consider again the discussion on the modular nature of machine learning software in Section 5.3. When modules in our software have well-defined interfaces that specify what their inputs and outputs are, and both inputs and outputs are serialised using standard formats, we can implement them in different languages. Model training and inference modules (Sections 5.3.4 and 5.3.5) are more computationally intensive and, therefore, should be implemented in compiled languages like C or C++. Modules that do not require as many resources like user interfaces, dashboards (Section 5.3.6) and often data ingestion (Section 5.3.3) may be implemented in interpreted languages like R or Python. Orchestration, model deployment and serving (Section 5.3.5), logging and monitoring (Section 5.3.6) are usually provided by third-party software; any glue code that complements them may be in a completely unrelated systems or scripting language. The isolation between the modules, and between the modules and the underlying compute systems, makes the choice of the language used internally in each module irrelevant for all the others. However, some degree of homogeneity in programming languages and module structures is desirable to make it easier for different people to work on the code (Section 5.2.4).

6.2 Naming Things

Carefully naming variables, functions, models and modules is essential to convey their meaning to other people reading the code [252, 369]. But who are those people in the case of machine learning software? They will be a combination of *final users*, *developers*, *machine learning experts* and *domain experts*. Each group will have a different view of what names are meaningful to them. Similarly, we will argue in Chapter 8 that we should complement software with documentation written from different perspectives to make sure that all the people working on it can understand it well.

Names that are most useful to users and domain experts describe what a function is supposed to do, what a variable contains or how it is supposed to be used, which model is implemented by a module, and so on. They can do that by leveraging the naming conventions of the domain the software is used in. Such names do not describe how a function works internally, what is the type of a variable or other implementation details: most users and domain experts will not be developers themselves, so this type of information will not be useful to them. They will mainly be interested in using functions, modules, etc. for their own purposes without having to understand the implementation of every piece of code they call. Doing so would increase the cognitive load involved in working with any complex piece of software beyond what is reasonable. For the same reason, we suggested using names that come from the domain in pseudocode (Section 4.1).

Names that describe the implementation details of what they refer to can be useful to other developers working on the same module. Similarly, short names that map directly to the mathematical notation used in the scientific literature will be most useful to machine learning experts. Both types of names assume familiarity with the mathematical and implementation details of the relevant models and algorithms, and assume that whoever is reading the code will refer to the literature to understand what the code does and why it does it that way. Such names are usually quite short, making for terse code. Users and domain experts are unlikely to be familiar with the notation and they will find such code impossible to understand without a significant amount of effort and the help of extensive comments (Section 8.1). On the other hand, people who are familiar with the mathematical notation can grasp the code much faster if the naming convention is the same as in the literature. This is advantageous when writing research code that will only be shared among collaborators working on similar topics. However, using mathematical notation can also be a source of misunderstandings because the same concepts are expressed with different notation and, vice versa, the same notation is used to represent very different concepts in different subfields of machine learning.

Therefore, in practice it is impossible to establish a single suitable naming convention across a machine learning pipeline: the code it contains is too varied, as will be the people interacting with it. (This is true more in general for any kind of coding convention, as we will see in the next section.) However, the general guidelines from Kernigham and Pike [180] apply even across naming conventions. *Use descriptive names for globals, short names for locals*: it may be fine to adhere to mathematical notation inside modules implementing machine learning models and algorithms because only developers and machine learning experts are likely to touch such code. Both the module scope and the comments it contains will narrow down the context (Section 8.1) and make short names as understandable as longer names would be (but faster to read). Variables and functions that can be accessed from outside the module, on the other hand, are better named following their domain meaning because they are likely to be used by final users and domain experts. Public interface documentation (Section 8.2) can help in fleshing out their relationships with models and data as well as expand on their meaning. *Be consistent*: code of the same type should follow the same naming convention across all modules in the machine learning pipeline, practising either the same ubiquitous language used in the comments, interface and architecture documentation (Section 8.3) or the same mathematical notation established in the technical documentations (Section 8.4). *Be accurate*: avoid vague names and names that can be misunderstood to mean different things to people from different backgrounds.[2]

6.3 Coding Styles and Coding Standards

Code clarity is also a function of its readability. At a low level, we can improve readability by adopting *code styles* that standardise how code is formatted (indentation, use of braces, name casing, line length, etc.) and that give it a uniform look across the whole machine learning software. The idea is that consistently using the same style makes code easier to read and to understand both by the person who wrote it and by others. Therefore, adhering to a coding style reduces the risk of mistakes and makes it easier to collaborate within and across teams of developers. All programming languages in common use in machine learning software including Python [128, 384], R [400] and Julia [38] have industry-standard code styles which apply well in this context. However, a machine learning pipeline will comprise code written in different programming languages (Section 6.1): we may want to consider making small changes to these

---

[2]Many technical terms have completely different meanings in software engineering: consider "test" (statistical test vs unit test), "regression" (the statistical model vs adversely affecting existing software functionality) or "feature" (a variable in a data set vs a distinguishing characteristic of a piece of software). Similar conflicts may happen with the terminology from other domains as well.

styles to make them more similar to each other and to reduce friction when working with more than one language at the same time.

At a higher level, we may want to adopt *code standards* that limit what programming constructs are considered safe to use and that lay out best practices to structure code at a local level (say, blocks within a function, or functions within a module). Such standards are language-agnostic and complement rather than replace code styles: for instance, they may describe how to handle exceptions, how inputs and outputs should be structured at the function and module level, how to track software dependencies, how code should be instrumented for logging and observability, and what code patterns to avoid for performance reasons. Lopes [199] shows how much of a difference these choices can make in practice. At an even higher level, code standards may also address software security concerns. Unlike code styles, there are no universal code standards: their breadth makes them necessarily application- or domain-specific. Combining both with a modular pipeline design (Section 5.3) allows us to make assumptions about the code's behaviour, which in turn makes it easier to read, to deploy, to maintain and to integrate with other code by reducing the need for refactoring (Section 6.7) and by making code easier to test (Section 9.4). They can be adopted systematically by having automated tools to check for compliance and by enforcing them during code review (Section 6.6).

The adoption of code styles and standards is, at the time of this writing, one of the low-hanging fruits to pick to improve machine learning software across the board. The prevalence of Jupyter notebooks [274] as a development platform encourages one-off code that does not need to follow any particular convention because it does not interact with other software and interacts with users in very limited ways. As a result, code in

Jupyter notebooks is not well organised into functions (which are 1.5 times more coupled compared to normal software, even though they are individually simpler), its dependencies are not well managed (twice as many undeclared, indirect, or unused imports), and, in general, code has more quality issues (1.3 times more) [136]. Even disregarding Jupyter notebooks, all systematic analyses of open-source machine learning code have found significant and widespread issues. After controlling for age and popularity, machine learning software has similar complexity and open tickets to other types of software. However, individual projects seem to have fewer contributors and more forks, suggesting code may not be reviewed as thoroughly [324]. Reproducibility and maintainability are problematic because software dependencies are often not properly tracked [383]: either they are not listed, they are vendored (Section 5.2.4), their versions are not pinned, or they are unresolvable because they are detected automatically and never vetted. Pylint's inability to reliably check local imports and imports in packages with C/C++ backends (that is, all foundational packages including TensorFlow, NumPy and PyTorch) makes this worse for Python projects. Furthermore, users are often unaware of the documented issues and pitfalls of the machine learning software they use [423], in part because they are only reported in independent blog posts if they are library-specific.

These general issues are made worse by several smells that are specific to machine learning code and that arise from how such code is developed. Many of the sources we have referenced [313, 324, 339, 383, 423] point out issues with module interfaces and functions having too many arguments (because they map to the mathematical notation of the underlying models too closely); duplicate code (because of experimentation by cut-and-paste and no pruning of dead code); functions being too long, with too many variables and too many branches (because they perform multiple tasks and were never refactored into smaller functions); and lack of configuration management (such as the experiment tracking and infrastructure-as-code approaches we argued for in Chapter 5). Some of these issues could be tolerated as inherent to machine learning code: we argued earlier (Section 6.2) that naming local variables after mathematical notation is fine even if names are not descriptive. However, most should not. To be fair, we acknowledge that many of these issues cannot be addressed on a purely technical level because they arise from wrong incentives. In academia, code is treated as a one-off throwaway [234, 340] because job performance is measured by the number of publications ("publish or perish!"), not by the quality of the code itself. The resulting software is typically neither maintained nor deployed to a production system. In the industry, many professionals working on machine learning pipelines have little or no background in software engineering [313] and companies have come to accept re-implementing machine learning code from scratch to use it in production as inevitable. A culture change is needed for the adoption of best practices such as code styles and code standards (as well as modular pipeline design) to become the norm.

6.4 Filesystem Structure

Keeping code organised into files and directories contributes to clarity by making it easier to find any specific piece of code. This is true for machine learning pipelines as much as for other types of software: functions performing related tasks should be stored together, and functions performing orthogonal tasks should be stored in separate parts of the filesystem. (The Single Responsibility Principle [369] applied to file hierarchies.) Each module should be stored in a separate directory, with functionality split coherently into files. Methods and variables exported from a module should be stored in a separate set of files than internal code, to make it easier for users to inspect them and to link them with interface documentation (Section 8.2). Unit tests for the module (Section 9.4.4) should be placed in a separate subdirectory but versioned alongside the code they test.

What is the best filesystem structure to use for a module in a machine learning pipeline? There is no single, universal standard: both language-agnostic [186] and language-specific proposals for Python [3, 134], R [42] and Go [284] are available and have been used in real-world software. They overlap substantially, broadly agreeing on the following set of subdirectories and files:

- An src directory for the source code of the module, possibly subdivided into further subdirectories.
- A build or dist directory to store the artefacts created during the build process, like object files, machine learning models and the files used for testing, deployment and CI/CD.
- A directory for the specification files for any containers used in CI/CD, say, docker for Dockerfiles [82]. Further configuration files controlling how containers are deployed and managed, such as Kubernetes [364] YAML configurations, may be placed in the same directory for convenience.
- A config directory containing the configuration files required to build and develop the module, including a complete list of versioned software dependencies (say, requirements.txt for Python modules) and IDE settings.
- A test directory for the unit tests and their reference outputs.

- A docs directory containing the module documentation, either in source or final form. Interface documentation can be stored alongside the code it refers to as discussed in Section 8.2 as an alternative.
- A vendor directory to store third-party code and software tools to build the module.
- A tools directory for the executable files built from src.
- An examples directory to store sample usage patterns and other documents describing algorithms and domain knowledge such as those discussed in Sections 8.4 and 8.5. Often in the form of Jupyter notebooks.
- A .secrets directory for credentials, certificates, authentication tokens and other privileged information that should be stored in encrypted form (for instance, using git-crypt [28]).
- The configuration file of the build system that produces the artefacts (stored in the build directory) and that runs the tests (in test). For instance, a .Makefile.
- A README file with short description of the module.
- A LICENSE file containing the copyright statement and the licence text if the module can be distributed as a self-contained, standalone piece of software.

It is also interesting to consider how these directories and files should be stored in a source version control system (Section 6.5). On the one hand, we can follow Google's "monorepo" approach [269] and store all of them (the code for the whole pipeline) in a single repository. This choice provides unified versioning with a single source of truth, simplifies dependency management, facilitates code reuse and large-scale refactoring spanning multiple modules, and increases code visibility by making it easier to collaborate between different teams of developers. Integration, system and acceptance tests (Section 9.4.4) become more straightforward to implement and to run as well. However, monorepos require more hardware resources and high-quality tooling to navigate code, to modify it and to keep it organised because of the size of the repository.

On the other hand, we can store each module in a separate repository. Cross-module code and configurations are stored in separate "parent" repositories implementing the orchestration and the deployment of the "child" repositories for the modules using tools such as git-repo [129] or meta git [395]. In other words, these "parent" repositories clone, set up and manage the "child" repositories (say, using docker-compose) to give the illusion of working with a monorepo. Individual "child" repositories will be smaller, requiring less hardware resources, and working on individual modules will not require any particular tooling. However, tracking the dependencies between the modules and keeping the dependencies on third-party software consistent across the whole pipeline cannot be automated as easily as in a monorepo: this is an important source of technical debt (Section 5.2) that we should address manually in the "parent" repositories. Navigating the codebase of the whole pipeline requires additional tooling to hide the boundaries between the repositories and to give the appearance of a unified repository. Any task spanning multiple modules is no longer atomic: moving code between modules, splitting or merging modules, or changing the interface of a module along with all the places where that interface is used in other modules can no longer be performed as a single commit in a single repository. Similarly, we are now required to create and maintain "parent" repositories to set up the environment to run integration and system tests. As with many other design choices, there is no optimal solution, just choices with different trade-offs: which one is best for a particular pipeline will depend on how large it is, on how many modules it contains, and on how models are trained and served.

6.5 Effective Versioning

Storing code in a version control system ("versioning" for short) has become a standard practice in software engineering [86, 105], and it benefits machine learning pipelines as much as traditional software. We can track the evolution of code over time, navigating its history and reverting it back to a functioning state if it breaks. We can also track the data, the models and the pipeline configurations together with the code as discussed in Section 5.2.3. Multiple developers can work on the code at the same time, merge their changes, resolve any conflicts that may arise with the help of dedicated tools and produce releases tagged with a semantic versioning scheme [271]. Versioning also ensures that all changes to the code are tracked (for code integrity and developer accountability) and applied by appending them to a read-only ledger of commits (to obtain immutable releases and snapshots). Therefore, versioning provides the "single source of truth" of our code that enables the automated workflows of MLOps (Section 5.3), continuous deployment (Chapter 7), software testing (Section 9.4) and refactoring (Section 6.7).

How can we use versioning to the best effect when working on a machine learning pipeline? Two practices from modern software engineering are especially relevant. Firstly, *keeping the gap between development and production code as small as possible* (often called "dev-prod parity" [406]) to use CI/CD development workflows to best advantage (Section 5.3). Introducing changes in *small, self-contained sets of commits* makes them easy to review (Section 6.6), easy to test for continuous integration (because only a fraction of all tests will be relevant) and makes it possible to merge them into the mainline branch very frequently (say, daily). As a result, changes to the code are immediately visible to all developers allowing them to collaborate effectively. Dividing code into modules stored in separate directories and storing functions implementing different functionality in separate files (Section 6.4) can drastically reduce the likelihood of conflicts: any two developers working on different features are unlikely to modify the same files. However, it cannot completely prevent higher-level problems such as correction cascades (Sections 5.2.2 and 9.1.2) that may arise as the behaviour of various parts of the pipeline change. The best way to both reduce conflicts and detect such problems early is to *only use short-lived branches* that are immediately merged into the mainline branch from which the production releases are cut. Incomplete changes should be hidden behind *feature flags* that prevent new code from running by default and that can be *toggled* easily using environment variables. In other words:

1. Place the existing code we would like to change behind a feature flag that controls whether it is run or not, switched on to keep the code running.
2. Introduce the new code behind the same flag, configuring it to run when the flag is switched off.
3. Test the machine learning software with existing unit, integration and system tests with the flag switched off, checking whether there are any regressions and whether the new code is an improvement over the existing code.
4. If the new code is suitable, remove the existing code and the feature flag. There are tools that do that automatically [376] when flags become stale.

This practice is known as "trunk-based development" [138] ("trunk" being a traditional name for the mainline branch, along with "master"). In the case of machine learning software, we should extend this approach to data and models as well. Versioning both data and models together with the code is crucial to reduce technical debt (Section 5.1) by allowing experiment tracking and reproducible model training. It also makes it possible to construct property-based tests in non-trivial settings by allowing us to match models, their inputs and their outputs (Section 9.4.2). Troubleshooting issues with the pipeline and reverting it to a known good release on botched updates (Section 7.6) also becomes possible, for the same reasons.

Secondly, it is important to *write commit messages that are informative and that follow established conventions*: the Linux Kernel [194] and Git [360] are great examples of how to do this well. A commit message should provide enough context to the changes it describes to understand *what* changes were made, *why* they were made and *why* (not how) they were made in that particular way [370]. Nontrivial code changes usually span multiple files, and often there is no single place where it makes sense to place a comment explaining their rationale. Duplicating that comment in all the places we modified increases the likelihood of stale comments (Section 8.1) because we must remember to update all the copies of that comment at once every time we revisit the code we changed. The natural place to put such information is in the commit message since the commit references all changed files [252]. In any long-running codebase, commit messages might be the only source of information left for future developers to understand changes to the code after the developers who originally made them have left. If practising trunk-based development, we can squash together the commits in our short-lived development branches and only write meaningful commit messages as we merge code into the mainline branch. Furthermore, we should write a short title summarising the change (say, 50–60 characters) followed by a more thorough description. Navigating the history of the code will be much easier because we can now skim through the commit titles and read the detailed commit messages only for those commits that are relevant to us. If we use modern code review practices (Section 6.6), we may also be able to read the comments of the developers who reviewed the commit: they are linked or included in the commit message by all current version control systems when the code is merged. Finally, we may want to include structured information: sign-off lines from the developers who performed code review, labels that identify the commit as part of a series, ticket numbers and their status. All this information can then be processed by CI/CD tools to automate merging and deploying the code in the commit. For reference, Tian et al. [370] discuss in detail the characteristics of "good" commit messages and of their contents for different types of commits.

6.6 Code Review

Code quality is crucial for the effectiveness of a machine learning pipeline: coding styles and standards (Section 6.3), versioning (Section 6.5), refactoring (Section 6.7), testing (Section 9.4), MLOps (Section 5.3) and continuous deployment (Chapter 7) all aim to minimise the number of defects. The increased risk of technical debt (Section 5.2) because of the interplay of data, models and code and because of their mutable nature (Sections 9.1 and 9.2) makes code quality all the more important.

However, the practices and the automated workflows described in this book are not enough in themselves: while they can significantly reduce the number of defects, there are classes of issues that can only be spotted and addressed by the developers themselves. This is the reason for *code review* [298]. Developers other than those who wrote a particular piece of code should inspect it and work together to ensure that:

- It implements the desired functionality.
- It is efficient and accompanied by software tests.
- It follows the spirit and the letter of coding styles, coding standards and naming conventions.
- It is well organised and documented.

The benefits are many:

- We ensure that each developer writes code that other developers can understand.
- Exchanging constructive criticism is a valuable way of teaching junior and future developers.
- More people working on the machine learning pipeline will have a practical understanding of its design, making it more likely to find ways to improve it.
- We encourage a feeling of collective ownership of the code.

Clearly, each module will have a primary "owner" who is ultimately responsible for it and controls what changes are merged into the mainline branch. That developer will be the ideal reviewer for changes to that module because he will be the person who knows its code and design best. However, other people should feel comfortable contributing to it, fixing it, and providing feedback on the quality and design of the code. At the same time nobody should be able to commit code without oversight, which code review provides.

Reviewing code is usually performed in two complementary ways:

- Taking advantage of *code review tools* [306, 372]: the developer proposing a code change prepares a commit and submits it to some software tool that tests it and then assigns it to one or more reviewers. The review itself is asynchronous and informal in nature, with developer and reviewers exchanging comments and refining code via the tool until they are satisfied with the commit's quality. The tool then merges the commit into the mainline branch, linking the comments in the commit message.

· Practising *pair (mob) programming* [267, 335] while developing software: two (or more) developers write, debug, or explore code together. One of the developers (the "driver") is responsible for the implementation, focusing on writing high-quality and error-free code. The other developer(s) (the "navigators") focus on the broader scope of the problem and on keeping the process on track. The navigator(s) in practice act as reviewers "live" as the code is written. At fairly short intervals (say, 30 minutes), the current "driver" commits the code it is working on and passes the role to another developer, who will pull the code and become the next "navigator".

Both approaches encourage writing small incremental changes and submitting them frequently, like in trunk-based development (Section 6.5): it is difficult to find experienced reviewers with a deep knowledge of larger portions of a machine learning pipeline, and it is more difficult for reviewers to find the time to review a large piece of code. Ideally, the code to be reviewed should address a single issue and do that completely, involving just one or two reviewers. This makes it easier to identify where errors were introduced if something goes wrong and to roll back just the offending change.

In a tool-based code review setting, the developer writing the code should first perform a personal code review in order not to waste the reviewers' time. Having code automatically tested by linters, static code analysers and our suite of software tests before sending it out for review will also speed code review iterations up: the reviewer will be presented with their outputs to help examine the commit. For the same reason, the developer should add comments to the code (Section 8.1) and write a descriptive commit message (Section 6.5) covering the reason for the proposed change, its possible impact and any relevant design decisions.

With pair and mob programming, repeatedly rotating the "driver" and "navigator" roles effectively ensures that the code is reviewed, and helps in engaging more developers with the code. Domain experts can be involved as well: even if they have only marginal familiarity with programming, they can be guided by developers when they are acting as the "driver"; and they can contribute their knowledge to the developer writing code when they are acting as the "navigator". However, this approach works smoothly only if development environments can be set up quickly and if pulling and pushing code is effortless: frequent and smooth role transitions are crucial in keeping everybody engaged and discussing with each other, which is the main point of this approach. Particularly hard coding tasks benefit the most from having more eyeballs looking at problems and collaborating on both the low- and high-level design of the code.

Both approaches to code review require effort and an initial investment to establish as a standard practice but they will pay themselves back by making developers more productive. And, perhaps unlike other practices, the overwhelming majority of programmers enjoy them [306, 411]! Tool-based review processes require the appropriate tooling to be well-maintained and scalable. Pair and mob programming require developers to coordinate and to spend time together working on the same piece of code. But that does not mean that the people involved will be less productive.

In the case of tool-based code review, one or at most two developers are sufficient to review a commit, and if the commit touches only one or two files, the reviewers can easily provide feedback within a few hours or a day at most [298, 306]. Developers will produce increasingly better code over time, resulting in faster reviews and fewer comments on each commit. Bugs and architectural issues will be identified quickly, so they will be easier and faster to fix [371]. As a result, we will reduce the need for large-scale refactorings and outright code rewrites, leaving more time to write better code, tests and documentation. (By definition, this means productivity will increase over time since we will make progress faster instead of running in circles.) In addition, senior developers will widen their understanding of the architecture of the machine learning pipeline as they review code for different modules. Furthermore, reviewing patches does not have to be time-consuming for the reviewer: at Google, developers review about 4 commits in 2.6 hours (median) per week, taking about 40 minutes per commit [306]; at Microsoft, developers devote 20 minutes per day (1.6 hours per week) on average to code review [161].

We can make similar considerations for pair and mob programming: several studies over the last 30 years [77, 321, 411], including some on machine learning software and data science applications [307], have found that they improve productivity and code quality. For them to be most effective, we need tasks that are complex enough to warrant the attention of more than one person (trivial tasks have little margin for errors) and enough experience to address them effectively in the pair (either a senior and a junior developer, or two "intermediate" developers) or in the mob [24, 267].

6.7 Refactoring

Formally, *refactoring* is the process of changing a piece of code in a way that does not alter its external behaviour yet improves its internal structure and clarifies its intent and assumptions [105]. Following Section 6.5, we do that with a sequence of small incremental changes which are individually validated by running our suite of tests (Chapter 9.4) with continuous integration tools. At the end of the process, we can squash all the commits together and submit them for review (Chapter 6.6) as we do for other code changes. We refactor when adding a new feature, to alter the design of the existing code and accommodate it. We refactor when attacking bugs, both to fix them and to accommodate the tests that exercise them (and ensure that they stay fixed). We refactor to improve compliance with naming conventions (Section 6.2), coding styles and coding standards (Section 6.3). Refactoring can make us confident that we start each commit from correct code, making it easy to track any bugs we might introduce, and that the code does not spend much time (if at all) in a broken state.

Fowler [105] provides an extensive catalogue of refactoring approaches. Depending on the programming language, some can be automated: for example, both PyCharm [166] and Visual Studio Code [220] have a "refactor" button for Python code. (This is another factor we may want to consider when choosing a programming language in addition to those we discussed in Section 6.1.) Only a few of them are commonly used for machine learning code, and there are refactoring approaches that are specific to it: Tang et al. [339] constructed a taxonomy of both from a large survey of machine learning software. Machine learning code is only a small part of a typical pipeline, so mastering the refactoring approaches from Fowler [105] is still valuable to address the code smells we discussed in Section 6.3. Refactoring approaches that are specific to machine learning code, on the other hand, keep in check the various types of technical debt we covered in Section 5.2.4. Tang et al. [339] point out three in particular: using inheritance to reduce duplicate configuration and model code; changing variable types and data structures to allow for performance optimisations (Sections 3.3 and 3.4); and hiding the raw model parameters and hyperparameters and exposing custom types that have a domain meaning to achieve better separation between training and inference on one side and general metaheuristics and domain rules on the other.

There is, however, an additional point that makes the code implementing machine learning models inherently different from other code as far as refactoring is concerned: we cannot slice and dice it in the process of refactoring it as easily as we would other code. Some models perform a single task (say, smoothing or prediction) and compose well with other code, but others are black-boxes that integrate multiple tasks (say, feature extraction and prediction) in ways that make it impossible to split them. Deep neural networks are a prime example of this. And even if we can refactor a model and the associated code into well-separated sub-models, it is not a given that we can change them as we would like. The probabilistic properties of each sub-model are inherited from the model we started from: we should make sure that the probabilistic properties of any new sub-model we introduce are compatible with those of the others. Failing to do so will produce outputs that are biased in ways that are difficult to diagnose and impossible to correct because they lack the mathematical properties we usually take for granted. (The same is true for swapping whole models in an existing pipeline.) A possibly obvious example: we should match a model that uses a quadratic loss function, such as most linear regressions, with feature selection and extraction that work on variances and linear correlations and with model selection strategies that evaluate models using the same quadratic loss function on a validation set. If we extract features in ways that do not necessarily preserve linear dependencies, we may lose information that the model could capture from the data. If we evaluate the model with a different loss function than that it was optimised for, we may end up with a fragile model that will misbehave easily on new data. In other words, *refactoring a machine learning model means refactoring both the code implementing it and its mathematical formulation at the same time.* We want to preserve both the external behaviour of the code and the probabilistic behaviour of the inputs and the outputs of the model. Property–based testing can help with the latter, as we will discuss in Section 9.4.2.

6.8 Reworking Academic Code: An Example

Consider the following piece of code used in teaching machine learning to graduate students at a top–10 university in the QS rankings [283]. It is fairly representative of what we can find in many GitHub repositories and in many answers in Stack Overflow, which end up imported or cut-and-pasted in machine learning codebases.

```R
f<-function(x,mu1,mu2,S1i,S2i,p1=0.5) {
  #mixture of normals, density up to constant factor
  c1<-exp(-t(x-mu1)%*%S1i%*%(x-mu1))
  c2<-exp(-t(x-mu2)%*%S2i%*%(x-mu2))
  return(p1*c1+(1-p1)*c2)
}
```

```
a=3
n=2000
mu1=c(1,1)
mu2=c(4,4)
S=diag(2)
S1i=S2i=solve(S)
X=matrix(NA,2,n)
X[,1]=x=mu1
for (t in 1:(n-1)) {
y<-x+(2*runif(2)-1)*a
MHR<-f(y,mu1,mu2,S1i,S2i)/f(x,mu1,mu2,S1i,S2i)
if (runif(1)<MHR)
x<-y
X[,t+1]<-x
}
```

Guessing what this code is supposed to implement is harder than it should be, because functions and variables have nondescript names that mirror some mathematical notation. This does not help in itself since there is no comment in the code giving a literature reference we could use to look up what the notation is. The only hints we have are a comment mentioning mixtures of normals and a variable named MHR.

Attending the lecture this code was presented in would tell us that this code implements the Metropolis-Hasting algorithm for sampling from a mixture of normals. Knowing this, we can give more descriptive names to both functions and variables: naming some of the variables after their *de facto* standard notation [say, from 204] is an acceptable trade-off between conciseness and clarity. We can now guess that MHR is the Metropolis-Hastings ratio used to accept or reject a new random sample from the mixture. At the same time, we can add spacing and indentation to make the code easier to read.

R

```r
dmix2norm = function(x, mu, Sigma, pi, log = FALSE) {

  Omega1 = MASS::ginv(Sigma[1:2, 1:2])
  Omega2 = MASS::ginv(Sigma[3:4, 3:4])

  elem1 = exp(-t(x - mu[1]) %*% Omega1 %*% (x - mu[1]))
  elem2 = exp(-t(x - mu[2]) %*% Omega2 %*% (x - mu[2]))

  return(pi[1] * elem1 + pi[2] * elem2)

}#DMIX2NORM

metropolis.hastings = function(mu, Sigma, pi, iter) {

  X = matrix(NA, 2, iter)
  X[, 1] = old = mu[1:2]
  for (t in seq(iter - 1)) {

    new = old + (2 * runif(2) - 1) * a
    acceptance.probability =
      dmix2norm(new, mu = mu, Sigma = Sigma, pi = pi) /
      dmix2norm(old, mu = mu, Sigma = Sigma, pi = pi)

    if (runif(1) < acceptance.probability)
      old = new
    else
      old = old

    X[, t + 1] = old

  }#FOR

  return(X)

}#METROPOLIS.HASTINGS
```

```
mu = c(c(1, 1), c(4, 4))
Sigma = diag(rep(1, 4))
pi = c(0.5, 0.5)
metropolis.hastings(mu = mu, Sigma = Sigma, pi = pi, iter = 2000)
```

We complete this first refactoring step by creating a temporary (local) commit and testing it. While better organised and easier to read, this code falls short of what it purports to do in two ways: the number of components in the mixture is hard-coded to two, and the densities themselves are hard-coded to be normals. Now that we have organised the code into functions, we can move on to the next refactoring step: adding two arguments to metropolis.hastings() to allow the user to control the definition of the mixture. We can call them density, for the density function to be called for each component of the mixture, and density.args, a list of additional arguments to that function. To keep the existing behaviour of the code, we update dmix2norm() to work with more than two components while making sure that its return value remains unchanged when the mixture has only two components. Furthermore, we do the same for the proposal function that generates the new random sample, adding two further arguments proposal and proposal.args to metropolis.hastings().

These changes make the code more flexible and more readable. The functional programming approach we have adopted allows us to rewrite metropolis.hastings() in such a way that it almost looks like pseudocode (Section 4.1). As a result, there is less of a need for comments on *what* the code is doing, apart from a reference to some textbook in which we can find the pseudocode for Metropolis-Hastings and an in-depth explanation of how and why it works. Comments on *why* the code is structured the way it is may of course still be useful, since they will contain information that

is specific to this particular implementation and that
cannot be found anywhere else.

```r
dmix2norm = function(x, mu, Sigma, pi, log = FALSE) {                    R

  nmix = length(mu)
  mixture.component.density = function(x, mu, Sigma)
    exp(-t(x - mu[1]) %*% MASS::ginv(Sigma) %*% (x - mu[1]))

  comp = sapply(seq(nmix), function(i)
          mixture.component.density(x, mu[[i]], Sigma[[i]]))

  return(sum(pi * comp))

}#DMIX2NORM

proposal.update = function(dim = 2, a) {

  return((2 * runif(dim) - 1) * a)

}#PROPOSAL.UPDATE

metropolis.hastings = function(density, density.args, proposal,
                              proposal.args, pi, start, iter) {

  X = matrix(NA, length(start), iter)
  X[, 1] = old = start
  for (t in seq(iter - 1)) {

    new = old +
      do.call(proposal, c(list(dim = nrow(X)), proposal.args))

    update.threshold =
      do.call(density, c(list(x = new, pi = pi), density.args)) /
      do.call(density, c(list(x = old, pi = pi), density.args))

    if (runif(1) < update.threshold)
```

```
      old = new
    else
      old = old

    X[, t + 1] = old

  }#FOR

  return(X)

}#METROPOLIS.HASTINGS

mu = list(c(1, 1), c(4, 4))
Sigma = list(diag(2), diag(2))
metropolis.hastings(density = dmix2norm,
  density.args = list(mu = mu, Sigma = Sigma),
  proposal = proposal.update, proposal.args = list(a = 3),
  pi = c(0.5, 0.5), start = c(2, 2), iter = 2000)
```

We create one more temporary commit and test whether
the code is still working. Finally, we want to make the
code more reusable. In order to do that, we store the
instance of the Metropolis–Hastings simulation we run
in metropolis.hastings() into a data structure that
contains both the random samples that we generated
and the functions that we passed via the density
and proposal arguments to generate them, along
with the respective argument sets density.args and
proposal.args. For convenience, we assign the class
name "metropolis-hastings" to this data structure to
be able to write methods for it later.

```
metropolis.hastings = function(density, density.args, proposal,      R
                               proposal.args, pi, start, iter) {

  [...]
```

```
  return(structure(list(values = X, call = match.call(),
           density = density, density.args = density.args,
           proposal = proposal, proposal.args = proposal.args,
           start = start), class = "metropolis.hastings"))

}#METROPOLIS.HASTINGS
```

If we are satisfied with how the code now looks (or we have other stuff to do), we can create one last temporary commit and squash it together with the previous two. A suitable commit message for the new commit could be:

```
Refactoring Metropolis-Hastings mixture of Gaussians.

* Clarify function and variable names, following Bayesian Essentials
    with R (Marin and Robert, 2014).
* Switch to a functional implementation that takes arbitrary density
    functions as arguments, each with separate optional arguments.
* Store the simulation in an S3 object, to allow for methods.
```

Before submitting this commit for code review, we should write some unit tests to exercise the new functional interface of metropolis.hastings(). We will discuss this topic at length in Chapter 9: for the moment, let's say we want to ensure that metropolis.hastings() only accepts valid values for all its arguments. For this purpose, we add code to sanitise them and to produce informative error messages along the lines of

```
if (missing(density))                                                    R
  stop("missing a 'density' a function, with no default.")
if (!is.function(density))
  stop("the 'density' argument must be a density function.")
```

and then we add tests to check that valid values are accepted and invalid values are rejected.

```
error = try(metropolis.hastings(density = dmix2norm, [...]))            R
stopifnot(!is(error, "try-error"))
```

```r
error = try(metropolis.hastings(density = "not.a.function", [...]))
stopifnot(is(error, "try-error"))
```

We should do the same for the function passed via the proposal argument. Furthermore, we should call both functions with the respective lists of optional arguments density.args and proposal.args to make sure that they execute successfully: individual argument values may look fine in isolation, but make metropolis.hastings() fail when passed together. As an example, the code to sanitise proposal.args may look like

```r
if (missing(proposal.args))                                           R
  proposal.args = list()
if (!is.list(proposal.args))
  stop("the 'proposal.args' argument must be a list.")
```

where we set proposal.args to an empty list as a fallback, default choice if the user does not provide it. The code to sanitise both proposal and proposal.args can then check that the proposal function runs and that its output has the right type and dimension.

```r
try.proposal = try(do.call(proposal, proposal.args))                  R
if (is(try.proposal, "try-error"))
  stop("the 'proposal' function fails to run with ",
       "the arguments in 'proposal.args'.")
if (!is.numeric(try.proposal) ||
    (length(try.proposal) != length(start)))
  stop("the 'proposal' function returns invalid samples.")
```

The tests that exercise this code should call metropolis.hastings() with and without valid proposal functions, and with proposal functions with valid and invalid sets of optional arguments.

As another example, we should check the number of iterations in the iter argument, picking again a sensible default value.

```r
  if (missing(iter))
    iter = 10
  if (!is.numeric(iter) || ((x %/% 1) == x))
    stop("the 'iter' argument must be a non-negative integer.")
```

The corresponding software tests can then try boundary values (0), valid values (10), invalid values (Inf) and special values (NaN) to confirm that the sanitisation code is working as expected.

```r
error = try(metropolis.hastings([...], iter = 0)
stopifnot(!is(error, "try-error"))
error = try(metropolis.hastings([...], iter = 10)
stopifnot(!is(error, "try-error"))
error = try(metropolis.hastings([...], iter = Inf)
stopifnot(is(error, "try-error"))
error = try(metropolis.hastings([...], iter = NaN)
stopifnot(is(error, "try-error"))
```

The sanitisation code should be included in one commit, and the tests in another: they will be in different files and have different purposes, so it would be inappropriate to commit them together. After doing that, our new implementation of Metropolis–Hastings is ready to be submitted for code review.

7

Packaging and Deploying Pipelines

Packaging machine learning models into artefacts is an important step in making pipelines reproducible. It also makes models easier to deploy, that is, to bring them into production (or another target) systems and to put them to use. Choosing the right combination of *packaging formats* and *deployment strategies* ensures that we can build on CI/CD solutions [86] to do that efficiently and effectively. Our ultimate goal is to ship a pipeline with confidence because we have designed (Chapter 5), implemented (Chapter 6), documented (Chapter 8) and tested it well (Chapter 9).

Models are part of a machine learning pipeline as much as code is, and are packaged (Section 7.1) and deployed (Sections 7.2 and 7.3) in similar ways to traditional software. However, their behaviour is less predictable (Sections 5.2 and 9.2): we should monitor them when they are deployed and when they are running in production (Section 7.4). We should also have contingency plans for when they fail (Section 7.5) so that we can restore the pipeline to a functional state (Section 7.6).

7.1 Model Packaging

Models can be stored into different types of artefacts, as we briefly discussed in Section 5.3.4. There are several ways in which model artefacts can be integrated into a pipeline, with varying degrees of abstraction from the underlying machine learning systems.

7.1.1 Standalone Packaging

The most minimalist form of packaging is simply the artefact produced by the machine learning framework that we used to train the model: for instance, a SavedModel file from TensorFlow [341] or an ONNX [247] file. Such files are easy to make available to third parties and convenient to embed in a library or in a (desktop or mobile) application with frameworks like Apple Core ML [21]. They can also be shipped as standalone packages via a generic artefact registry such as those offered by GitHub [113], GitLab [115] or Nexus [328]. Tracking the version of the trained model, its parameters, its configurations and its dependencies is delegated to the configuration management platform supporting the pipeline (Section 5.3.5).

7.1.2 Programming Language Package Managers

Python has become the most popular programming language in machine learning applications because of the availability of mature and versatile frameworks such as TensorFlow [341] and PyTorch [259] (Section 6.1). As a result, it is increasingly common to ship models as Python packages to simplify the deployment process, and to make the model depend on a specific version of the Python interpreter and of those frameworks. Doing so throughout the pipeline helps avoid the technical debt arising from polyglot programming (Section 5.2.4). In practice, this involves distributing packages, modules and resource files following the Python standard (known as "Distribution Package"), using tools like Setuptools [278] and Pip [280] to install them, and possibly

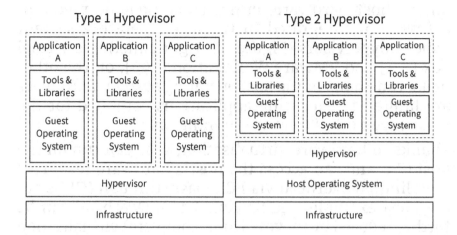

FIGURE 7.1 Type-1 and type-2 hypervisor virtualisation architectures.

uploading them to the central Python Package Index to make them easily accessible.

7.1.3 Virtual Machines

All modern CPUs (Section 2.1.1) implement instruction sets to support hardware virtualisation: for instance, Intel CPUs have Virtualisation Technology (VT-x) and AMD CPUs have AMD-V. This has made *virtual machines* (VMs, also known as "guest operating systems") a convenient choice on local hardware and resulted in the wide availability of cloud instances. VMs run on top of a *hypervisor*, a specialised software allowing multiple guest systems to share a single compute system (the host hardware). A VM is like a normal compute system: the main difference is that its CPU, memory, storage and network interfaces are shared with the underlying hardware through the hypervisor which allocates them to the guests as needed. vSphere [389], KVM [249] and HyperV [219] are some examples of type-1 hypervisors (Figure 7.1, left panel): they run directly on the host hardware, either as standalone pieces of software or integrated in the host operating system. Type-2 hypervisors (Figure 7.1, right panel) like Virtual box [251] and VMware Workstation [390], on the other hand, run on top of the host operating system. Both types are limited to executing applications compiled for the same type of CPU they are running on.

Thanks to hardware virtualisation, VMs can run on the host CPU and can access the host's hardware resources with limited overhead via PCIe pass-through (GPUs are a typical example, see Section 2.1.1). Overhead can be further reduced by moving from (complete) virtualisation to *paravirtualisation*, which trades off complete isolation of the guests for better throughput and latency. The guest operating system is now aware of running in a virtualised environment, and it can use a special set system of calls (*hypercalls*) and I/O drivers (especially for storage and networking) to communicate directly with the hypervisor.

VMs are the second type of artefact we mentioned in Section 5.3.4. We can either create them from scratch, installing and configuring the operating system and all the libraries we need, or we can start from *pre-baked images* that come configured with most of the software we need. For the former, we have tools like Hashicorp Packer [143] or Vagrant [146], which can install the operating system, and configuration management software like Ansible [18], which can install the models as well as the software stack they depend on. As for the latter, a vast selection of pre-baked images is available from cloud providers: an example is the catalogue of Amazon Machine Images (AMIs) [13]. VM configurations and images are typically stored in a standardised open format such as the Open Virtualisation Format (OVF) [81]. Finally, VMs can be managed automatically by the orchestrator of the machine learning pipeline through the hypervisor and the associated software tools, which can create, clone, snapshot, start and stop individual VMs.

VMs offer three main advantages:

- They are *flexible to operate*: we can run multiple instances of different operating systems and of different software stacks on the same host, consolidating their configurations using pre-baked images and managing them centrally as individual entities.
- They can also be easily scaled to deal with peak loads, both by starting new ones (*horizontal scalability*) or by increasing the hardware resources they have access to (*vertical scalability*, Section 2.4).
- They can be moved to another host (*portability*) and are easy to snapshot, facilitating disaster recovery in the case of hardware failure.

However, VMs have one important disadvantage: they contain an entire operating system and therefore require large amounts of hot storage. As a result, the deployment time of a VM can range from tens of seconds (in the best case) to minutes (in the average case) [139], depending on the cloud provider or the on-premises hypervisor configuration.

7.1.4 Containers

In contrast, *containers* are more lightweight [93] because they only virtualise the libraries and the applications running on top of the operating system, not an entire machine learning system (Figure 7.2). Instead of a hypervisor, they are managed by a *container runtime* (sometimes called a "container engine") like Docker [82] which controls the access to the hardware and to the operating system of the host.

Container runtimes are typically built on top of a set of Linux kernel capabilities [297]:

- *Namespaces*: an isolation layer that allows each process to see and access only those processes, directories and

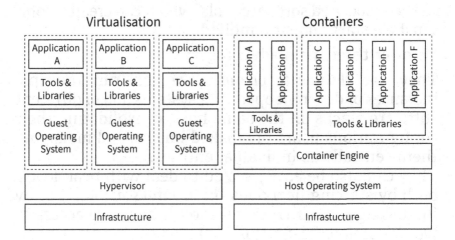

FIGURE 7.2 Virtualisation and containers high-level architectures.

system resources of the host that are bound to the same namespace it is running in.

- *Cgroups (control groups)*: a resource management layer that sets and limits CPU, memory and network bandwidth for a collection of processes.
- *Seccomp (secure computing)*: a security layer that limits a container to a restricted subset of system calls (the kernel's APIs).

As was the case with VMs, containers can package machine learning applications with all the associated libraries, dependencies and tools in a single self-contained artefact: a *container image* which is immutable, stateless and ephemeral by design.[1] In the case of Docker, we commonly refer to it as a *Docker image*. Container

---

[1]Containers are *ephemeral* in the sense that they should be built with the expectation that they may go down at any time. Therefore, they should be easy to (re)create and to destroy, and they should be *stateless*: any valuable information they contain will be irrevocably lost when they are destroyed. These characteristics make them a key tool in "The Twelve-Factor App" [406] and other modern software engineering practices.

images are created from declarative configuration files, also known as Dockerfiles, that define all the necessary commands. Each command produces an immutable *layer* reflecting the changes that the command itself introduces into the image, allowing for incremental changes and minimising disk space usage. The starting point of this process are *base images* that provide a stripped-down environment (not a complete operating system, as was the case for pre-baked VM images) to which we can add our models and the libraries, tools and applications that complement them.

Below is an example of a Dockerfile that creates an image for a FastAPI RESTful application (a framework to create web services and APIs). For reproducibility, both the Dockerfile and the requirements.txt file it references should be stored under version control in a configuration management platform (Section 6.4).

```
FROM python:3.10.6-bullseye                              Docker

WORKDIR /app

COPY requirements.txt .
RUN pip3 install --no-cache-dir -r requirements.txt

COPY . .

CMD [ "uvicorn", "main:app", "--host=0.0.0.0"]
```

Firstly, the Dockerfile explicitly identifies the system dependencies of the image it generates. The first line, "FROM python:3.10.5-bullseye" identifies a base image with the stable release of Debian GNU/Linux, codenamed "Bullseye", and version 3.10.5 of the Python interpreter. Secondly, it identifies the Python packages we depend on. The third and fourth lines, "COPY requirements.txt ." and "RUN pip3 install -r requirements.txt", copy the file requirements.txt which lists the Python dependencies into the image and uses the Python package manager (pip) to install them. It is important that all dependencies are listed and pinned to the exact versions we have tested, to avoid accruing technical debt (Sections 5.2.4 and 6.3). If we upgrade one or more dependencies, the corresponding container layer is invalidated. Docker caches layers as they are created: those that have not been affected by our changes will be taken from that cache instead of being re-created from scratch. The second line ("WORKDIR /app") changes the working directory to that containing the application files, the fifth line ("COPY . .") copies them into the container image, and the last line defines the command that is run when the container is started.

After a successful build, we can store containers into a *container registry* such as Docker registry [83] or Harbour [140]. Container registries are server applications that provide a standardised API for uploading (push), versioning (tag) and downloading (pull) container images. The registry structure is organised into repositories (like Git [360]) where each repository holds all the versions of a specific container image. The container's runtime, registry and image specifications are based on the Open Container Initiative (OCI) [248], an open standard by the Linux Foundation, and are therefore highly portable across platforms and vendors.

Like any other software artefact, container images may have security vulnerabilities [39] inherited from vulnerable libraries in an outdated base image, rogue images in an untrusted container registry or a vulnerable Dockerfile. To identify these vulnerabilities, we should enforce *compliance and security checks* to validate both the Dockerfiles, with tools such as Hadolint [361], and the resulting images, with static analysis and image scanner tools such as Trivy [22]. Cloud providers such as Amazon AWS [316] and Google Cloud [126] have public container registries with secure and tested base images ranging from vanilla operating system installations to pre-configured machine learning stacks built on TensorFlow [341] and PyTorch [259].

Container runtimes integrate with orchestrators to allow for a seamless use of container images. The orchestrator is responsible for managing a fleet of containers in terms of deployment, scaling, networking and security policies. The containers are responsible for providing different pieces of functionality as modular and decoupled services that communicate over the network, that can be deployed independently and that are highly observable. This is, in essence, the microservices architecture [239]. In addition, container runtimes integrate with CI to enable reproducible software testing: base container images provide a clean environment that ensures that test results are not tainted by external factors (Section 9.4 and 10.3).

Kubernetes [364] is the de facto standard among orchestrators.[2] Orchestrators specialising in machine learning pipelines integrate Kubernetes with experiment tracking and model serving to provide complete MLOps solutions: two examples are Kubeflow [363], which is more integrated, and MLflow [420], which is more programmatic. Container runtimes enhance them by implementing a GPU pass-through from the physical host to the container (with the "--gpus" flag, in the case of Docker). Kubernetes can use this functionality to apply the appropriate *label selector* [365] to each container and to schedule training and inference workloads on machine learning systems with the appropriate hardware (Section 2.1.1).

---

[2]A group of one or more containers that encapsulates an application is called a "pod" in the Kubernetes documentation.

7.2 Model Deployment: Strategies

A *deployment strategy* or *deployment pattern* is a technique to replace or upgrade an artefact or a service in a production environment while minimising downtime and impact on users. Here we will focus on how we can deploy machine learning models (Section 5.3.5) without impacting their consumers, that is, the final users and the modules in the pipeline that depend on the models' outputs. Clearly, there are similarities to how traditional software is deployed: we want automated and reproducible releases via CI/CD, in most cases using containers as artefacts (Section 7.1.4). Furthermore, parts of a machine learning pipeline are in fact traditional software and are deployed as such.

Model deployment can take advantage of modern software deployment strategies from *progressive delivery*. A pipeline will usually contain multiple instances of each model (say, version A) to be able to process multiple inference requests and data preparation queues in parallel. Therefore, we can initially replace a small subset of these instances with a new model (say, version B). If no issues emerge, we then gradually replace the remaining instances: the new model has effectively passed acceptance testing (Section 9.4.4). If any issues do arise, our logging and monitoring facilities (Section 5.3.6) will have recorded the information we need to troubleshoot them. We can also deploy multiple models at the same time to compare their performance in terms of accuracy, throughput and latency. As a result, progressive delivery speeds up model deployment (by reducing the amount of pre-deployment testing), decreases deployment risk (because most consumers will not be impacted by any issues that may emerge in the initial deployment) and makes rollbacks easier (Section 7.6).

We can implement progressive delivery with a number of related deployment strategies [373]:

- The *blue-green* deployment pattern [153] assumes that we are using a router (typically a load balancer) to spread requests over a pool of instances that serve the version A of a machine learning model (Figure 7.3, left). When we deploy a new version B of the model, we create a second pool of instances that serves it and send a subset of the new incoming requests to this new pool. If no issues arise, the router will then gradually send more and more requests to the pool that serves model B instead of that serving model A. Existing requests being processed by model A are allowed to complete to avoid disruptions. The pool serving model A will eventually not be assigned any more requests and may then be decommissioned. If any issues arise, rollback is simple: we can send all requests to the pool serving model A again. Keeping the two pools in separate environments or even separate machine learning systems will further reduce deployment risk.
- We already mentioned the *canary* deployment pattern [153] in Section 5.3.4: the main difference with the blue-green pattern is that we deploy instances with model B in the same pool that is already serving model A (Figure 7.3, top tight). The router will redirect a small number of requests to the instances with model B, taking care of session affinity.[3] Other requests act as our *control group*: we can inspect and compare the performance of the two models without any bias because they run in the same environment. Again, if no

---

[3]Each consumer or user is always served the same version of the model. This happens implicitly in the blue-green deployment pattern because each consumer or user is assigned to a pool, and all instances within each pool serve the same model.

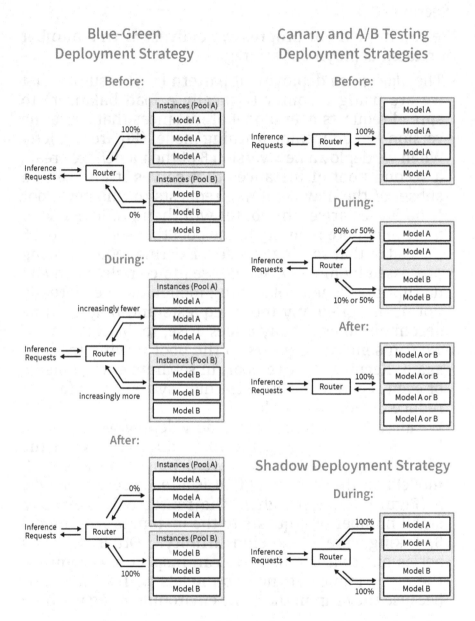

FIGURE 7.3 Blue-green (left), canary and A/B testing (top right) and shadow (bottom right) deployment strategies.

issues arise we can gradually retire the instances with model A. Canary deployments are typically slower than other deployment patterns because collecting enough data on the performance of model B with a small number of instances requires time. However, they provide an easy way to test new models in production with real data and in the same environment as existing models.

- In a *shadow* deployment [218], a new model B is deployed in parallel to model A and each request is sent to both models (Figure 7.3, bottom right). We can compare their accuracy using the outputs they produce from the same input, as well as their latency and any other metric we collect through logging and monitoring. In fact, we can deploy several models in parallel to test different approaches and keep only the model that performs best. Shadow deployment therefore requires us to set up a different API endpoint for each model we are testing, and to allocate enough hardware resources to handle the increased inference workload. However, it allows for testing new models without disturbing operations.
- In the *rolling* or *ramped* deployment pattern, we simply replace the instances with model A in batches on a pre-determined schedule until all the running instances are serving model B. Rolling deployments are easy both to schedule and to roll back.
- Another deployment pattern we mentioned elsewhere (Sections 5.3.4 and 9.4.3) is *A/B testing* [7, 425]: the router randomly splits the requests 50%–50% across two models A and B, we evaluate the relevant metrics for each model, and we promote model B if and only if it outperforms model A. The key difference from canary deployments is that in the latter only a small proportion of the requests is sent to instances with model B to reduce deployment risk: the split is 90%–10% or at most 80%–20% (Figure 7.3, top right).
- *Destroy and re-create* is the most basic deployment strategy: we stop all the instances with model A and

we create from scratch a new set of instances with model B to deploy in their place. As a result, the pipeline will be unavailable and consumers that are performing multiple requests in a sequence may receive inconsistent outputs.

We can integrate these deployment patterns by adding feature flags (Section 6.5) to our models: then models A and B can share large portions of code. In this way, we can easily create new models just by switching different combinations of flags, without building and deploying new artefacts at all. However, both models will be served at the same time during the progressive delivery process: all consumers should support both their APIs or model B should be fully backward compatible with model A.

7.3   Model Deployment: Infrastructure

In a machine learning pipeline, model deployment is the part of the pipeline orchestration that enables models to be deployed and served in the development, testing and production environments (Section 5.3.5). Ideally, it should be completely automated via CI/CD to avoid catastrophic failures like that at Knight Capital [317] which we touched on in Section 5.2.3.

The nature of the continuous deployment part of CI/CD can vary depending on the type of artefact (Section 7.1) and on the type of compute systems (Section 2.4) we are deploying to. Our artefacts may be container images that wrap and serve our models through APIs: we can deploy them locally by manually invoking Docker, or remotely by instructing Kubernetes to call an automated script stored in the pipeline's CI/CD configuration. In both cases, the image is fetched from the registry at deployment time if it is not available locally. Our artefacts may also be VMs: continuous deployment can then leverage configuration management tools like Ansible [18] to deploy and upgrade them. In both these cases, the CI/CD pipeline standardises the deployment process, hiding the differences between local and cloud environments (Section 2.3) and shifting complexity from glue code to declarative configuration files (Sections 5.2.3). This has standardised the deployment process to the point where it is largely the same to target orchestrator platforms like Kubernetes [364] and commercial providers like Amazon AWS ECS.

We may also run machine learning pipelines on top of an integrated MLOps platform: model deployment then depends entirely on the platform's opinionated work-flows. For example, an MLOps platform like Databricks [76] integrates many open-source components through MLflow [420] and wraps them with APIs that support multiple deployment targets. These APIs present a stan-dardised interface similar to that of Docker and Kuber-netes regardless of what target we choose. Machine learning platforms from cloud vendors ("Machine Learning as a Service") like Azure ML [214] or Amazon AWS SageMaker [11] provide a much higher level of abstraction. On the one hand, they give us little control over how the pipeline is implemented and how models are deployed. On the other hand, they are accessible for teams that do not have the skills or the budget to manage their own CI/CD, monitoring and logging infrastructure. They also provide an experiment tracking web interface (with an API to use it programmatically) to test new models and to visualise them along with their parame-ters and performance metrics.

7.4 Model Deployment: Monitoring and Logging

We should track automated model deployments through all their stages with our logging and monitoring infrastructure to achieve the observability we need to diagnose any issue we may run into (Section 5.3.6). All continuous deployment platforms allow that: MLflow [420] has MLflow tracking, Airflow [348] can use Fluentd [359] and general-purpose CI/CD solutions like GitLab have built-in mechanisms for issuing metrics and log events as well as support for Prometheus [275]. It is essential to log every entry and exit point of every module, as well as any retries and the successful conclusion of all tasks in the pipeline: we should be able to construct descriptive activity reports that include comprehensive stack traces. Machine learning pipelines have many moving parts and can fail in many different places and in ways that are difficult to diagnose even with that much information (Sections 9.1, 9.2 and 9.3). Furthermore, logging should automatically trigger external notification systems like PagerDuty [255] to become aware of any issues during deployment as early as possible.

After a model is deployed, we should check that it is being served, that it is ready to accept inference requests (readiness) and that it produces correct results (liveness). The software that we use to serve the model may expose a health-check API (like the readiness and liveness probes in Kubernetes [364]) which the orchestrator can use to only route inference requests to models that can to process them. The monitoring client inside the model itself can serve the same purpose by exposing metrics to check that performance has not degraded over time. As we discussed in Section 5.3.6, we should locate the logging and monitoring servers on dedicated systems to make sure that they are not affected by any of the issues caused by or affecting the models and that they can be used to perform a root cause analysis of what went wrong.

7.5 What Can Possibly Go Wrong?

Many kinds of issues can arise when we deploy a new model, for different reasons: lack of control or observability for either the deployment process or its targets (Section 2.4); manually executing pre- or post-deployment operations (Section 5.2.3); or a critical defect in a model or in a module slipping through our software test suite (Section 9.4). We can minimise deployment risk by taking advantage of CI/CD (Chapter 5) and following modern development practices (Chapter 6), but some problems cannot be fully resolved or even detected automatically.

Hardware resources may be unavailable. The environment we are deploying to may be running on machine learning systems that have inadequate resources (say, not enough storage space or memory), hardware faults or network connectivity issues (say, the systems themselves are unreachable, or they cannot access remote third-party resources needed by the model).[4] These problems can occur both in local (on-premises) and remote (cloud) environments; in the latter, scheduling a new deployment will typically solve them since the underlying hardware will change (Section 2.3).

Hardware resources may not be accessible. The machine learning systems may be fine, but there are access restrictions in place that prevent us from using them. Firewalls may be preventing us from connecting to them across networks; file permissions may be preventing us from reading data and configurations from their storage. This is a common issue with cloud instances and managed

---

[4]Connectivity issues between compute systems, clusters or data centers due to the failure of network devices or network connections are also called "network splits" or "network partitioning" [5].

services because their identity and access management (IAM) policies are difficult to write and to understand. In fact, it is often only possible to test the configurations controlling authentication and authorisation to those services interactively which makes it easy to break them accidentally. As a result, there have been many instances of machine learning engineers removing too many access restrictions and leaving S3 buckets full of personal data publicly accessible on AWS (Twilio [368] and Switch [394] are two notable examples from recent years). This is also clearly undesirable, but it can be prevented by writing IAM policies according to the *principle of least privilege*, by tracking them with configuration management tools (Section 11.1) and by including them in code reviews (Section 6.6) before applying them.

People do not talk to each other. Model deployment is when we actually put to use the models we trained and the code that supports them. Therefore, it is also when defects arising from the lack of communication between domain experts, machine learning experts, software engineers and users may come to light. Scoping and designing the pipeline (Section 5.3), validating machine learning models (Section 5.3.4) and inference outputs (Section 5.3.6), designing and naming modules and their arguments (Section 6.2), code reviews (Section 6.6) and writing various forms of documentation (Chapter 8) should all be collaborative efforts involving all the people working and using the pipeline. When this collaboration is not effective, different people will be responsible for different parts of the pipeline and the resulting lack of coordination may cause issues at the boundaries of the different areas of responsibility. Machine learning engineers may develop models without consulting the domain experts ("Are the models meaningful? Do we have the right data to train them?") or the software engineers ("Can the models run on the available systems and produce inference with low enough latency?"). Domain experts may fail to get across their expert knowledge to machine learning engineers ("This model class cannot express some relevant domain facts!") or to software engineers ("This variable should be coded in a specific way to make sense!"). Software engineers may take liberties in implementing machine learning models that change their statistical properties without the machine learning engineers noticing ("Maybe I can use this other library... or it may be faster to reimplement it myself!") or structure the code in ways that make it difficult for a domain expert to understand ("What does this theta_hat argument mean again?"). The segregation of roles is an organisational anti-pattern that should be avoided at all costs in favour of the shared responsibility and constant sharing of skills and knowledge originally advocated by DevOps [153].

Missing dependencies. The deployment of a module may fail because one or more of its dependencies (inside or outside the pipeline) is missing or is not functional. For instance, if module A requires the outputs of module B as inputs, we should ensure that module B is present and in a working state before deploying module A. In practice, this requires a *coordinated deployment* of the two modules, which is an anti-pattern when we strive for modules to be decoupled from each other. We can, of course, also implement appropriate retry policies in module A to make it resilient to module B being temporarily offline. On Kubernetes [364], we can use liveness and readiness probes (Section 7.4) together with "init containers" (specialised containers that run before app containers in a pod) for this purpose.

Incomplete or incorrect configuration management. Configuration management tools (Section 10.1 and 11.1) promote and automate the reuse of templates, environment variables and configuration files. However, this means that we should be careful to store those that correspond to different environments separately, and to keep them clean and complete at all times. In a complex pipeline with many modules and environments, it is easy to mistakenly use the configuration of a different environment than what we intended. In the best case, what we are trying to do will fail and an exception will be logged. In the worst case, we will apparently succeed in what we are trying to do but the results will be silently wrong because we are accessing different resources than we think we are. For instance, we may inadvertently cause an information leakage by accessing training data instead of validation data. Similar *misconfiguration* issues may involve any part of the pipeline (training, software testing, inference, etc.) and any of the entities tracked by configuration management (database references, secrets, model parameters, features, etc.).

7.6 Rolling Back

When a model that is deployed in production fails to meet the required performance and quality standards (Section 8.3), we have two choices: either we replace it with a previous model that is still fit for use (*rolling back*) or with a new model that we train specifically to address the reason why the current model is failing (*rolling forward*). In the following, we will focus on rollbacks, but our discussion will be as relevant for rolling a model forward.

Model rollbacks are only possible if the model APIs are backward compatible between releases. Then every version of our model can be restored to any previous version at any given moment in time without disrupting the rest of the pipeline because we can guarantee that the model delivers the same functionality, with the same protocol specifications and the same signature. Achieving backward compatibility requires a significant amount of planning and effort in terms of software engineering. In addition to wrapping models in a container that abstracts and standardises their interface, encapsulating their peculiarities and their implementation, we also need an experiment management platform that versions the pipeline modules, the models and the respective configurations. At a minimum, such a setup involves a model registry (Section 5.3.4) and a version control system for the code (Section 6.5).

Sometimes maintaining backward compatibility is simply not possible: if we replace a model with another from a completely different model class, or if the task the model was trained for has changed, the APIs should change to reflect the new model capabilities and purpose. We can *transition between the two different sets of APIs by versioning them*. For example, the old set of APIs may be available from the URL path https://api.mlmodel.local/v1/ while the new ones may be made available from https://api.mlmodel.local/v2/, and the old APIs may raise a warning to signal that they are deprecated. (OpenAPI supports deprecating API "Operations" [326]). We can then deploy new, incompatible models with the strategies we discussed in Section 7.2, and the pipeline modules will be able to access both sets of APIs at the same time and without any ambiguity about what version they are using. This in turn makes it possible to update individual modules in an orderly transition.

If a model is shipped with a built-in configuration that is versioned along with its APIs, the function that loads it should support the older versions. Similarly, if a model is stateful and needs to access a database to retrieve assets and configurations, the function that accesses these resources should be able to deal with different database schemas. Our ability to perform rollbacks will then depend on our ability to perform database migrations.

Whether rollbacks should be manual (that is, triggered by a human-in-the-loop domain expert) or automatic (that is, triggered by the pipeline orchestrator on the basis of the metrics collected by the monitoring infrastructure) is not a simple decision to make. From a technical perspective, we should evaluate the impact of the deployment strategy we plan to use in terms of how long it will take to return the pipeline to a fully functional state. From a business perspective, domain experts may want more solid evidence before asking for a rollback: they may be fine with an underperforming model while they acquire more data points and they better understand the underlying reason why the model is no longer accurate. Machine learning experts can help during that time by deploying alternative models with a canary or shadow deployment strategy to investigate their performance and compare it with that of the failing model. The only case in which an automatic rollback is clearly the best option is when the model's poor performance is not caused by changes in the data or in the inference requests but by issues with the hardware and software infrastructure underlying the pipeline. (For instance, a newly deployed model uses too much memory or becomes unresponsive.) Even in such a case, the decision to roll back should be supported by monitoring and logging evidence (Section 5.3.6).

8

Documenting Pipelines

Ideally, the code we write should be self-explanatory: everyone should be able to understand how it works and why it was implemented the way it was just by reading it. In practice, this aspiration is impossible to achieve for real-world codebases of any significant size even if we put effort into making code as clear as possible (Chapter 6). Hence we need *documentation*: a living, natural-language explanation of the machine learning systems and of the pipeline that evolves along with them.

Documentation is not a single entity, but rather a collection of information with different scopes, levels of detail, technical levels and audiences: comments explaining the "whats" and especially the "whys" of different chunks of code (Section 8.1); documents describing the public interface of each module and how to use it (Section 8.2); a holistic description of how the pipeline is structured and of how its parts fit together (Section 8.3); white papers detailing what machine learning models have been implemented and why, and what business or academic needs they address (Section 8.4). To complement these pieces of information, we should showcase how we envisage the machine learning pipeline will be used in practical day-to-day operations (Section 8.5).

8.1   Comments

There is no consensus among software engineers about the need to include comments in the code, nor about their frequency and contents. Some argue that "comments are, at best, a necessary evil [...] to compensate for our failure to express ourselves in code" [205]; some that "too many comments are as bad as too few, and you can achieve a middle ground economically" [206]; and others that "good code has lots of comments [...] keep the low-level knowledge in the code, where it belongs, and reserve the comments for other, high-level explanations" [369]. The only things that everybody agrees on are that comments can easily become out-of-date as the code they refer to changes over time, and that comments that do not provide any additional information over the code itself are redundant.

Machine learning pipelines can be reasoned about from three different perspectives (Section 5.3.1): the domain they operate in, such as the business operation or the academic field that generates the data it will process; the software architecture, that is, the engineering effort of organising the software in separate modules that can be worked on efficiently and that have a well-defined purpose; and the models that power them with their probabilistic properties. The interplay between these perspectives determines both low-level and high-level design decisions in ways that are extremely difficult to represent in the code. We choose machine learning models considering the characteristics of the data they will process; performance optimisations (Sections 2.2 and 2.4) may (or may not) be worthwhile depending on the combination of models and compute systems; and our efforts to structure the software into modules (Section 5.3) and data structures (Sections 3.3 and 3.4) must reconcile the conflicting goals of representing abstract mathematical concepts and real-world domain concepts at the same time.

As a result, the idea that comments should focus on complementing code by stating the "whys" (say, the rationales for particular design decisions and how non-obvious low-level optimisations work and why they are needed) and that they should leave the code itself to illustrate the "whats" (say, the sequence of steps that produces the outputs of a function) is much more nuanced than it is in either enterprise or academic software. In both these settings, modern development practices ensure that domain experts and software engineers have a shared conceptual model of the key domain concepts and, in doing so, establish a *ubiquitous language* [96] to identify and discuss them. This language is used throughout all documentation and in the code (to name classes, methods and variables), so that all the people involved have a common understanding of the "whats" and the "whys" of what the code is doing. However, it is difficult to establish such a ubiquitous language in the context of machine learning software (Section 6.2) because the backgrounds of the people involved are more varied: it is rare for any single person to have a broad enough background to be able to understand the machine learning systems and software well from a domain, software and machine learning perspectives at any given time. The rise of professional figures such as domain (data) analysts (domain + machine learning) and machine learning engineers (software engineering + machine learning) who can work on pipelines from two different perspectives is partly a response to this issue.

Therefore, we believe that there is value in annotating code with comments describing both the "whats" and the "whys" but that do so from a perspective that is different from the one the code is written from. Code implementing models (Section 5.3.4) should be structured well enough for a machine learning engineer to understand its behaviour clearly: comments should focus on how the parameters of the model and its outputs map to domain concepts, and they can also state how optimising the model for a compute system's hardware led to the use of specific data structures. Code that pre-processes inputs to a machine learning pipeline (Section 5.3.3) and post-processes its outputs for consumption by third parties (Sections 5.3.5 and 5.3.6) should be clear to domain experts, since it is just encoding domain concepts into data structures and vice versa; but it is worthwhile to comment on the statistical properties we expect those inputs and outputs to have, and to relate them to the machine learning models they are produced from or fed to. Finally, code that orchestrates the modules in the pipeline (either directly or by configuring a third-party MLOps solution, see Section 5.3) should be clear from both domain and machine learning perspectives because it is linking different models in a data processing pipeline designed after domain workflows. However, the algorithmic complexity of particular models and the hardware characteristics of the compute systems the models run on can influence how the code is organised into modules and how the modules are connected to each other in ways that should be documented because they may not be readily apparent.

Other than that, the advice in [96, 105, 252, 369] on how to write comments applies well to machine learning software. The goal of comments is to ensure that the structure and the behaviour of the software is obvious to the readers: other developers, so that they can modify the code quickly and with confidence, and users, so that they can understand it and use it appropriately. The readers could eventually deduce such information by reading the code, but the process would be time-consuming and error-prone: especially when they are approaching the code from a different perspective than the one from which the code was written. Comments should be concise and located close to the code: for instance, prefacing a block of code performing a particular task with a description of the implementation issues that were considered and the probability results that shaped it. (This may also help in relating tests to the code, see Section 9.4.2. Additional information that does not belong in any single place in the code may be found in commit messages as discussed in Section 6.5.) They should be written just before or at the same time as the code to ensure that they are written in the first place and that any design issues are still fresh in the developer's minds. For the same reason, they should be updated along with the code whenever the code is modified. This approach may also help in refining the architecture of the code early on (Sections 5.3.1 and 5.3.2) by making it easier to discuss pros and cons of different designs and by allowing domain experts to look into the implementation of key domain concepts to some extent. Finally, expressing the same idea twice, in the code and in the comments, and from different perspectives can have similar benefits to code review (Section 6.6) because it forces developers to rethink what they are doing from the point of view of a user of the software.

8.2 Documenting Public Interfaces

In addition to augmenting blocks of code inside functions and modules, we should use comments to document module interfaces, their methods and their general behaviour. In particular, each module should come with a high-level description of what it does and of the situations in which it makes sense to use it. Both should be written from the point of view of a prospective user: in the spirit of abstracting away complexity and reducing cognitive load, users should be able to use the module without reading its implementation [252]. As discussed earlier, people working on and using machine learning pipelines will come from a variety of backgrounds, and many may struggle to read code written from a perspective far from their own. Therefore, comments prefacing module interfaces should describe them from all relevant perspectives to make them approachable in the same way as other comments (Section 8.1). These descriptions, together with the method signatures, should provide all the essential information on the modules: the meaning of the methods and of their arguments as well as any constraints, side effects and preconditions they may have. If we find it difficult to put such information in writing in a clear and concise way, it may well be that the interface is not a good abstraction and that the module should be refactored (Section 6.7) to give it a better sense of purpose. The documentation that describes it should be changed at the same time to remain up-to-date.

Documenting individual functions in a similar way may make sense for those few functions that are not completely encapsulated inside a single module. Other functions are either not visible to the module users, so they only need to be documented to the extent that is required by the developers of that module; or they are visible to the module users, and they should be documented among its methods.

In order to keep this type of documentation close to the code it refers to, so that it is easier to keep the two in sync, we can annotate each module with a long-form comment covering the information above. These comments should be structured in a standard format, possibly with additional in-house conventions, to ensure consistency and to make it more straightforward to write them. Tools such as Doxygen [382] can enforce comment formats for all programming languages typically found in machine learning pipelines (namely, C, C++, R and Python), which is convenient because different modules may be implemented in different languages (Section 6.1). They can also generate documents in common formats such as HTML, PDF and DOCX from the comments. This is especially convenient for keeping documentation up to date as interfaces change, because we can just update the comments along with the code and regenerate those documents as needed. We can also use language-specific tools such as Roxygen [401] in R or Sphinx [49] in Python if either language is dominant in the machine learning pipeline.

What should we write in these long-form comments in practice?

1. What we can expect from the module: the signatures of the methods, its semantics and its behaviour in both success and failure scenarios. These include the meaning and the data types of exported variables as well as a list of all the possible error conditions and how they are handled.
2. What problem the module solves, and a brief summary of why it was designed the way it was. This might include a discussion of alternative solutions that have been evaluated and discarded (Section 5.3.1) to avoid re-evaluating them unless we are changing the module in a fundamental way. However, such decisions typically span across module boundaries and are better documented in the architecture documentation (Section 8.3).
3. Short examples of how the module is used, possibly in combination with other modules, are also nice to have.
4. Pointers to the relevant sections of the technical documentation (Section 8.4) and to books or

papers that describe the algorithms used in the module.

Popular open-source machine learning software provides many examples of how to do this well. Take, for instance, Scikit-learn. We can access the documentation of its module interfaces from the landing page of its website [311] via a link labelled "API". All modules are listed in alphabetical order, from sklearn.base all the way to sklearn.utils. For each of them, we have a short description summarising what algorithms, models or general functionality it implements, links to long-form documentation that gives further details and shows typical usage patterns, and a list of all the attributes and the functions it exports. The page documenting each class further details its methods and their arguments as well as any variables it exports. All this documentation is generated by Sphinx from comments in the Scikit-learn code. The source files in which the comments appear are linked from each page, making it easy to explore the code the page describes.

For example, consider the documentation of the module implementing the DBSCAN clustering algorithm [310]. The online documentation is shown in Figure 8.1. The Sphinx comment the module description is generated from appears just before its declaration and it is enclosed in triple double-quotes ("""). Section headers are marked by ten dashes (----------) and the lists of parameters and attributes are formatted using indentation.

```
class DBSCAN(ClusterMixin, BaseEstimator):
    """Perform DBSCAN clustering from vector array or distance
    matrix.

    DBSCAN - Density-Based Spatial Clustering of Applications with
    Noise. Finds core samples of high density and expands clusters
    from them. Good for data which contains clusters of similar
```

FIGURE 8.1 An abridged version of the online documentation generated by Sphinx from the comments in the DBSCAN module of Scikit-learn.

```
Attributes
----------

core_sample_indices_ : ndarray of shape (n_core_samples,)
    [...]


See Also
--------

OPTICS : A similar clustering at multiple values of eps. Our
    implementation is optimized for memory usage.


Notes
-----
[...]


References
----------
[...]


Examples
--------
[...]
"""
```

The "Notes" section links further examples and illustrates the computational complexity (Chapter 4) of DBSCAN, complementing the pointers to similar functionality in the OPTICS module and the layman's explanation of how DBSCAN works in the User Guide.

In addition, the documentation of DBSCAN provides a list of all the exported methods along with a short description of what each of them implements, of its arguments (including their types and default values) and of its return value. The comment generating the documentation of the fit() method, for instance, is the following.

```
def fit(self, X, y=None, sample_weight=None):
    """Perform DBSCAN clustering from features, or distance matrix.
```

```
    Parameters
    ----------

    X : {array-like, sparse matrix} of shape (n_samples, \
        n_features), or (n_samples, n_samples)
        Training instances to cluster, or distances between instances
        if ``metric='precomputed'``. If a sparse matrix is provided,
        it will be converted into a sparse ``csr_matrix``.
    y : Ignored
        Not used, present here for API consistency by convention.
    sample_weight : array-like of shape (n_samples,), default=None
        Weight of each sample, such that a sample with a weight of at
        least ``min_samples`` is by itself a core sample; a sample
        with a negative weight may inhibit its eps-neighbor from
        being core. Note that weights are absolute, and default to 1.
    Returns
    -------

    self : object
        Returns a fitted instance of self.
    """
```

Unfortunately, the comment conflates function arguments with the parameters of the underlying models and algorithms: this is not ideal because it implies that they can be reasoned about interchangeably (which is not true, for instance, for floating point variables, see Section 3.1.2) and because it suggests that function arguments should map one-to-one to parameters (which depends entirely on how the machine learning pipeline is structured, see in particular Sections 5.2.3, 5.2.4 and 5.3.4). On the good side, however, it specifies what is the expected type for all arguments, which is a useful detail for module users to have in a dynamically-typed language like Python. Types can be enforced using a type checker such as mypy [367], effectively turning Python into a statically-typed language for any function with type annotations.

Another example of documenting interfaces at scale is the infrastructure that CRAN [70] uses to distribute and enforce quality standards on R packages. Each package has a dedicated web page on CRAN's website, which includes a short description of the functionality provided by the package and links to its Changelog, to relevant web pages and to its reference manual. Its entries follow a structured "R Documentation" format, based on a subset of LaTeX, with predefined sections ("Description", "Arguments", "Details", "Examples", "References") that package authors are required to fill for each function they export from the package. R Documentation files can be generated by including comments in the Doxygen format in the code and processing them with Roxygen: CRAN does not require that, but cross-checks that function names and arguments are consistent between the code and the documentation, and it executes all the examples to make sure they run. Furthermore, CRAN reports the status of any tests shipped with the package on its web page. The package's web page also links long-form documentation that provides further details on relevant algorithms and models and that showcases them with comprehensive examples. These long-form documents, known as *vignettes*, are notebooks interleaving R code with Markdown or LaTeX prose whose sources are part of the package. CRAN will compile them to make them available alongside the package sources.

A popular R package that contains all these types of documentation is rstanarm [230], which implements a suite of Bayesian regression models on top of Stan [58]. The authors provide both the reference manual and a set of vignettes illustrating how to use it. Its web page on CRAN links the GitHub repository with the package's source code where we can easily see the Doxygen comments the reference manual is created from. For instance, the comment prefacing the stan_mvmer() function looks as follows.

```
#' Bayesian multivariate generalized linear models with correlated
#' group-specific terms via Stan
#'
#' Bayesian inference for multivariate GLMs with group-specific
#' coefficients that are assumed to be correlated across the GLM
#' submodels.
#'
#' @export
#' [...]
#'
#' @param formula A two-sided linear formula object describing both
#'    the fixed-effects and random-effects parts of the longitudinal
#'    submodel similar in vein to formula specification in the
#'    \strong{lme4} package (see \code{\link[lme4]{glmer}} or the
#'    \strong{lme4} vignette for details). [...]
#' [...]
#' @param data A data frame containing the variables specified in
#'    \code{formula}. For a multivariate GLM, this can be either a
#'    single data frame which contains the data for all GLM
#'    submodels, or it can be a list of data frames where each
#'    element of the list provides the data for one of the GLM
#'    submodels.
#' [...]
#'
#' @details The \code{stan_mvmer} function can be used to fit a
#'    multivariate generalized linear model (GLM) with group-specific
#"    terms. The model consists of distinct GLM submodels, each which
#'    contains group-specific terms; within a grouping factor (for
#'    example, patient ID) the grouping-specific terms are assumed
#'    to be correlated across the different GLM submodels. It is
#'    possible to specify a different outcome type (for example a
#'    different family and/or link function) for each of the GLM
#'    submodels. [...]
#'
#' @return A \link[=stanreg-objects]{stanmvreg} object is returned.
#'
```

```
#' @seealso \code{\link{stan_glmer}}, \code{\link{stan_jm}}, [...]
#'
#' @examples
#' [...]
```

The Doxygen comment is identified by the fact that each line starts with a single quote. The first paragraph gives the title of the entry in the reference manual for the function, which is declared to be public by the @export. The second paragraph is the "Description", the @params are the "Arguments", and the @return describes the return value of the function. The text that follows the @details ends up in the "Details" section, and the code after the @examples provides short examples.

Longer examples and technical discussions that are too cumbersome to include in the reference manual are shipped as a set of vignettes, which in the case of rstanarm are R Markdown documents. Unlike the reference manual, vignettes can include figures and mathematical equations typeset in LaTeX, and they can easily be converted to PDF, HTML and DOCX documents using the knitr package [414]. The R Markdown format differs from plain Markdown only in its YAML header, which tells knitr the type of document the file should be compiled into and some of its metadata. For instance, in glmer.Rmd:

```yaml
---                                                        YAML
title: "Estimating Generalized (Non-)Linear Models with" >
       "Group-Specific Terms with rstanarm"
author: "Jonah Gabry and Ben Goodrich"
date: "`r Sys.Date()`"
output:
  html_vignette:
    toc: yes
---
```

Code chunks are delimited by triple backticks, followed by the language label (R in this case) and by a list of options that will be evaluated by knitr when compiling the document.

```
```{r, results = "hide"}\n',
post1 <- stan_nlmer(circumference ~ SSlogis(age, Asym, xmid, scal)
                  ~ Asym|Tree,
         data = Orange, cores = 2, seed = 12345, init_r = 0.5)
```
```

Note that, by default, knitr executes all code every time the document is compiled, in the order in which it appears. Therefore, we cannot have the issues with out-of-order execution and inconsistent state that affect Jupyter notebooks [274] (Section 10.2.2).

8.3   Documenting Architecture and Design

Architecture documentation binds together the public interface documentation of the individual modules to give an overall view of how the machine learning systems and the pipeline are structured as a whole. It summarises the rationale of the decisions made when designing them, the properties of their (hardware and software) components and their interactions, and how they relate to the requirements for the pipeline [64] (Section 5.3.1). All this should be written in the same ubiquitous language as the comments and the module interfaces documentation, and for the same reasons: the architecture is the primary means of evaluating how the pipeline and the underlying systems work, whether they can be modified in specific ways, and whether they meet current or new requirements we may have. These activities necessarily involve discussions among domain experts, software engineers and machine learning specialists that greatly benefit from the clarity brought by the ubiquitous language. In particular, architecture documentation should document all those cross-module design decisions that do not belong in any single module interface documentation: a prime example is the design and workings of glue code (Sections 5.2.3 and 9.2.4), which is often the least documented part of a machine learning pipeline.

A natural starting point to document the architecture and the design of a machine learning pipeline is the DAG that describes its paths of execution (Section 5.3). The nodes in the DAG represent the modules that implement the different processing stages the data go through, and an explanation of their roles in the pipeline should be linked to the documentation of the respective interfaces. The presence of arcs linking the nodes suggests that the corresponding modules have been designed to be interoperable, and the design decisions that make it possible should also be documented. Furthermore, arcs determine the temporal sequence of the processing stages and may be associated with event triggers (say, pull updated models for serving as they become available), scheduled tasks (say, retrain a model after a certain amount of new data becomes available) or human inputs (say, for model validation). Accommodating future needs that are not yet made explicit in the form of arcs in the DAG may have influenced the design of module interfaces, and such considerations should be documented as well.

This is, however, just one possible perspective from which we can describe a machine learning pipeline. Its design is likely to be influenced by the combination of the local and remote compute systems it runs on or it may run on in the future because individual modules will have different requirements (Section 2.4). How the overall functionality of the pipeline is structured into modules may be influenced by the domain or the business it operates in. For instance, a machine learning pipeline that uses computer vision for supporting clinicians in diagnosing diseases from medical images (like the use case example in Section 8.5) may have the DAG patterned after the tasks performed by different specialists and after the progression of clinical information in the diagnostic process. Or, in a business context, different parts of the pipeline may be under the supervision of different units within the company, with clear boundaries to avoid overlaps for personnel and budget reasons. The interplay of the models and of various algorithms at a probabilistic level provides one more view of the machine learning pipeline as an overarching, hierarchical model whose components may or may not be related to how the code is organised into modules.

Thorough documentation of the architecture and of the design decisions behind a machine learning pipeline and the underlying systems will naturally comprise a set of documents written from different perspectives to provide different conceptual views. Using the ubiquitous language (Section 8.1) across all documents will help cross-referencing them and make them accessible to all the people working on or using different modules. Cross-referencing the documents with each other and with the interface documentation of each module will allow readers to navigate them and to jump from one document to another to view related pieces of information. Describing a real-world pipeline and the systems it runs on in a single document is not practical: the result would be unwieldy and difficult to keep up to date.

Overall, the DAG can provide a suitable outline of the structure of the whole documentation for the machine learning pipeline and a map to navigate it. A systems diagram like Figure 2.1 can serve a similar purpose for documenting the machine learning systems. Domain concepts can then be organised informally with a diagram of some sort; it will rarely be worthwhile to use a formal graphical specification such as UML [104]. Ideally, all these graphical representations will share some similarities and will be meaningful to all of domain experts, machine learning experts and software engineers. If the domain experts do not understand the architecture of the system, there may be something wrong with it: they can communicate any issues they may have using the ubiquitous language, and discuss them while we iterate project scoping (Section 5.3.1) and prototyping (Section 5.3.2) until everybody is comfortable with the design.

For obvious reasons, it is difficult to find public, detailed examples of design documentation because companies consider their machine learning pipelines to be valuable assets that give them a competitive advantage. Much of that information, however, is available on the engineering blogs of companies like Uber [377] and Spotify [330]. We will use them as sources to outline an example of how design documentation and mission statements (Section 8.4) should be organised.

Consider the machine learning pipeline for early fraud detection at Uber [422]. After briefly describing what business problem the pipeline is solving, the blog post illustrates the pipeline from each of the domain, machine learning and software architecture perspectives. We show each of them in Figure 8.2:

· The domain perspective (top panel): Uber receives from its customers a constant stream of orders which will be initially screened by a machine learning model for frauds. If found to be suspicious, they will be passed to a human expert for manual validation and either approved or rejected (Section 5.3.6). The decisions made by the human experts are then fed back into the machine learning model doing the automatic screening to improve its performance over time and to prevent issues with data drift (see Sections 5.2.1 and 9.1.3).

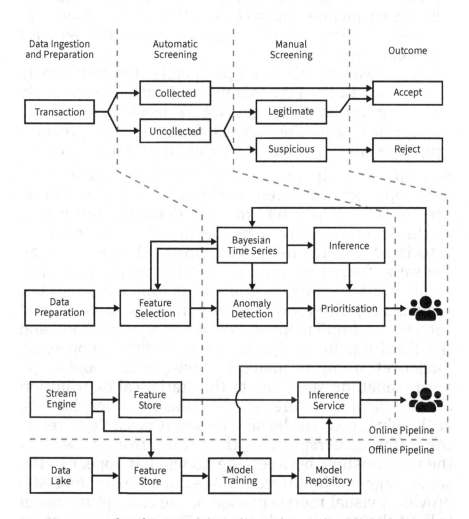

FIGURE 8.2 Uber's machine learning pipeline for early fraud detection, based on [422]: the domain DAG (top), the machine learning DAG (middle) and the software architecture DAG (bottom).

- The machine learning perspective (middle panel): the data flows through different pre-processing algorithms, including feature selection, to the models tasked to detect suspicious transactions. The same models will prioritise such transactions and schedule them for manual review.
- The software architecture perspective (bottom panel): each node in the DAG is a piece of software (possibly running on specific hardware) implementing the algorithms and the models found in the previous pipeline, storing data, or moving information around.

Each of these pipelines will be easier to reason about for people with different backgrounds, and it can be used to provide pointers to more detailed information on the data processing steps, the models or the modules associated with the individual nodes. All pipelines span the same four stages (data ingestion and preparation, automatic screening, manual screening, outcome) but provide very different views and insights on how fraud detection is implemented. For instance, the second and the third pipelines highlight the feedback loop tying model retraining to manual review, which doubles as a data labelling step, and to the statistical distribution of the relevant features in the data. However, looking at the pipelines side by side makes it possible to relate the different perspectives they come from as well as the relationships between the nodes that appear in the same stage but in different DAGs. In a sense, the DAGs provide a visual representation of the conceptual model behind the ubiquitous language. Their main limitation is the inability to describe the semantic meaning of the arcs effectively, as is the case for UML: this information is what the various documents in the architecture documentation provide, complementing what we can see from the DAGs.

8.4 Documenting Algorithms and Business Cases

The documentation of individual modules and of how they work together in the machine learning pipeline should be supplemented by two other documents:

1. a *technical report* detailing the relevant probabilistic and statistical properties of the machine learning models; and
2. a *mission statement* describing, at a high level, what is the goal of the machine learning pipeline from a domain or business perspective.

There are several reasons for preparing a technical report covering the relevant facts about the algorithms and the models. Firstly, we can establish a coherent mathematical notation that agrees with the ubiquitous language (Section 8.1) and with the variable naming scheme used by our modules (Section 6.2), and that can be related to that of any external libraries we may be using. Different parts of the scientific literature have different notation practices: the same concepts may be expressed with different notation or have different definitions, or the same notation may have different meanings. This is likely to cause some confusion because of the variety of approaches involved in a real-world machine learning pipeline. Secondly, a technical report will reduce the need to access the academic literature, which can become difficult over time because journal papers, conference proceedings and their supplementary materials can be locked behind paywalls or simply vanish from the Internet when their authors change employers. Thirdly, we can limit ourselves to the properties of the models and of the algorithms that are relevant to us, and we can concentrate on documenting those properties well and in an approachable way. (It is not common for the canonical reference for a model to be its clearest illustration, especially in machine learning where 8-page conference papers represent a fair share of the literature!) In particular, we can focus on the pros and cons of any models and algorithms we evaluate for use in the pipeline with respect to the specific domain that is relevant to us. This will be more informative than most benchmarking efforts based on reference data sets from the literature. Finally, we can easily cross-reference the technical report with both module interface (Section 8.2) and design documentation (Section 8.3).

A mission statement, which [64] calls a "domain vision statement", is a brief document of 1-2 pages identifying the core domain of the machine learning pipeline and its aims as established during project scoping (Section 5.3.1). It serves two purposes: evaluating whether the pipeline is fit for its intended purpose and guiding its evolution at a strategic level. By stating its purpose, the mission statement tells us what outcome we should judge. In turn, this allows us to define a scale of measurement ranging from "bad performance" to "good performance" according to how effectively and efficiently the pipeline fulfils its purpose. At the same time, it can serve as a high-level guideline for evolving it. The compute systems, the machine learning models and the domain concepts the pipeline is built upon will inevitably change over time. With each change, we can plan at the tactical level how to evolve it by pinpointing which components we should update and how. However, all these local changes should be consistent with a long-term strategy that ensures that the pipeline evolves coherently as a whole over time as its intended purpose changes. In other words, the mission statement is the "aspirational" counterpart of the more technical design documentation (Section 8.3) and of the more practical use cases (Section 8.5).

For example, consider the mission statement behind the machine learning pipeline powering Spotify's home screen [90]. Firstly:

"At Spotify, our goal is to connect listeners with creators, and one way we do that is by recommending quality music and podcasts on the Home page. Machine learning is central to how we personalize the Home page user experience and connect listeners to the creators that are most relevant to them."

The pipeline is a recommender system that matches users with contents. This requires tracking the users' listening data and Spotify's catalogue of music and podcasts, which has implications in terms of hardware, data ingestion and data processing capabilities in the pipeline. Both user data and the catalogue will change over time, as will their features: hence the models predicting which music and which podcasts the users may like should be updated at regular intervals. How often will depend on how quickly the catalogue changes, on how quickly the size of the users' listening data grows and on what models we will use, so it is not appropriate nor possible to recommend a schedule for the updates. For the same reason, what features of the data will be used to provide the recommendations is left unstated. Furthermore, the exact definition of "quality" and "relevant" will depend on the specific technical criteria putting them into numbers, on how engagement will be measured, on the models, and on how their accuracy metrics relate to revenue.

Secondly, the two final outputs of the pipeline are introduced in domain terms:

"Stage 1: Candidate generation: The best albums, playlists, artists, and podcasts are selected for each listener. Stage 2: Ranking: Candidates are ranked in the best order for each listener."

The pipeline is expected to present the users with recommendations ranked in terms of (predicted) preference. Again, details such as how many items are recommended and how they are ranked are implementation details that are bound to change over time and thus do not belong in the mission statement. The outputs are then described in more detail:

> "The Podcast Model: Predicts podcasts a listener is likely to listen to in the 'Shows you might like' shelf. The Shortcuts Model: Predicts the listener's next familiar listen in the Shortcuts feature. The Playlists Model: Predicts the playlists a new listener is likely to listen to in the 'Try something else' shelf."

The statement does not specify which models will be used, nor how many. It does not even state that they will be machine learning models: in fact, it later says that "some content is generated via heuristics and rules and some content is manually curated by editors." Which models or heuristics are appropriate will depend on what features will be available in the data, on what state-of-the-art models will be available from the literature, and on what software and hardware will be needed to provide recommendations in real time.

Thirdly, how the outputs of the pipeline are presented to the users:

> "The Home page consists of cards — the square items that represent an album, playlist, etc. — and shelves — the horizontal rows that contain multiple cards."

Note how the statement introduces the metaphor the user interface will be based on, but without describing any implementation details. It would not be appropriate to do it here: we will want to change the interface over time in response to any insights from usability studies and from usage patterns collected by telemetry. Furthermore, different platforms and operating systems will have different capabilities and will require at least some levels of customisation. For instance, it is often impossible to design a user interface with good ergonomics on both mobile and desktop systems.

8.5 Illustrating Practical Use Cases

Last but not least, topical examples showcasing the machine learning pipeline in action can be very valuable. Pipelines are built to address some need like automating and speeding up analyses or improving products: the best way to motivate their development, use and maintenance is to show that they can address that need effectively and efficiently in the context of the domain or of the business line of the prospective users. Users will then be able to relate to the problems the machine learning pipeline is tackling and they will be in a position to appreciate the advantages of using it. The types of documentation presented in the previous sections are either too technical, too abstract or too focused on the inner workings of the pipeline for this purpose.

An example of a very effective use case is the InnerEye project [222] from Microsoft Research Cambridge (UK), which aims to develop machine learning pipelines for medical imaging. The video linked in the reference talks about the specific application of performing image segmentation in 3D medical images taken from cancer patients scheduled to be treated with radiotherapy.

1. *It states the need in clinical terms*: speeding up the segmentation in magnetic resonance (MR) and computerised tomography (CT) scans while retaining a sufficient degree of accuracy.
2. *It states the problem in a way prospective users can relate to*: radiologists do segmentation manually,

outlining the tumour in a sequence of dozens of cross-section images with a visual tool to obtain a 3D contour. This is a slow process, and the precision of the contour is limited. It takes hours of preparation to map tumours and healthy tissues to target treatment for the former and to limit exposure for the latter.

3. *It states how the machine learning pipeline can address the need from the perspective of the user*: automatic or human-assisted segmentation. The video shows the user interface that would be used by the radiologists, to give them a feeling of how it would fit in their everyday work. This makes it possible to contrast, live, the time it takes for manual, automatic and human-assisted segmentation as well the level of detail and precision of the segmentation.

4. *It states the value of the solution to the user*: it takes minutes instead of hours to prepare a treatment plan for a patient with the desired accuracy. Furthermore, the same tools can be used to track how cancer is responding to therapy. These improvements will lead to better treatments and better outcomes.

Note that the video does not make any quantitative statements about running times nor about the statistical accuracy of the segmentation as neither would be easily interpretable for radiologists. Instead, the InnerEye project has a web page linking all the scientific publications where we can find these numbers. Machine learning engineers can use them to evaluate the pipeline from the perspective of their own discipline. Furthermore, the InnerEye project news page highlights that the machine learning pipeline has been deployed and is currently used on actual patients at Addenbrooke's Hospital in Cambridge. The implication that it obtained regulatory approval and that a radiology department finds it worthwhile to use it are strong indications that the machine learning pipeline is not an academic endeavour but something that provides value in real-world clinical practice.

Finally, we would like to point out that practical use cases may also be instrumental in gathering feedback from prospective users. Illustrating them will provide a natural venue for users to discuss how the machine learning pipeline would be useful (or not) and what their strong (weak) points appear to be from their perspective.

9

Troubleshooting and Testing Pipelines

Troubleshooting machine learning software is complicated for several reasons: the data may be huge (Section 9.1.1), may be collated from a number of different sources fed by different pipelines (Section 9.1.2) or may change over time (Section 9.1.3). Models may be too large for mere humans to interpret their parameters and eyeball incorrect behaviour patterns (Section 9.2.1) especially in the case of black–box models (Section 9.2.2). The time and cost of training them may also limit our ability to investigate any issues that require updating models (Section 9.2.3), especially if we are using several of them chained together in the pipeline (Section 9.2.4).

Software testing is a natural complement to troubleshooting: once we know where trouble lies (Sections 9.1 and 9.2), we can either actively prevent it by "defining errors out of existence" [252] or we can put in place tests to detect it before it can meaningfully degrade our software's performance. While every bug is unique, some patterns of behaviour are indicative that something is amiss that we should be aware of (Section 9.3). When expected and observed behaviour are markedly different, it is worth looking into it! What we should test (Section 9.4.2) depends on the data (Section 9.4.3), but it should span local and global behaviour (Sections 9.4.4) as well as conceptual and implementation errors (Sections 9.4.5 and 9.4.6).

9.1 Data Are the Problem

Machine learning models effectively compile data into code and dictate to a large extent the behaviour of the software they are embedded in (Section 5.1). Hence it is only logical that issues in the data will impact the software by affecting model training or predictions. Before we do anything else, we should make sure that the data are correctly recorded, properly labelled and without duplicates: only 3% of data are acceptable in this respect even with pretty loose quality standards [179] and technical debt arising from data is a common issue (Section 5.2.1).

The shape of the data and how the data are collected can result in very different types of issues. For the former, we may have *tall data* (large sample size, few variables), *wide data* (small sample size, many variables; also known as "small n, large p") and *big data* (large sample size, many variables, changing over time and possibly unstructured [178]). For the latter, we should distinguish between *experimental* and *observational* data. Experimental data are collected following some experimental design [225] that involves identifying a limited set of variables of interest from available knowledge (domain experts, the literature, small-scale preliminary experiments, etc.) and a small number of variables we wish to intervene on (like giving targeted discounts and recommendations or administering specific medical treatments). Eligible data points are chosen based on their characteristics to ensure that the conclusions we draw from models apply to the population of interest, and are randomly assigned different interventions. Randomisation ensures that all types of individuals are observed with different interventions and prevents confounding to some extent. (More on this later.) In contrast, observational data are collected as they arise. Often individuals are added to the data as their information is recorded, without taking their characteristics into account. This, along with the fact that we are not performing any randomised intervention, can bias the models we learn from observational data: either we do not observe data points with certain characteristics (enough of them, or at all) or we do not observe them in a wide-enough range of situations to model their behaviour. This issue is called *sampling bias* (Section 5.3.1) and affects many applications of machine learning. For instance, 96% of participants in genome-wide studies were of European descent in 2009; while new studies performed on Asian populations have reduced that figure to around 80% by 2016, other ethnicities remain chronically underrepresented [266]. The practical consequence of this disparity is that personalised medicine treatments currently under development will not benefit individuals from those backgrounds.

9.1.1 Large Data

Consider the three possible dimensions of data mentioned above: the sample size, the number of variables and the number of time points. The larger the data are in at least one of these dimensions, the more difficult it is to troubleshoot the models we learn from them.

If the data are wide, changes in one variable may induce changes in the contributions of other variables to the model: this phenomenon is called *entanglement* [312, 313]. As the number of variables grows ("why not add one more input?"), it becomes increasingly likely that multiple variables will express the same information in different ways. The parameters that encode that information in the model will then be jointly determined by those variables. If the distribution of one such variable changes, making it a *legacy feature* that is no longer significant in the model, the effects of the other variables will increase to compensate. And even if it still retains some degree of statistical significance, it may become an *epsilon feature* that contributes so little to the model that it is not worth the effort of including it in the first place. (Both legacy and epsilon features should in principle be dropped from models, but they are often not when they are included as a bundle with features that are actually useful.) In other words, "changing anything changes everything" [312], as we discussed in Section 5.2.2 with respect to technical debt. This is all the more true for time series data because, in addition to different variables being entangled with each other, each variable is entangled with itself at previous time points (Section 9.1.3).

As a side effect, entanglement makes it difficult to identify true causal features[1] within a set of correlated features. This is problematic because it prevents us from keeping models simple and small without a significant amount of feature engineering.

The other problem in troubleshooting large data is latency: accessing the data takes time and computational resources, which in turn slows down our iteration speed. This is particularly true for models like deep neural networks that require GPUs and TPUs, which have limited bandwidth and memory (Section 2.2). One possible solution is to choose a good-quality, representative subset of the data and work with that (more in Section 9.1.2), keeping in mind that (repeated) subsampling also has a cost. Another is taking the last known-good snapshot of the model and working on it with a subset of recent data as if we were doing online training.

---

[1]That is, a feature that is built on a variable with a (direct) causal effect on the target variable of interest.

9.1.2 Heterogeneous Data

Furthermore, we must consider that data may be *heterogeneous*, comprising variables encoded with different data types and complex data structures. Data ingestion and preparation (Section 5.3.3) then require several algorithms and auxiliary models to filter out poor-quality data points, impute missing data and extract relevant features. Additional models may also be required to post-process the outputs of the core machine learning models. If one input variable changes, it is bound to affect one or more of these models: their output will in turn affect even more models in what we called a *correction cascade* [312] in Section 5.2.1. In a sense, we can see it as a form of entanglement that spans multiple models (Section 9.1.1); or as a form of coupling between models that are (sometimes undeclared) consumers of each others' outputs, effectively making them work as a single large model (Section 9.2.1).

Heterogeneous data are difficult to subsample as well: choosing data points at random is unlikely to yield a subset that is representative of the overall data set. Observations belonging to less-frequent classes in imbalanced data are unlikely to appear in a random subsample in sufficient numbers or at all: our estimates of predictive accuracy for the machine learning models can remain high even if they are consistently mispredicted. Subsets are also likely to have a different distribution (as captured by summary statistics) compared to the overall data, which may trigger calibration issues. Outliers that may be causing trouble in the original data are likely to be dropped, making it difficult to replicate the issues we are troubleshooting (reliably or at all). All these problems become more and more pronounced as the difference in size between the original data and the subsamples grows.

9.1.3 Dynamic Data

The data, the models, the code and the architecture can all be sources of technical debt in a machine learning pipeline (Section 5.2). The data sources we use to feed our machine learning models, in particular, are often outside of our control. Hence data dependencies are more costly than code dependencies [313]: it takes more effort to troubleshoot their behaviour and to quantify and mitigate their potential impact on the performance of our pipeline.

Data may change slowly over time, either following a medium- to long-term trend or in periodic patterns. (The former is known as *data drift*, and the latter is called *seasonality* in statistics.) Both can be encoded in machine learning models at the cost of increasing model complexity. However, models take time to adapt to change: if change is sudden or drastic enough predictions will be miscalibrated. Using dynamic thresholds that are updated regularly and frequently allows models to adjust to change, but there may be a noticeable lag. Setting such thresholds, however, will require additional, dedicated models thus introducing additional complexity. Any fixed threshold, whether implicit or explicit, will require domain experts to constantly monitor (Section 5.3.6) the inputs and outputs of data ingestion and preparation modules (Section 5.3.3) to keep it up to date, possibly introducing an even longer lag. (This is an instance of the human-in-the-loop approach we recommended in different places in Chapter 5).

A type of change that is particularly difficult to identify is when a feature we are using in our models stops correlating with a causal feature. If we include the former instead of the latter by mistake (Section 9.1.1), we suddenly lose access to the information that the causal feature was indirectly providing to the models. Recovering that information may require re-evaluating our data sources and an extensive re-engineering of our data ingestion and preparation modules. And it may be difficult to understand what happened: if two features showed a significant degree of association at the time the models were trained, but gradually drifted apart over time, the (non-causal) feature we included may suddenly become irrelevant for no apparent reason.

9.2 Models Are the Problem

Machine learning models tend to be complex beasts: this is especially the case for deep neural networks but holds for many Bayesian hierarchical models as well. Our ability to troubleshoot models with a large number of parameters estimated from data (and with hyperparameters as well, usually) is severely limited by the sheer number of moving parts we need to track.

9.2.1 Large Models

Firstly, it is difficult to map the effect of any change in the model behaviour or in the data to individual parameters because parameters interact with each other. In order to capture complex patterns of behaviour from the data, machine learning models mix the information present in individual input variables in many (linear and non-linear) ways that are encoded in different parameters. As a result, any change in even a single variable will affect multiple parameters at the same time in ways that may be difficult to understand. Changing the values of some parameters in a way that locally improves some part of a model may have a knock-off effect on the parameters in other parts of the same model. Both these effects compound across the models in a pipeline as we discussed in Sections 5.2.2 and 9.1.2.

Secondly, dealing with a large number of parameters makes it impractical to investigate them individually. Each parameter may have little or no real-world meaning by itself. As we just discussed, its behaviour will be intertwined with that of other parameters: they should be grouped and each group investigated as a single, meaningful entity. Hence we have to resort to an auxiliary model that investigates the parameters for us: it may be something simple like a diagnostic plot based on summary statistics, or something more complex like a second, independent machine learning model. However, summary statistics by their nature lose information, making bugs easily go undetected, and adding a second machine learning model may not be worth the additional complexity of ensuring that model is also working properly. It is troubleshooting all the way down!

9.2.2 Black-Box Models

Thirdly, most large machine learning models are effectively black boxes. Individual parameters are mathematical constructs that often have no real-world meaning, even when considered in groups. An entire research field, focusing on *explainability* and *interpretability*, has sprung up in an effort to relate changes in the model inputs to changes in the model outputs. Ideally, we want to do that in a way that can make these relationships meaningful to a domain expert: for instance, visualising word relevance in NLP [191] and pixel relevance in computer vision [325] or splitting images into layers with semantic meaning [296]. Observing the behaviour of a model around key input values with local approaches like LIME [296] and SHAP [201] can also provide insights: both approaches work by perturbing the inputs and checking whether the outputs are stable, and mapping any instabilities to specific subsets of parameters.

9.2.3 Costly Models

Fourthly, training large machine learning models is expensive and time-consuming. This makes for slow iterations and may very well make troubleshooting impractical. Among recent deep neural network architectures for NLP, Google's XLNet [418] costs an estimated $61,440 to train, taking 2 ½ days with 512 TPU v3 chips (Google's proprietary AI coprocessors); University of Washington's Grover-Mega [421] takes two weeks and $25,000; Google's BERT [78] costs between $500 and $6,912 and takes 4 days to 2 weeks to train. It is currently unknown how much OpenAI's GPT-2 [285] originally cost to train, but the open-source OpenGPT-2 [66] took $50,000. And this only covers training: hyper-parameter tuning can easily involve training 10-100 models before finding a well-performing one. A recent study from the American Medical Association has found that simply reproducing one of these models using publicly available resources can cost between $1 million to $3.2 million [34].

The numbers above represent a worst-case scenario. Deep neural networks for applications other than NLP are typically much smaller and thus much cheaper and quicker to train. For instance, the ResNet-50 architecture for computer vision tasks can be trained in minutes for a few dollars [338] because it only has 25 million parameters (Grover-Mega and GPT-2 have 1.5 billion, XLNet has 340 million). And we rarely have to retrain models from scratch: it is common to use the current model as a pre-trained starting point or to buy a pre-trained model from a commercial vendor. (However, this practice may produce technical debt at the model level as discussed in Section 5.2.2.) We can also trade training speed for cost and vice versa: slower solutions are cheaper, and their prices have been steadily falling in recent years. We may also be tempted to reduce the overall computing costs with lazy code execution but that may introduce non–deterministic behaviour and make troubleshooting even harder. Using cloud resources as massive parallel compute facilities to divide–and–conquer training may complicate things rather than make them easier because remote debugging in the cloud comes with its own set of problems (Section 2.3).

Finally, let's not forget that there are machine learning models other than deep neural networks: random forests and gradient-boosted trees [233] are much faster and cheaper to train and quite often achieve competitive performance, especially on tabular data.

9.2.4 Many Models

As we mentioned in Section 9.1.2, dealing with complex data may require a complex machine learning pipeline involving several models linked by an orchestrator and to some extent by glue code. On the one hand, such code may be helpful in isolating the peculiarities of the different models and of the libraries that are used to implement them. On the other hand, glue code may introduce bugs in how models interact. Such bugs are not easily detected without extensive integration tests, and are common in the "pipeline jungles" we discussed in Section 5.2.3. Unit tests would cover the correctness of individual models, but not the correctness of how they are wired together. The more models we include in our pipeline, the more difficult it is to troubleshoot their interactions because the number of possible pipeline configurations explodes combinatorially as the number of models increases. This may be compounded by the presence of dead and experimental code paths that are not essential to the functioning of the machine learning models (Section 5.2.4).

Another issue, which we covered in Section 5.2.2, is that the more models we have in our pipeline, the more likely it is that they will create feedback loops or correction cascades.

9.3 Common Signs That Something Is Up

How can we tell whether one or more of the issues discussed above are affecting the performance of our machine learning pipeline? There are so many (combinations of) things that can go wrong that it is difficult to compile an exhaustive list of signs that something is up. There are, however, some common patterns of behaviour that should be regarded as suspicious.

Predictive accuracy is really bad. Models may be unable to capture enough relevant information from the training data to be able to predict new data points. The data may not contain such relevant information in the first place. That information may not be usable without further effort into engineering a suitable set of features. Or the information may be there, but the models fail to capture it due to computational issues or because they make the wrong assumptions on the distribution of the data. If any of these is true, we should focus our troubleshooting efforts on data preparation (Section 5.3.3) and model training (Section 5.3.4) modules. We should also re-evaluate our data sources: were there any changes that made (some of) them no longer useful?

Predictive accuracy is really good. If the models we are implementing are appropriate for the problem they are tasked to solve, and if the data provide relevant information to train them, we would expect them to perform "well". How well is "well" depends on a combination of these two factors, and on how we chose the problem and the metrics with which we define success (Section 5.3.1). Narrowly-defined tasks are easier to put into precise mathematical terms, making them easier to optimise for. On the other hand, tasks with broad definitions typically conflate multiple subtasks with different requirements and goals that may conflict with each other. However, if a task is nontrivial we should treat extremely high performance (say, like 99.9+% classification accuracy) as a possible red flag. Unbalanced data sets in which not all the classes we are trying to predict are well represented may result in unrealistically high accuracy if the models always predict the most common 1-2 classes and miss the rest. The different types of feedback loops we discussed in Section 5.2.2 may have a similar effect. Finally, high accuracy may be indicative of an information leakage between what we are trying to predict and the data we use to train our models, for instance because one of the variables is an alias[2] of the prediction target.

Furthermore, data leakage will also happen when part of the training set is implicitly used in the test or validation sets. This may involve different data points originating from the same individual or from related individuals being included in either data set. For instance, these may be two sentences from the same page of text, two web product accounts opened by the same person or by people in the same family, health information from siblings or online questionnaires administered to the same person at different times. In any of these cases, instead of validating the machine learning models with a realistic simulation of the production setting they will work in (completely new data points), we are validating them against data points they already know about at

---

[2]*Data leakage* arises when information from outside the training data set is used to learn a model, typically because one or more variables carry the same information as the prediction target but in different form. Such variables are sometimes called *aliases* in the context of linear regression models.

least to some extent. Hence our assessment will give us a biased estimate of the models' predictive accuracy and overconfidence in their capabilities.

Predictive accuracy suddenly changes. Mathematical models of reality, including machine learning models, make various regularity assumptions that encode the idea that reality varies smoothly: small changes in the inputs of the models should produce small changes in their outputs; and the larger the changes in the inputs, the potentially larger the changes in the outputs. Any marked change in a model's behaviour that cannot be immediately linked to a known real-world event may be indicative of an incorrect model that just happened to work and finally broke down, making it apparent that it was wrong in the first place. (Losing any connection between the training data and unobserved causal features as described in Sections 9.1.1 and 9.1.3, for instance.) It may also be indicative of some inputs changing in a fundamental way (changes in the variable types or meaning, feedback loops, etc.) or becoming unavailable (Sections 5.2.1 and 5.2.2). The only way of troubleshooting such issues is to put in place comprehensive monitoring facilities covering all the modules in the pipeline and to aggregate all metrics in a monitoring server, where they can be correlated and cross-referenced across time (Section 5.3.6).

The resources required to train the models or to make predictions with the machine learning pipeline are at odds with the computational complexity of the algorithms it implements. As we discussed in Section 4.6, real-world resource usage is not a perfect reflection of big-O notation: it does not take constant factors and different hardware capabilities (parallel execution, cache sizes, etc.) into account, nor can it easily incorporate all the optimisations performed by modern compilers and language interpreters. There should be, however, some discernible relationship between the two. Large discrepancies suggest that training data or input features may be breaking some of the assumptions on the model, or that there are too few data points. In either case, model training and hyperparameter tuning will struggle to identify an optimal model, taking more time than expected. Large clusters of related variables (Section 9.1.1) may have a similar effect, because model training will struggle to separate their (overlapping) effects. Prediction, by comparison, is less likely to be problematic. As before, we should be able to point out any anomalies in resource usage by a combination of monitoring and logging across modules.

9.4   Tests Are the Solution

Current practices from software engineering strongly suggest that the most reliable way of identifying defects in software is *testing*. Much has been written on this topic in classic books such as "The Pragmatic Programmer" [369] and "Test–Driven Development" [35]. Few resources touch on the topic of testing machine learning software: among them are Alice Zheng's "Evaluating Machine Learning Models" [425], the "ML Test Score" rubric from Google Research [51] as well as a few survey papers in academic literature [48, 424]. We will do our best to give an overview of all the facets of testing machine learning pipelines in the remainder of this chapter, complementing our discussion of software testing from Chapters 5 and 6. We will also rely heavily on the automated and reproducible deployment practices we discussed in Chapter 7: we should run each test in a clean environment to make sure that its results are not influenced by external factors (including other tests). That is typically implemented by using the base container images we use for our production systems in our continuous integration setup.

9.4.1 What Do We Want to Achieve?

Following [424], we can summarise our goals as:

- *Model correctness*: if input data follow the distribution we expect them to, outputs should be correct and predictions should be accurate with high probability.
- *Empirical correctness*: outputs should be correct and predictions accurate for new data points, that is, the empirical performance of the models should be reliably above the threshold we set for our metrics (Section 5.3.1).
- *Model relevance*: models should be able to represent the distribution of the data and to fit them well without overfitting.
- *Robustness*: models should handle invalid or extreme inputs gracefully.
- *Adversarial robustness*: models should also handle malicious inputs that are crafted to be hard to detect and to produce specific outputs.
- *Efficiency*: model training and inference should use the least possible amount of compute and memory that produces the desired level of predictive accuracy.
- *Interpretability*, *fairness* and *privacy*: as discussed in Section 5.3.1.

Tests should strive to ensure that these goals are met by investigating a variety of valid and invalid inputs and outputs for both individual models and the machine learning pipeline as a whole. They should give confidence in the ability of the pipeline to perform its assigned task well for common inputs and to degrade gracefully otherwise.

9.4.2 What Should We Test?

In principle, a comprehensive test suite should cover:

- The *raw data*, covering invalid or missing values, variable representations (scaling, one–hot encoding, etc.), variables that are of little to no use along with those that are redundant because they encode the same information (legacy and epsilon variables). We should also have offline and online tests for:
    - Insufficient sample size: Do we have enough data points to (re)train the model? Is the sample size large enough to make it possible to observe infrequent configurations of the variables?
    - Data drift: Does new data have a distribution comparable to that of the data the model was trained from?
    - Outliers: Are there any data points with values different enough from the rest that we may think of them as recording errors?
- The key components of the *models*:
    - Models: Are they appropriate for the data? Can they regularise (smooth) noisy outputs?
    - Parameters: Are parameter values unusually large or small? Are there parameters that have no effect on predictions (for instance, because they are equal to zero)?
    - Hyperparameters: Do they encode expert knowledge correctly? Or, conversely, are they really non-informative? Do they restrict the range of models we can learn?
    - Loss functions: Do they express meaningful properties of the model outputs (Section 5.3.4)? Can they differentiate between models well, picking models that predict well and that capture the key relationships between the variables?
    - Optimisers: Can they explore a wide range of models efficiently? Do they converge reliably or are they prone to settling for suboptimal models?

- The *post-processed data* and *inference outputs* to spot features that become problematic or are not worth keeping and to ensure that predictions are accurate enough to be fit for purpose.
- Any *glue code* that is used to wrap models, to help access their inference capabilities or to orchestrate them (Sections 5.2.3 and 5.2.4).

This is, of course, in addition to any tests required to ensure that the underlying infrastructure is working, feeding inputs to the pipeline and putting its outputs to use. For this to be possible, we must be able to track data, models, predictions, hyperparameters and parameters simultaneously through configuration management under version control (see also Sections 5.1 and 5.2).

Even if we can effectively test all the above, a crucial problem remains: how do we determine whether a test should pass or fail? In order to do so we must be able to determine what is the expected behaviour of each individual model and of the pipeline as a whole, which is difficult when dealing with the stochastic nature of machine learning models. Typically, we do not have access to an oracle:[3] we do not know in advance what the "correct behaviour" should be or we would not need the models in the first place! The models give us some clues in their assumptions and their mathematical and probabilistic properties: the former determine what valid inputs are, the latter suggest what output we should get for a given input. Model invariants (that is, changes in the inputs that should not change the output) give more theoretical properties that should be empirically satisfied. This is a form of *property-based testing* in which the properties to test are mathematical statements that we

---

[3]A *test oracle* is a mechanism for determining whether a test has passed or failed; it has no relationship with oracle properties from the statistics literature.

can derive from model definitions. If we are using models that have multiple implementations, we can also compare the output of the implementation we are using to that of other implementations. If they agree up to some tolerance threshold, and we trust those other implementations to be correct, we can take them as pseudo-oracles and validate our models. This practice is called *differential testing*, and can supplement property-based testing for models without easily-testable properties like black-box models (Section 9.2.2).

9.4.3 Offline and Online Data

Tests based on *offline data* and *online data* are quite different.

Offline data are mainly used for tuning hyperparameters and training models, and they are collected by combining historical data and new data points into a static sample until its size is large enough (Section 5.3.4). These data will then be labelled to obtain a ground truth to train the model. Images will be tagged based on which items they display; sentences will be tagged by their main topic(s); lab samples will be tested to detect the phenomena we would like models to identify. (Note that in many cases a label is a discrete, categorical variable, but it needs not to be. It can be an ordinal variable, such as age brackets, or a numeric value.) The labelling process acts as a pseudo-oracle: it is expensive, time-consuming, and with a non-zero error rate, but it is the closest thing to ground truth we can access in most settings. In a sense, it allows us to train a model and compare its performance against human performance (assuming labelling is done by domain experts, see Section 5.2.1).

Therefore, testing model training and hyperparameter tuning with offline data together with the offline data themselves is relatively straightforward. We have a large sample, which allows us to test the pre-processing of raw data and feature engineering to ensure that they produce suitable inputs for the models. In the spirit of property-based testing, we can test that the models behave correctly when they are fed features that satisfy their assumptions; and that they either report errors or degrade gracefully otherwise. From the empirical distributions of the data and the model assumptions, we can identify both corner cases to test limit behaviour and cases that are well-spaced in the sample space and cover a variety of typical behaviour. Thanks to the labels, we can estimate the model's predictive performance with some sort of train-test-validation data split, making it possible to perform hyperparameter tuning and to rank different model choices. The accuracy observed during training will also serve as a benchmark to monitor the performance of the models in production (Section 5.3.6).

Online data are generated as a constant stream from external sources in the form of individual data points or small batches. Therefore, testing takes the form of online monitoring, A/B testing (which is covered in depth in [425]) or one of the other strategies outlined in Section 7.2. Online data often come without labels, so we cannot directly assess whether models handle them correctly. We can test whether the data we see in production follow the same distribution as the training data by collecting data points across a short period of time and testing whether their empirical distribution is different from what we would expect. If the data are unlabelled, we will be limited in doing so either by the availability of domain experts to perform the labelling in a short time frame or by the limited accuracy of machine learning models at this task. We can then set dynamic thresholds to detect both sudden and gradual losses in accuracy. Similarly, we can test for changes in the distribution of input features. In either case, we can flag the test to be reviewed by a domain expert or assume that the model is now out of date and must be retrained automatically. In practice, such tests can fail in benign ways for a number of reasons, so keeping a human in the loop to check why failing tests are failing is preferable (Section 5.3.4).

If we do not have enough data to both train the models and to test them, we can generate more either by resampling or by stochastic simulation. Both bootstrap and cross-validation make it possible to create new data sets by resampling an offline data set (see, for instance, [188] for a brief introduction and several examples). They both start from the idea that data are sampled from the population of interest, hence the distribution of the variables in the data is an empirical approximation of their distributions in the population. Sampling again from the data can be implemented so that the bootstrap samples and cross-validation splits preserve this property. The resulting data sets are perturbed versions of the original containing a subset of its data points: 63.2% in case of bootstrap, in proportion to the fold structure in the case of cross-validation. The remaining data points can then be used to build test and validation sets to evaluate the models, as in random forests [52, 53].

Preserving the empirical distribution of a variable while resampling is a simple endeavour if all data points are independent, but it can become very complicated very quickly when the data have some kind of structure such as spatial and temporal dependencies. Using stochastic simulations may be more straightforward in such cases. A simple approach is to perturb data points with either stochastic noise or randomly-chosen deterministic transformations (addition, subtraction, multiplication, etc.). Small perturbations should not alter the outputs of a model if the model is sufficiently robust for practical use. They make overfitting less likely by effectively smoothing the data in the same way as ridge regression [40], which will help us in identifying whether our models are overfitting or are singular in places. Using deterministic transformations, on the other hand, facilitates testing model invariants and some types of model properties. If a transformation is invariant, the model and its outputs should not change: the original and transformed data belong to the same equivalence class, in the sense that they result in equivalent models.[4] If a transformation is not invariant, we may still be able to map the transformed inputs to the corresponding parameter estimates and predictions based on the properties of the model. For instance, models constructed using linear functions of the data, like linear regression models, are closed against linear transformation: multiplying a variable by a constant will result in an equivalent change in the associated regression coefficient; adding a constant to a variable should not change the associated regression coefficient, which expresses the change in the response for a unit change in the variable; and adding a constant to all variables will shift the intercept of the model by the same amount. These are all properties that are easy to test and that our model implementation must satisfy. If we think of including and excluding data points as a deterministic transformation of the data, we can consider bootstrap and cross-validation themselves as stochastic simulations! Which makes intuitive sense if we consider that they use random sampling with and without replacement, respectively.

A more complex approach to stochastic simulation is to train a generative model on the data, and use it as an auxiliary model that generates new data points to build tests with. If the generative model captures the

---

[4]There may be other equivalence classes beyond those we can identify in this way: domain knowledge about the data may help in identifying them.

distribution of the data well, the data points that it generates should follow the same distribution and thus be a valid substitute. Generative Adversarial Networks (GANs) [123] are a popular choice, but graphical models [314] may provide an alternative that is simpler to learn and that requires fewer data to train. The advantage of this approach is that it is more flexible than those we discussed above: it can be tweaked to generate outliers and adversarial data points as well as data points with the expected distribution. We can also make sure that the generated data sets are sufficiently different from each other to test the model under various scenarios. However, training a generative model requires a significant amount of data, and it adds to the complexity of the machine learning pipeline (see Sections 9.2.1 and 9.2.4). If nothing else, it means more models to test. A cheaper alternative may be an interpolation algorithm like SMOTE [100], which is more computationally efficient at the cost of being more limited in the data points it can generate.

9.4.4 Testing Local and Testing Global

We can only understand the emergent properties of a machine learning pipeline by considering it as a whole, which suggests that testing the whole pipeline is as important as testing the individual models it orchestrates. Hence the following classes of tests are all equally important to implement:

- *Unit tests:* testing that the individual models display the theoretical properties we know they have, including their resource usage based on big-O notation.
- *Integration tests:* testing that all models accept valid inputs, reject invalid inputs, produce valid outputs, and generate errors instead of producing bad outputs. We want to make sure that if models are wired up properly they will not trip each other up.
- *System tests:* feeding raw data to the pipeline and testing that the final output is correct, insofar as we can

determine that from theoretical considerations (like model evaluation in Section 5.3.4).

- *Acceptance tests:* checking whether the final outputs of the pipeline are of sufficient quality for their intended use (like model validation in Section 5.3.4).

This list broadly follows standard naming conventions for different types of tests established in *Code Complete* [206], but requires some clarifications to make sense in the context of machine learning pipelines. First of all, what is a "unit"? The traditional definition is "a complete class, routine, or small program that has been written by a single programmer or team of programmers". In our case, we consider that to be a single model in the pipeline or a module performing associated tasks like data ingestion or data preparation (Section 5.3.3) or inference (Section 5.3.5). Often we will be able to use models that are already implemented in third-party libraries, in which case unit tests should be provided by their developers. (Given the realities of the software produced in academia, that may very well not happen, leaving all the testing to us.) If we are implementing any machine learning models ourselves, we can make model evaluation code double as a suite of tests as well.

Integration testing is "the combined execution of two or more classes, packages, components or subsystems that have been created by multiple programmers or programming teams". Since we are treating each machine learning model and each module as a unit, we should test that their outputs are valid inputs for the modules that consume them. In particular, integration tests involving data ingestion and data preparation together with models ensure that our quality gates are effective (Section 5.3.3). Often these tests can only be very basic, because even with property-based testing we may only have some very general knowledge about what a module inputs and outputs look like. As for machine learning models, their sample and parameter spaces are both very large and difficult to test in a comprehensive way.

This leaves system testing, "the execution of the software in its final form" focusing on "security, performance, resource loss, timing problems, and other issues that can't be tested at lower levels of integration". Ideally we can implement it by starting from a limited, representative set of data and tracing how the data is acted upon by all the modules in the pipeline, all the way from data ingestion (Section 5.3.3) to reporting (Section 5.3.6). Or we can do the same with randomly generated data. System testing provides the most realistic assessment of the correctness and the performance of the pipeline, especially if we are using real-world data to seed the test. It allows us to test the propagation of errors, meaning both programming errors (like incorrect code and floating point errors) and stochastic errors (errors in the distributions of intermediate outputs that are taken as input by other models). Even in the absence of errors, we usually do not know what the distribution of the output of a model looks like, so it is difficult to simulate it to build integration tests.

If a machine learning pipeline passes unit, integration and system testing, we may have some degree of confidence that it works like it is supposed to. This, however, does not necessarily mean that it will prove to be useful to the people it was designed for, be they scientists trying to figure out how nature works or marketing people trying to make people click on ads. That is what acceptance testing is for: checking whether the pipeline solves the problem that motivated its development during project scoping (Section 5.3.1) and whether it meets all its targets. The software may be too slow, while users need real-time feedback; it may be too resource intensive, so it does not scale well enough to work on future data sets; or it may not be accurate enough in its predictions to meet service-level agreements or relevant regulations. The difference between being technically correct and being useful is, in a sense, a reflection of the difference between statistical significance and practical significance. Even if one machine learning model performs better than another, and even if the difference is statistically significant, it does not necessarily mean we should pick that model over other alternatives. The metric we are measuring may not correlate well with the task we are trying to model; the difference between the two models may be real but too small to matter in practice; or the better model has some undesirable characteristics that make it difficult to deploy it. None of these issues are, per se, the concern of unit, integration or system tests. Nevertheless they are real issues for the users of the machine learning pipeline and thus we should give them serious consideration.

9.4.5 Conceptual and Implementation Errors

What types of errors do we expect to catch with tests? If we exclude issues with infrastructure and input data, one way we can think about them is in terms of *conceptual errors* and *implementation errors*.

Machine learning models with a closed-form formulation, from simple logistic and ridge regression models [147] to hierarchical Bayesian models implemented via variational inference [43], often have closed-from estimators for their parameters and the respective distributions (for a given choice of the hyperparameters) as well as for loss functions and key statistical tests. The algebraic derivations involved in constructing them are prone to human errors. Some of these errors will be incorrect algebraic manipulations that can be spotted, albeit with difficulty, either by machine learning experts or by software for the symbolic manipulation of mathematical expressions. Errors involving modelling choices are more difficult to catch: for instance, incorrect assumptions on model inputs, approximations that prove to be too coarse, asymptotic considerations that do not work out or the inability to capture particular patterns of dependence between variables. These kinds of conceptual errors may require an experienced machine learning expert or two and much eyeballing to identify, and they are especially difficult to detect when the model uses stochastic optimisation for hyperparameter tuning or inference because stochastic noise tends to hide errors with relatively small magnitudes.

On the other hand, many machine learning models have an implicit formulation that relies on numeric or stochastic optimisation to learn a model that has some set of properties for some loss function. It is less common for such models to be affected by conceptual errors, simply because their mathematical formulation is not explicit and thus requires fewer algebraic derivations or probabilistic assumptions. However, implicit models are more prone to implementation issues. In order to make optimisation computationally feasible, or to be able to use commercial solvers, their implementation often looks nothing like their theoretical specification. For example, in the last 20 years many machine learning models have been reimplemented on top of CUDA [244] to leverage the parallelism of GPU linear algebra operations. To benefit from parallelism, model training had to be refactored in as many small, independent operations as possible. On top of that, mathematical operations were restricted to those implemented in silicon on GPUs and TPUs which means, for the most part, linear operations on vectors and matrices.[5] GPUs and TPUs have limited memory,

---

[5]This is not as severe a limitation as it may seem. Non-linear models are mathematically harder to work with, so most have linear formulations that operate on transformed inputs to encode non-linear relationships. A common example are kernel-based methods [176].

which has encouraged the use of single-precision floating point instead of the more common double-precision and made floating point errors and rounding a pressing issue to consider. They also have limited bandwidth, so the code they run had to be designed not to require frequent interaction with the main program running on the CPU. And given limited memory and bandwidth, models were also required to operate on limited subsets of the data and collate the results instead of loading all data into memory. Another example is implementing machine learning models as distributed models over cheap cloud compute instances. (More on this in Chapter 2.)

9.4.6 Code Coverage and Test Prioritisation

Then, the more tests we put in place, the better? Not quite. Each test comes at a cost. Software tests are themselves software: they involve writing code, troubleshooting it and ensuring that it is correct. We should also keep them in sync with the modules they are testing and with the machine learning pipeline. Every time we introduce a new model or a new module, remove or modify one, and every time we revisit how they are wired up, we should also review the associated software tests. In other words, every time the specification of the pipeline in our configuration management platform changes (Section 5.1), continuous integration will re-run all the tests (Section 5.3) and we will have to revisit those that fail. Furthermore, running tests to check whether they pass or not can take a significant amount of time and hardware resources.

We walk a fine line between having enough tests to ensure the pipeline works well and having as few tests as we can get away with. Given the constraints of what hardware we have available and of how much time is acceptable for the tests to complete, we should aim for the tests to cover as much of the functionality of the pipeline as possible. How can we prioritise tests to achieve the best possible *coverage* with limited resources?

For traditional software, the answer is to measure *code coverage* [231]: the proportion of the code executed by the tests. The goal is to make sure that as many functions, conditional branches and code paths are executed as possible so that it is difficult for bugs to remain undetected. Implicitly, what we are saying is that the algorithms and the logic we are implementing in the software are encoded in the code, hence the more code we test, the more we can ensure that the expected behaviour of the software matches our expectations. At the same time, we want tests to overlap as little as possible in terms of what they cover so as to implement as few as possible.

Machine learning software, however, differs from traditional software in that its behaviour is determined by data as much as by code (Section 5.1). Using different data for training, or predicting data points that are markedly different from what the models expect, may very well exercise the same code paths as "typical data" while producing pathological outputs. Hence code coverage is not a useful measure of how much of the functionality of the pipeline is being tested, because code is only part of the story. Sample space, for both inputs and outputs, parameter space and model space coverage are more meaningful indicators. This is not to say that code coverage is useless: but it is orthogonal to measures of coverage built on data, models and parameters. By all means, we should test code paths to be working to specification if in use, and remove them as dead code if not.

What does that mean in terms of choosing and prioritising tests? Sample space, parameter space and model space are effectively infinite in size so we cannot fully cover them. We can, however, make sure that we test a good selection of *boundary values, typical values* and *invalid values* [369]. In a very limited way, this is what we did at the end of the refactoring example in Section 6.8.

Boundary values are data points or parameter values that are close either to the boundary of their domain or to a decision boundary. The former are typically corner cases that produce some sort of limit behaviour, like hugely inflated or biased values in prediction or singular models in training. In general, limit behaviour is never desirable because extreme predictions will be wrong in most cases; and because singular models are overfitting the training data and will have a very poor predictive accuracy. The latter are values which make a model's outputs unstable because a small change in such values will lead to the model producing outputs that lead to a different course of action. This is common in classification models, where we map continuous inputs (the variables in the data) to a discrete output (the class set) by dividing the input space in regions separated by hard thresholds. If one or more variables take values close to the boundary for a data point, a small change in their values will make the model choose different classes for practically identical data points.

Typical values are data points or parameter values that the model should handle well, without displaying any kind of pathological behaviour. They are mainly useful to implement property-based tests verifying that the theoretical properties of the model hold in its software implementation. Ideally, we would like to cover the space of typical values with a grid such that each point in the grid is sufficiently different from its neighbours and that all regions in the space are tested. This would ensure little or no duplication in the tests while ensuring coverage of the sample space (in the case of data points) or of the parameter space (in the case of parameter values). We can choose grid points either deterministically (a regular grid) or stochastically (by sampling them at random); the latter may be easier to implement if the space of typical values is high-dimensional or if we are making assumptions on the distribution of the typical values (say, prior distributions for the parameters). A practical example of this approach is the TensorFuzz debugging library for neural networks [246]. TensorFuzz implements coverage-guided fuzzing: it samples possible inputs to a neural network from a corpus of test data, creates new inputs by changing them using a set of possible transformations, and checks which neurons are activated by the transformed inputs. If the transformed inputs result in a pattern of activations that is too similar to that of one of the inputs already in the corpus, as established by an auxiliary nearest-neighbour model [147], then they are discarded because they are deemed not to increase coverage. If, on the other hand, the pattern of activations is sufficiently different from those we have already observed, the transformed inputs are added to the corpus. Therefore, TensorFuzz gradually builds a corpus of inputs that contains data points with typical values for all variables and that puts the neural network in a variety of states, increasing the likelihood of finding instances of misbehaviour that would not be caught by the original test data.

Finally, invalid values lie beyond the boundaries of the acceptable inputs or outputs of a model. If valid values are limited to an interval, that means any values outside of that interval. Values that are of the wrong type (say, a character string when a real number is expected) and special values like NaN, +Inf or -Inf (Section 3.1) should also be considered. NA may or may not be invalid depending on the context: it is certainly desirable for machine learning models to be able to handle missing data, and if they are able to do so, NA should be treated as a boundary value. Otherwise, we should ensure that the output is NA if any input is NA, that is, that we are propagating missing values correctly; or the model should fail with an error. In general, we test invalid values to verify that model performance degrades gracefully and to make sure errors are generated when no meaningful output can be produced.

Testing a good selection of boundary, typical and invalid values will provide insights on the behaviour of our machine learning software. Testing both typical values and corner or invalid values, we can ensure that models are robust and display the expected theoretical properties. Testing pairs of values for data and parameters (in addition individual values in isolation) increases the probability of finding bugs from 67% to 93% [187]; testing higher-order combinations produces quickly-diminishing returns and may not be worth the effort in applications that are not life-critical. As a side effect, we can also achieve some degree of code coverage: if different code paths map to different regions of the sample and parameter spaces, testing both well will execute many code paths.

Part III

Tools and Technologies

10

Tools for Developing Pipelines

In Part II we discussed how we may adapt software engineering practices to the development of machine learning pipelines. Practices are predicated on the tools we adopt to implement them, which will be the focus of Part III.

In this chapter, we present an up-to-date selection of tools for data exploration, experiment tracking (Section 10.1), for developing code (Section 10.2) and for building, testing and documenting it (Section 10.3). Together, these tools provide a development environment suitable for creating machine learning pipelines. We will then move to those used to manage pipelines in production and maintain them (Chapter 11). We fully expect that the tools available at the time of this writing will consolidate over time, as has happened to other types of productivity tools in software engineering and systems administration.

10.1 Data Exploration and Experiment Tracking

Many issues in machine learning pipelines can be traced to data that are not sufficiently clean or well-structured and therefore are not suitable for training or inference. Early exploratory analyses, together with domain experts, will improve our understanding of the data and can help us improve their quality to the point where we can address the issues we discussed in Section 5.2.1 and 9.1. The code we write in these explorations is the initial prototype that, after much polishing and refactoring, will become the data ingestion and preparation modules of the pipeline (Section 5.3.3). Using a programmatic approach to data exploration, cleaning and transformation is always preferable because it provides reproducible results and enables code versioning (Section 6.5). The code we produce should be tested using property-based testing (Section 9.4.2) with sample data to check whether it works correctly; the same tests can be reused as quality gates for new data during the pipeline lifetime. We will suggest different tools to write such code in Section 10.2: notebooks like Jupyter [274]; IDEs like RStudio [301]; Python libraries like NumPy [141] and Pandas [207]; R packages like dplyr [402], tidyr [403] and janitor [101] are just a few examples. In addition, most integrated MLOps tools incorporate experiment tracking, so we can save these explorations in a centralised and versioned repository and then compare different approaches and their parameters on the basis of the metrics that we chose (Section 5.3.1) for model evaluation and validation (Section 5.3.4).

In addition, high-level visual tools to explore and clean the data may be useful to involve domain experts who may not be comfortable with programming. Some examples are:

- Openrefine [250]: an open-source client-server solution that provides a collaborative web interface for working on data, as well as client libraries to automate tasks using the API exposed by the server.
- Trifacta [374]: a commercial solution that provides an easy-to-use interface to work on data quality, data transformation and data processing pipelines in general. It is designed for non-technical users and supports deployment on all major cloud providers.

- Tableau Prep Builder [337]: offers a straightforward interface to interactively clean, format and visualise data from different sources. It is available both as a local, graphical application and as a web application.
- Web solutions like Airtable [102], which provides the functionality of a database combined with the features of a spreadsheet, may also be suitable for working on small datasets in a collaborative manner.

Data exploration is an iterative process: interactively visualising its outputs as they change is essential. We can do that directly from the Python and R code we use to explore the data if we are using either Jupyter or RMarkdown [415]. As an alternative, we can produce a dedicated interactive dashboard from Python, R, Julia or Bokeh [46] code and from Jupyter notebooks with a visual tool like Tableau [337] or with a programmatic tool like Dash [262] that can generate one. We will discuss more tools in Section 11.3.

If the data are too large for the tools above to handle, we can store them using "big data" frameworks based on Hadoop [350] like Cloudera [65]. We can then use tools like Apache Pig [352], Apache Hive [351], Apache Impala [20] and Apache Spark [353] to manipulate them and implement our own data ingestion and cleaning; or we can use integrated cloud-based solutions like Snowflake [327] and Databricks Lakehouse [76]. The advantage of these integrated solutions is that they handle all the aspects of data management as well as machine learning applications development and delivery, supporting integration with data engineering, data science and machine learning open-source projects.

Databricks, for instance, includes many open-source components. One is Delta Lake [355]: an abstraction layer for existing data lakes and object storage like S3 which is fully compatible with Apache Spark and which supports features such as ACID transactions, schema enforcing and data versioning. Databricks also offers a managed version of MLflow [420] an open-source library-agnostic platform to manage machine learning pipelines which we will describe in more detail in Section 11.2.

DVC (Data Version Control) [158] is an open-source tool that applies GitOps principles to data.[1] DVC manages data and machine learning models through metadata stored in text files, and it uses Git [360] to version them and to track their provenance. DVC is both a command-line tool and a library, and is language- and framework-agnostic.

DVC and MLflow [420] implement experiment tracking in two different ways. DVC organises experiments within Git projects using commits, branches and tags. It automatically tracks data dependencies, machine learning code, parameters and model artefacts: we can compare different experiments through the associated metrics using either its command line or its web interface. MLflow instead provides a tracking server and client libraries that can be integrated into Python, R and Java code as discussed in Section 5.3.6. The tracking server stores the metadata, parameters, metrics and tags collected by the clients for each experiment run into a file or a database. Larger outputs like data files, images and model artefacts are saved separately, for instance, in an object storage.

In addition, there are also proprietary SaaS offerings with experiment tracking and model registry functionalities, to name a few: Neptune [238], Comet [67] and Weights & Biases [397]; more details on this type of software are in Section 11.2.

---

[1]GitOps is an application of DevOps practices such as version control, collaboration, compliance, and CI/CD, and applies them to automate infrastructure management [118].

10.2 Code Development

Modern software development is a collaborative effort based on knowledge sharing, constant iteration and continuous feedback. Distributed version control systems and Git [360] in particular make all this possible by setting the standard for code versioning and collaborative development and by powering popular platforms such as GitHub and GitLab. Our ability to deliver and deploy software using DevOps relies heavily on Git together with semantic versioning [271] and commit tags. Therefore, Git is a tool that every software engineer should be familiar with. Machine learning and data science professionals should be familiar with it as well because it is used in and influences the design of software like DVC that is used to work with pipelines.

Choosing the right set of tools for writing code is a matter of prior experience with specific tools and personal taste. It may be a decision made either by individual developers or at the level of the team, research group or company the developers belong to in order to standardise on a predetermined set of software. In either case, to work efficiently on a machine learning pipeline we will need support for:

- the programming languages that we will use (Section 6.1);
- enforcing coding standards (Section 6.3);
- automated refactoring (Section 6.7);
- integrations with source code versioning (Section 6.5);
- running software tests and summarising their results (Section 9.4);
- interactive debugging (Section 9.4);
- managing the containers (Section 7.1.4) that encapsulate the developing environment, and the ability to remotely work within them.

Ensuring that all developers use similar tooling is useful for compliance, to simplify the training of new developers and to improve reproducibility. (For the same reasons, we should avoid polyglot programming as discussed in Section 5.2.4). There is a wide variety of tools to choose from, falling into the following categories:

- modern and relatively lightweight *code editors* such as Atom [27] and Visual Studio Code [215, also known as VS Code] that can be extended to provide the features above with the use of third-party extensions;
- *integrated development environments* (IDEs) such as Eclipse [88] and JetBrains IntelliJ IDEA [165];
- *shared interactive computing platforms* such as Jupyter notebooks [274].

10.2.1 Code Editors and IDEs

The main difference between an IDE and a code editor is the amount of functionality that is built-in and configured with sane defaults. On the one hand, IDEs integrate most functionality out of the box on a single programming language. For instance, PyCharm [166] offers features such as code inspection, code completion, syntax highlighting, version control, debugging, refactoring, test execution and container integration like other major IDEs, but also supports the Python REPL and provides introspection into the objects created by scientific computing libraries such as NumPy and Pandas. The reference IDE for the R language is RStudio [301], which integrates a console, an editor that supports syntax highlighting and direct code execution, tools for plotting and inspecting R objects as well as history, debugging and workspace management.

On the other hand, code editors are more limited out of the box, but they can reach feature parity with IDEs by installing and configuring third-party extensions. For example, VS Code can provide similar functionality to PyCharm by using a language server like the *Python Language Server* [256] that is compliant with the language server protocol specification [217]. Other alternatives are Mypy [367], Pylance [212] (based on the Pyright [277] static type checker from Microsoft), Pytype [29] (from Google) and Pyre [210] (from Facebook). The same level of integration can be accomplished with the languageserver package [189] and the VS Code R extension [291] for R and with LanguageServer.jl [169] and the VS Code Julia extension [170] for Julia.

Both code editors and IDEs can also run as web applications: a web browser session connects to a cloud instance replicating a common, unified development environment. This approach has two advantages: it reduces technical debt arising from polyglot programming (Section 5.2.4) and makes it possible to develop in environments that are too complex or too resource-intensive to run locally (Section 5.3.2). Code editors like VS Code provide web interfaces [221] to navigate files and repositories and to commit small code changes, while IDEs like GitHub Codespaces [111] and AWS Cloud9 [10] provide complete cloud development environments backed by virtual machines (Section 7.1.3). We also have the option to self-host them using Docker [82] and Kubernetes [364]: base container images are readily available for Eclipse Che [87], Eclipse Theia [89] and GitPod [119]. As for R, RStudio Server [302] makes available the same features as the RStudio IDE through a browser-based interface that is connected to R sessions running on a remote server. We would also like to point out DagsHub [75] as a collaboration platform: it provides a shared work environment for data science and machine learning projects that follows the development patterns and the practices presented in this book. It integrates with GitHub, DVC, MLflow, Jenkins [164] and many other open-source tools.

Finally, we would like to mention one last set of code editors: Vim, Neovim [237] and Emacs [120]. They are valued by developers who prefer to create a modular development environment that fits their specific needs. Both editors provide full support for R, Julia and Python through plug-ins that communicate with the respective language servers. Although their learning curve is steep at first, they allow for unparalleled speed of action on code bases of any size in the long run.

10.2.2 Notebooks

In recent years, notebooks have seen widespread adoption in machine learning projects and, more in general, in scientific research. They are typically implemented as Jupyter notebooks [274, from the programming languages *Ju*lia, *Py*thon and *R* they support], an interactive development tool that is ideal for building proofs of concept. Jupyter notebooks are designed to quickly test ideas, to evaluate the trade-offs of different alternatives and to share code, results and figures intermixed with documentation in Markdown format. They can be executed interactively directly from GitHub and GitLab, from a dedicated collaboration platform such as Google Colaboratory [131, also known as Colab] or from MLOps platforms such as Amazon SageMaker [11] or Azure Machine Learning [214].

Despite considerable programming language support and a significant adoption by the scientific community, the use of Jupyter notebooks has several shortcomings in the context of modern development practices (Chapter 6, in particular Section 6.3). The Jupyter notebook file format stores code, outputs, images and Markdown text in a single huge JSON object to produce a self-contained, portable artefact. This architectural choice has four major shortcomings:

1. It is challenging to version a notebook correctly because stochastic outputs change every time it runs.
2. Representing code in "cells" that can be executed in any order is at odds with the imperative nature of the programming languages used in machine learning software.
3. Dividing code into cells to interleave their outputs and the surrounding text impacts code modularity and code reuse and reduces our ability to produce good abstractions. We can accept some level of coupling between cells (because they run code in a shared, hidden global environment) and add glue code to make things work, but that leads to an increase in technical debt (Sections 5.2.3 and 5.2.4).
4. Notebooks do not have any built-in support for automated testing (Section 9.4) or deployment (Chapter 7). While this can be acceptable for exploring data and prototyping models (Section 5.3.2), it makes them unsuitable for developing production-level software.

In particular, executing cells in a non-linear order can lead to inconsistent results because cells affect each other's environment, effectively creating a "hidden state" that is very difficult to track. The only way to achieve reproducibility is to always execute all the code in the notebook from the top in a clean environment. For these reasons, we cannot use notebooks directly to serve machine learning models in a production environment. However, this may change in the future: there are ongoing efforts to develop tools for diffing and merging (nbtime [4] and nbstripout [289]), automatic testing (testbook [242] and nbval [69]), automation (Papermill [241]) and quality assurance (nbQA [235]).

RMarkdown and Julia notebooks are fully reproducible because they execute all the code in the notebook from the top in a clean environment by default, so there is no state inconsistency after we change the code in a cell and re-run it. Furthermore, both are easier to version and to diff than Jupyter notebooks because they store text, outputs and figures in a separate Markdown, PDF or HTML file when compiled. RMarkdown notebooks are well supported by RStudio, which provides code auto-complete, linting and suggestions, but they can be edited with any text editor and compiled through the command line as well. We can also enhance them with the workflowr R package [44], which combines literate programming (with knitr [414]) and version control (with git2r [405]) to generate shareable HTML pages containing time-stamped, versioned code blocks and outputs. For reproducibility, each analysis is run in a new R session.

Given how Jupyter notebooks are geared towards prototyping, we suggest that they should be integrated in a modern development workflow as follows:

1. Experiment and build a prototype of the code using notebooks.
2. When the prototype is complete, move the code to a new Git repository and start refactoring it using an IDE or a code editor to make it modular and scalable. At the same time, add software tests.
3. Add docstrings [124] to the code using the text in Jupyter Markdown as a base.
4. Package your artefact using pip [280] and setuptool [278] (Section 7.1.2) for later use as a module within the machine learning pipeline or as a library that will be imported by other Jupyter notebooks.

10.2.3 Accessing Data and Documentation

Quickly accessing documentation during development is invaluable when working on complex code bases. We can use offline documentation browsers such as Velocity [323] or Dash, or the open-source Zeal [356]. All three can automatically download the *docsets* (HTML documentation archives for offline usage) for major programming languages and machine learning frameworks, and also integrate with the leading IDEs and code editors. Overall, they are interchangeable in terms of features.

As for accessing data, object storage like AWS Amazon S3 is becoming the de facto standard for data interchange in data science and machine learning. Therefore, it is very useful to integrate code editors and IDEs with libraries capable of abstracting the listing, downloading and uploading of data into object storage buckets across multiple cloud vendors. A popular example is MinIO [223], which is fully compatible with the S3 APIs and provides an open-source SDK for multiple languages.

10.3 Build, Test and Documentation Tools

Using appropriate tools for building, testing and performing software quality assurance is important to improve ergonomics and reduce the likelihood of errors. In addition, we may want to use the same set of tools in all environments (developer workstations, staging and production environments) and in all stages of development, both to avoid inconsistencies and to maintain a common environment shared by all the people who work on the pipeline.

Currently, containers (Section 7.1.4) are the most common way of packaging the modules of a machine learning pipeline: either individually with Docker, in groups with Docker compose [84] or Podman [354], or as a single-node Kubernetes with Minikube [366] or MicroK8s [57]. All these solutions build on Docker, with different trade-offs in terms of architecture and functionality, and therefore support the deployment practices described in Chapter 7.

One of the points of using containers is to isolate different modules and applications from each other. We can further decouple our code from the software installed within each container by using pipenv or pip [280] plus virtualenv [279] to create isolated Python environments and to manage dependencies on packages and on specific versions of the Python interpreter (without collisions with the globally installed ones). We can install and switch between multiple versions of Python using pyenv [417] or Poetry [173], or a more general-purpose tool like asdf [203] that supports multiple runtime versions for the most used interpreters, compilers and development tools. If our needs are too complex for this approach, we might consider tools such as Pipenv [294] and Conda [16]. Conda in particular has a broad support for machine learning and data science applications [15] but is rather cumbersome to use. The R counterpart of Pipenv is the packrat package [380], which also uses a locally installed R interpreter.

Automated tests are another key feature of modern practices for developing (Section 6.5), refactoring (Section 6.7) and maintaining software (Section 9.4). Each test should be run in a clean environment such as a container that is re-created at each run: we want to avoid the execution of one test influencing the results of another. (The automated and reproducible deployment practices we discussed in Chapter 7 are a key enabler of automated testing!) Test results should be included as pass/fail by the CI/CD pipeline to facilitate code review (Section 6.6) and to ensure that the pipeline is always in a functioning state. There are many frameworks and libraries that we can use to implement the types of tests described in Section 9.4. For individual modules, we can use the unittest [282] and doctest [281] packages in the Python standard library, the testthat R [404] package and the Julia test module.

We should also test that the machine learning pipeline as a whole works as expected. Tools like Airflow [348], DVC and Pachyderm [254] use the DAG that maps the dependencies between the modules to allow for local, iterative testing. In DVC and Pachyderm, dependencies are specified in a declarative configuration file (say, dvc.yaml for DVC) which can be either written manually or built programmatically using helper commands. DVC does not have any built-in support for testing, so we should instrument modules ourselves (for unit tests) and embed the whole pipeline in a testing framework (for integration, system and acceptance tests). In Airflow, the pipeline is implemented in Python code and dependencies are encoded in a dedicated DAG object: this makes it easy to test individual modules with unittest and to validate data with frameworks such as Great Expectations [334]. As for pipelines running on GitHub, GitLab or Jenkins, we can use actions and runners [116, 163, 236] that, albeit with some limitations, can run the complete pipeline or some of its parts using containers. Another alternative is to validate the pipeline directly by iteratively committing changes to a test branch and pushing them to the mainline branch to force the CI to run any tests that may be relevant. Jenkins also provides a testing framework for implementing unit tests on the configuration and on the conditional logic of the pipeline code and a command-line tool for linting the pipeline. GitLab provides APIs to trigger validation and linting for the same purpose.

Enforcing code styles and standards, which we discussed in Section 6.3, is a crucial complement to testing to ensure that we produce maintainable, working software.

Pylint [197] is the reference static code analyser and linter for Python: it is based on PEP-8 (Python Enhancement Proposal 8), the official document that contains the guidelines and best practices on how to write Python code. An alternative is Flake8 [331], which builds on other tools such as pycodestyle (a style guide checker), pyflakes (a source files checker for errors) and mccabe (a tool to check the complexity of the code). A comprehensive linting step for Python code should apply a sequence of tools such as the following:

1. isort [72] to sort imports alphabetically and separate into sections by type;
2. black [190] to format the code;
3. flake8 to check the code style;
4. pylint as the final step to run static code analysis.

The styler package [228], which enforces compliance with the tidyverse style guide [400], and the lintr package [150], which performs static code analysis and which identifies syntax errors and possible semantic issues, fill the roles of the Python packages above for R code. Both lintr (see `vignette("continuous-integration")`) and styler support CI/CD integration [229], accept user-provided code style policies and integrate with RStudio.

Writing documentation and keeping it up-to-date is also key to maintaining machine learning pipelines over time. Documentation should be versioned like code and kept as close as possible to the code it refers to. Documentation on module, function and class interfaces or on method definitions can placed in both Python [124] and Julia [185] code using structured comments in the docstring or native Sphinx format; Sphinx [49] can then compile those comments into documents in various file formats via the Sphinx `autodoc` extension (see Section 8.2 for an example). Sphinx can also be used to (re)compile documentation automatically using CI (with "Read the Docs" [290]) and to render OpenAPI specification files as static HTML pages [175]. The OpenAPI specification files can in turn be automatically generated from docstrings using Sphinx [174], Apispec [200] or a framework such as FastApi [286] and Flask [257].

In R, we can use comments in the Doxygen [382] format for the same purpose: they can be parsed by the Roxygen2 package [401] to generate R documentation in various formats as discussed in Section 8.2.

11

Tools to Manage Pipelines in Production

The production environments of machine learning pipe-lines often have more moving parts than those of traditional software, and the MLOps software to manage them is a broad and fast-moving field with many platforms, projects and tools. The underlying infrastructure may be more complex (Section 11.1), and the combination of data, code and models that makes up the pipeline is certainly more heterogeneous (Section 11.2). In addition to the tools and technologies we need to manage them, we also discuss those that we may use to complement pipelines with the dashboards and reporting capabilities that are common in data science (Section 11.3).

11.1 Infrastructure Management

Successfully running a machine learning application in production goes beyond just implementing a pipeline: it involves managing different local and remote compute systems and integrating different pieces of software that communicate with each other through various APIs. Confusingly enough, the literature often refers to both as "systems", meaning anything that requires configuration, takes some inputs and produces some outputs in response. With such an abstract definition, compute systems, the GitHub organisation that hosts our code, the Amazon AWS EC2 instances that run part of it in the cloud and the Kubernetes cluster than manages the resources of our local systems are all systems. Considering the prominent role hardware plays in a machine learning application (Chapter 2), we find this definition unhelpful because it is too abstract to reason about the architecture and the performance of the application itself (Chapter 5). The same goes for the even-more-abstracted view that "everything is just an API".

Managing the compute systems and the software in a real-world pipeline either manually or with a few simple scripts (which would qualify as glue code, Section 5.2.3) is often too burdensome: there are too many of them, they follow different conventions (because they are produced by different vendors), they are not backward compatible and their configuration files use different languages and formats. Configuration management is the only possible approach to keep this complexity under control and to ensure that the pipeline is reproducible and auditable.

One of the most widely-used tools for this task is Terraform [144], which defines itself as a tool to achieve "infrastructure as code". Terraform is essentially an abstraction layer for a wide range of services [145] and platforms including Amazon AWS, Microsoft Azure, GitHub, GitLab and Airflow. Each platform is exposed as a service "provider" that communicates through APIs that we control, effectively decoupling our infrastructure from the APIs of the original service. Terraform takes care of initialising resources in the original service and of configuring them. For instance, we can use it to create remote resources such as an EC2 instance on Amazon AWS, an object storage on Azure or a VM on a local vSphere [389]. However, it does not handle the installation or the configuration of operating systems and software packages.

Cloud instances, VMs and development machines based on Vagrant [146] and Packer [143] can be installed and configured using specialised tools such as Ansible [18], Puppet [276] and Chef [273]. All three tools provide a complete solution to configuration management: we can define all resources and their configurations as code and store that code in a version control system. They also have modules for testing the configuration management code, for validating changes before applying them to a specific target environment, and for identifying manual modifications or tampering of the configuration files. As a result, they are convenient to integrate and automate in a CI/CD pipeline. Furthermore, Ansible, Puppet and Chef can all be invoked on instances and VMs created by Terraform on their first boot by software like cloud-init [56]. However, they have different learning curves and they require different technical skills to operate. Ansible is written in Python, uses YAML declarative configuration files and has an *agentless* architecture (that is, it can be run without installing anything on the instances we want to configure). Puppet and Chef use Ruby-based domain-specific languages and have a *master-slave* architecture (that is, we install "agents" on the instances to configure them).

As for containers, the de facto standard management tool is Kubernetes [364], an open-source orchestration system originally developed by Google and now maintained by the Cloud Native Computing Foundation (CNCF). Kubeflow [363] extends Kubernetes by integrating it with popular machine learning frameworks like Tensorflow, notebooks like Jupyter and data pipelines like Pachyderm: the result is an integrated platform specifically geared towards managing, developing, deploying and scaling machine learning pipelines. Kubeflow can be deployed on managed Kubernetes services like Amazon EKS [12], Azure AKS [213] or Google Kubernetes Engine [127] as well as on local Kubernetes clusters. The latter, which are admittedly more complex to run, can be set up with CNCF-certified open-source solutions like the Kubernetes Fury

Distribution [322] and Typhoon [268]. Both are based on Terraform and Ansible and integrate with other CNCF components like software-defined networking, monitoring and logging (Section 5.3.6) to facilitate the interoperability between cloud and local deployments.

11.2   Machine Learning Software Management

Machine learning applications can be designed, tested, maintained and delivered in production using integrated MLOps platforms that blend tooling and practices from DevOps (Section 5.3) with data processing (Section 5.3.3), model training and serving (Sections 5.3.4, 5.3.5 and 7.2). This is a very recent trend at the time of this writing, so the label "MLOps platform" (or "Machine Learning Platform") has been attached to quite a variety of tools. At one end of the spectrum, we have online platforms like AWS Sagemaker [11], Vertex AI [130], Tensorflow Extended [347], Databricks [76] and Neptune [238]. At the other, we have more lightweight solutions like Airflow, MLflow and DVC that are built on top of a collection of smaller open-source tools that are not specific to machine learning applications. On top of that, we have established CI/CD platforms such as GitLab that are working on MLOps features [117] which overlap with those of the platforms above. We expect it will take a few years before MLOps platforms consolidate into a small number of clear categories. In the meantime, we are choosing between tools that are not mature and have different, unclear trade-offs: there certainly is no one-size-fits-all solution at the moment! However, we can safely mention one trade-off: integrated platforms are limiting because they are often opinionated (they make it difficult to support configurations and workflows other than those envisaged by the authors) and because they are opaque (their components are not visible from the outside). Adopting them early in the life of the pipeline may limit our ability to change its architecture at a later time, may prevent us from exploring different configurations to explore their trade-offs, and may limit our ability to develop software engineering skills. In contrast, manually integrating smaller open-source tools gives us more freedom but requires more work and some level of software engineering skills up front.

Solutions based on Kubernetes such as Kubeflow and Polyaxon [265] integrate and compose different tools, including Jupyter notebooks; model training (on both CPUs or GPUs) and experiment tracking for TensorFlow and other frameworks; and model serving with different solutions such as TensorFlow Serving [345], SeldonCore [315] and Kserve [362]. Kubeflow focuses on managing machine learning workflows end-to-end, while Polyaxon complements it by providing distributed training, hyperparameter tuning and parallel task execution. Polyaxon can also schedule and manage Kubeflow operators and track metrics, outputs, models and resource usage to compare experiments. If a solution like Kubeflow is over-complicated for managing our pipeline, we can also consider replacing it with Argo Workflow [23], a simpler orchestrator that can run parallel jobs on a Kubernetes cluster.

The architecture of Kubeflow builds on the same key ideas as Kubernetes, in particular operators and namespaces. In fact, each machine learning library that is supported by Kubeflow (TensorFlow [341], PyTorch [259], etc.) is encapsulated in a Kubernetes operator that can run local and distributed jobs. Pipelines are executed inside separate namespaces: each user can leverage the Kubernetes namespace isolation to prevent others from accessing notebooks, models or inference endpoints without proper authorisation (Section 5.2.2).

Seldon core [315] and KServe [362] are specialised MLOps frameworks to package, deploy, monitor and manage machine learning models as custom resources on Kubernetes [364]. Both encapsulate models stored in binary artefacts or code wrappers into containers that expose the models' capabilities via REST/gRPC APIs with auto-generated OpenAPI specification files. Furthermore, both integrate with Prometheus [275] and Grafana [133] (for monitoring metrics), with Elasticsearch [91] or Grafana Loki [132] (for logging), and with other tools (for features like detecting data drift and performing progressive deployments, which we discussed in Section 5.2.1 and 7.2). Two other options with a similar architecture are BentoML [37] and MLEM [160]. The former is a Python framework with a simple object-oriented interface for packaging models into containers and creating HTTP(S) services. The latter, which is from the same authors as DVC, stores model metadata as plain text files versioned in a Git repo, which becomes the single source of truth.

Tensorflow Extended [347, also known as TFX] is a platform to host end-to-end machine learning pipelines based on Tensorflow. TFX is designed to run on top of different platforms (Google Cloud via Vertex AI, Amazon AWS) and orchestration frameworks (Apache Airflow, Kubeflow and Apache Beam [349]), supports distributed processing (with frameworks like Apache Spark), and allows for local model and data exploration using TensorBoard [346] and Jupyter notebooks. The TFX pipeline is highly modular and is structured in different components along the lines of those we discussed in Chapter 5, all tied together by dependencies represented as a DAG. The metadata required for experiment tracking are saved using the ML metadata library [344, also known as MLMD], along with monitoring information and the pipeline's logs, in a data store that supports relational databases. All this functionality comes at the cost of complexity and lack of flexibility in certain areas: choosing whether to use TFX requires a careful evaluation of our use case before deciding whether to adopt it or not.

Unlike Kubeflow (built around Kubernetes) or TFX (built around Tensorflow), MLflow [420] is a library-agnostic platform written in Python that can be integrated with any machine learning library through lightweight APIs. The goal of MLflow is to support MLOps by providing four key features:

- a project packaging format built on Conda [16] and Docker [82] which guarantees reproducibility and which makes projects easy to share;
- an experiment tracking API to log parameters, code and results together with an interactive user interface to compare models and data across experiments;
- a model packaging format and a set of APIs for deploying models to target platforms such as Docker, Apache Spark and AWS Sagemaker; and
- a model registry with a graphical interface and a set of APIs to work collaboratively on models.

As we mentioned earlier, we can implement machine learning pipelines using general-purpose open-source orchestrators like Airflow and Luigi [329] or using more integrated tools such as Dagster [92] and Prefect 2.0 [270]. Both Dagster and Prefect 2.0 implement pipelines in Python as modules linked in a DAG, and they provide a web interface that makes it easy to visualise pipelines running in production, to monitor their progress and to troubleshoot them. Monitoring is outsourced to Prometheus in both Airflow and Luigi. Pachyderm, unlike Airflow and Luigi, supports unstructured data like videos and images as well as tabular data from data warehouses. Furthermore, it can trigger pipelines automatically based on data changes, version data of any type and scale resources automatically (since it is built on containers and runs on Kubernetes).

We can implement experiment tracking using more lightweight tools than Kubeflow: two examples are MLflow Tracking and DVC (integrated with a CI/CD pipeline such as Gitlab's or Jenkins), which we discussed in Section 10.1. A related tool is CML [157], which is developed by the same authors as DVC: an open-source command-line tool that can be easily integrated into any CI/CD pipeline to add auto-generated reports with plots of model metrics in each pull request/merge request. In order to do that, CML monitors changes in the data and automates model training and evaluation as well as the comparison of ML experiments across project iterations. Neptune [238] is also designed specifically for storing and tracking metadata across multiple experiments. It implements the practices we presented in Section 5.3.4: in particular, saving model artefacts in a model registry along with references to the associated data, code, metrics and environment configurations.

The other option we have is using managed cloud platforms such as Sagemaker and Vertex AI. Their strength is the deep integration with Amazon AWS and Google Cloud, respectively, which makes it straightforward to implement progressive delivery techniques, to centralise logging and monitoring, and to train and serve models using GPUs. AWS also offers integrations with Redshift [8] and with Databricks to access data; Vertex AI does the same with BigQuery [125], and supports working with feature stores as well. Both platforms support Jupyter notebooks for interactive exploration, and both support pipelines: Sagemaker via a custom Python library, Vertex AI via Kubeflow and TFX. In addition, Vertex AI allows us to develop machine learning models in Jupyter notebooks, to deploy models saved in object storage buckets, and to upload them to a dedicated model registry. In conclusion, both platforms are chasing each other's features, and they are very comprehensive: but they can be confusing because of that.

Finally, feature stores are increasing in popularity in MLOps for storing and cataloguing frequently used features and for enabling feature reuse across models, thus reducing coupling and duplication. They are available from open-source tools such as Feast [98] and Hopsworks [152], Vertex AI and Databricks.

11.3 Dashboards, Visualisation and Reporting

Data visualisation is an essential part of data science and machine learning: it helps explain complex data and makes them understandable by users and domain experts, allowing them to participate in the design and maintenance of the pipeline (Chapter 5). As in Section 11.2, we can choose to implement it with a spectrum of solutions, from low-level libraries for data exploration to more comprehensive visualisation platforms that create interactive dashboards and data reports.

The decade-old Matplotlib [155] library is the most widely adopted Python package for basic data visualisation, followed by its descendant Seaborn [396], which tries to tackle some of the complexity of Matplotlib while producing figures with a more modern look.

At a higher level, we have Plotly [264], Bokeh [46] and Altair [6] for Python, and the ggplot2 package [399] for R. These libraries have similar features and aesthetics, and they can create static, animated and interactive visualisation. Plotly, Bokeh and ggplot2 are programmatic; Altair uses the declarative JSON syntax of the Vega-Lite [309] language and a simple set of APIs to implement the "Grammar of Graphics" [410], which has inspired the design of ggplot2 as well. Ggplot2 has a Python port called Plotnine [182] and Altair has an R wrapper [202] based on the reticulate package [379].

These packages are the foundation upon which more advanced web dashboards like Dash [263], Bokeh Server and Shiny [62] are built. Dash provides interfaces for Jupyter notebooks and for multiple languages such as Python, R and Julia, while Bokeh only supports Python. Both libraries are good starting points for creating dashboards, although Plotly has a faster learning curve. Shiny, on the other hand, is the de facto standard for creating web-based interactive visualisations in R due to its deep integration with RStudio and R Markdown. Other open-source options are Voillà [391], Streamlit [333], and Panel [151]. Voilà can turn Jupyter notebooks into standalone applications and dashboards, which is useful when generating quick data analysis reports. Streamlit and Panel build web dashboards that interact with data by composing widgets, tables and plots from Plotly, Bokeh and Altair, as well as viewable objects and controls. Panel has better support for Jupyter notebooks compared to Streamlit and Voilà.

Applications for visual analytics and business intelligence like Tableau [337] and Microsoft PowerBI [216] are also suitable for creating dashboards, and are especially useful to management or domain experts who need to create their own dashboards but who may not be as familiar with programming. Tableau can execute Python code on the fly and display its outputs within Tableau visualisations via TabPy [336]. PowerBI, on the other hand, does not yet have a complete integration with Python: it only allows reports to be placed within Jupyter notebooks but without a direct connection between the data in the notebook and the PowerBI report.

Finally, we can leverage standard monitoring and reporting tools such as Prometheus [275] and Grafana

[133] to display metrics related to data, features and models. We discussed in Section 5.3.6 how important it is to monitor every part of the pipeline: this makes it likely that we are already using Prometheus and Grafana to monitor other things, and we may as well use them to track and compare data and models across environments in addition to other metrics. This approach is certainly robust: it uses highly-tested components. However, it requires a significant engineering effort to integrate the training and serving modules with Prometheus and to integrate the dashboards into the server-side infrastructure. We can build a similar setup with a more opinionated approach using the TFX validation module on Google Vertex AI, which implements training-serving skew detection [347], or using Amazon Sagemaker with its Monitor [9].

Part IV

A Case Study

12

Recommending Recommendations: A Recommender System Using Natural Language Understanding

In collaboration with Carlo Lipizzi, Teaching Associate Professor & Program Lead, School of Systems and Enterprises, Stevens Institute of Technology.

In Part I we covered the foundations underlying machine learning pipelines; in Part II we discussed how to create and maintain them well; and in Part III we provided a brief overview of the tools and technologies involved. We now put all this material into context by discussing an abridged version of a real-world machine learning pipeline that Carlo Lipizzi built for the U.S. Department of Defense. We base our discussion on Lipizzi et al. [195] and the references therein. An adapted version of the pipeline code and configurations is available at

https://github.com/pragprogml .

We first define the scope of the pipeline and put it into the appropriate domain context (Section 12.1). We then outline the machine learning models involved and how we can think of them as a data processing pipeline (Section 12.2). Finally, we sketch a suitable hardware and software infrastructure for the pipeline to run on (Section 12.3) and the modules that are most interesting from a software engineering perspective (Section 12.4).

12.1 The Domain Problem

The first step in creating a machine learning pipeline is to define its scope, starting with the problem it will try to solve (Section 5.3.1). Lipizzi et al. [195] frame it as follows:

> "a system to determine what are the most relevant recommendations that stakeholders are providing to the Defense Acquisition community [...] extracting user-specific relevance from text and recommending a document or part of it."

In other words, we envisage that users will submit one or more documents and that the machine learning pipeline will rank them in terms of overall relevance, highlighting the most relevant passages in each document at the same time. This would be an ideal opening in the mission statement document (Section 8.4).

The domain metrics that Lipizzi et al. [195] focus on are the *relevance of each document*, which is defined as:

> "By counting the number of words with a similarity more than a threshold (such as 0.50) and normalising it with respect to the number of the words in each document, an average similarity measure is calculated that presents the level of similarity of the entire document with respect to the entire benchmarks. [...] A document with a higher measure is more relevant or like the benchmarks."

and the *relevance of individual passages*, which is defined as follows:

> "To determine the relevant parts of each recommendation, the document was looked at in segments of words. [...] It was found that with a window of 20 words from the similarity matrix, the actual document (which includes the raw text) would have a

window of 35 words that would make up important and relevant recommendations. To assure high-
quality moving average windows, the threshold of
average similarity is set to 0.75. Any window of words
above that threshold is then traced back to the original
document and is highlighted."

What is the threshold for success? From a domain
perspective, we want relevant documents to be ranked
consistently higher than unrelated documents.

"A good indicator that the model learned is that the
control document's similarity (0.25) was significantly
lower than the worst recommendation document (0.5).
This means that the model did an accurate job of
learning the domain of recommendations and finding
the parallels in the documents."

In statistical terms, we can evaluate the performance
of the pipeline using any of the popular measures of
rank agreement. If we have access to a set of documents
labelled by domain experts as either relevant or unrelated,
a simple but effective choice may be the hit ratio among
the top k documents:

$$\text{HR} = \frac{\text{number of relevant documents among the top } k}{k}.$$

Firstly, we may assume that users will only look for
relevant results among the first k of documents: after
all, 70%–90% of users never go beyond the first page
of Google results [318]. Therefore, the accuracy of
the ranking of later documents is not as important
from a domain perspective. Secondly, the labelling of
the documents will inevitably be noisy (Section 5.2.1):
different domain experts will produce different rankings.
Hopefully, we can estimate HR using a subset of
documents that all experts agree are either highly
relevant or unrelated. Granular measures of rank
agreement such as Kendall's τ or Spearman's ρ may

not be robust against the noise in the labels, limiting our ability to contrast the performance of different machine learning models. In turn, this may impact the ability of the monitoring infrastructure (Section 5.3.6) to automatically trigger model retraining (Section 5.3.4) or rollbacks (Section 7.6).

For the ranking to be well-defined, we should specify what "relevant" means. Lipizzi et al. [195] base the pipeline design on the *room theory* framework developed in their previous work [196]. The key idea behind this framework is that we need to make machine learning models aware of the context they operate in to achieve a semantic understanding of the documents they analyse. The same word may have different meanings in different domains: disambiguating them and their relevance is essential to move from natural language processing (NLP) to natural language understanding (NLU). Lipizzi et al. [196] propose to achieve NLU by having domain experts carefully select the documents the models will be trained on to form a knowledge base for a specific topic. In addition, experts identify the key terms in the domain and give them weights to encode their relative importance. New documents will be compared to this knowledge base, as distilled by a machine learning model: the more similar they are to those in the knowledge base, the more they are considered relevant. Clearly, this approach does not work if we train our models on a large general-purpose data set like the Wikipedia corpus: as we argued in Section 5.3.1, identifying what data we need to collect is essential for the pipeline to perform well. In the case of Lipizzi et al. [195], these data are a corpus of documents on a specific type of goods or services that is within the purview of the procurement processes of the U.S. Department of Defense. The corpus should be large enough to cover all the relevant information on that type of goods or services: if it is too small, it may not contain all key terms and phrases or it may not allow us to model their relationships accurately. On the other hand, if it is too large, it may lack focus and it may lower the quality of the rankings produced by the models. We should train the machine learning models in the pipeline using only documents on the exact same topic as those that the pipeline will be ranking (Section 9.1). Limiting the focus of the pipeline in this way may also help in preventing models from becoming stale (Section 5.2.1) as quickly, since there will be fewer relevant terms and they will only be used with a specific technical meaning.

12.2 The Machine Learning Model

The pipeline in Lipizzi et al. [195] is relatively straightforward from a machine learning perspective because it includes just a single model. As a result, it is not susceptible to model feedback loops (Section 5.2.2) and is robust against correction cascades (Sections 5.2.2 and 9.1.2). The data and the models interact in the pipeline as follows:

1. The documents that encode the domain knowledge on the acquisition of a specific type of goods or services are ingested and prepared (Section 5.3.3) using standard NLP techniques including those described in Section 3.1.3. They are a static data set that is used for training (Section 5.3.4).

2. The domain knowledge is distilled from the documents into word embeddings using word2vec [299] and the list of key terms with the associated weights provided by the domain experts. The embeddings represent what Lipizzi et al. [196] call the "room" and are the core of our machine

learning model. The key terms are the vocabulary we pass to word2vec.

3. Inference (Section 5.3.5) involves users submitting new documents which are then prepared in the same way as those in the training set. The relevance of each document is measured as the degree of similarity with the "room" by pooling cosine distance and scaling it by the document's length. Therefore, the machine learning model outputs a scalar number between 0 and 1 which is then used to rank the model.

4. At the same time, the model parses each new document sequentially, identifies sequences of words with high relevance and highlights them. Therefore, each inference request also returns a modified version of the document that was submitted by the user.

Training and inference are both computationally efficient. The time complexity (Chapter 4) of training varies between $O(N \log(V))$ and $O(NV)$, where N is the number of documents and V is the number of words in the vocabulary, depending on the implementation of word2vec. Inference is $O(N)$ both for estimating relevance and for highlighting relevant portions of text, and it can be implemented as a single pass over each document. In addition, word embeddings can be updated when new documents are available [172]: there is no need to relearn them from scratch when the embeddings become stale.

In practice, Lipizzi et al. [195] limit V by asking the domain experts to provide a list of a few hundred key terms: manually assembling such a list is feasible because we are targeting a single type of goods or services as discussed in Section 12.1. The sample size requirements of word2vec are dramatically reduced for the same reason [85], so both N and V are limited for practical purposes. We can, however, expand the scope by extending the pipeline to include an ensemble of models (one for each type of goods or services) in which the appropriate model is selected either (manually) by the user or (automatically) by matching the new document to the closest "room". The latter task can reuse the inference module that computes document similarity, so it has linear time complexity and should not noticeably impact the time complexity of the pipeline.

The inputs and outputs of each of data ingestion, data preparation, model training and inference have well-defined characteristics that make it easy to construct a suite of software tests based on property-based testing (Section 9.4) and to monitor their behaviour in production (Section 5.3.6). The models and the algorithms involved are easy to replace with new ones that have better performance in model evaluation and validation (Section 5.3.4) because we can demonstrate them to be functionally equivalent to those we are currently using. In particular:

- Data ingestion takes PDFs containing text as inputs and outputs the words therein as a vector of strings.
- Data preparation takes a vector of strings as input, performs the operations discussed in Section 3.1.3 and outputs a second vector of strings containing only the key terms in the list provided by the domain experts.
- Model training takes the output from data preparation as an input and outputs the word embeddings, which can be either a sparse or a dense matrix (Sections 3.2.3 and 4.5.2).
- Inference takes the word embeddings and one or more new, preprocessed documents as inputs and outputs a relevance score (a scalar) and a document with highlights as outputs. The outputs may or may not be ordered in order of reverse relevance, depending on whether they are meant for programmatic use rr for a dashboard.

We should test that data ingestion correctly handles well-formed PDFs, and either fails outright or degrades gracefully when handed malformed PDFs or PDFs with structured data that cannot be parsed as text (for instance, tables and equations). Optionally, we could augment data ingestion with bitmapping and OCR to try and salvage such documents. Data preparation should handle text related to the goods or services within the scope of the pipeline, dropping unrelated words and rejecting texts in a language different from English. We should also test that model training and inference complete successfully for boundary and valid inputs (say, documents with no relevant keyword, just one relevant keyword, all relevant keywords) and to fail for invalid inputs (say, empty documents, NA strings). Finally, we should add integration and system testing to examine the stability of all outputs and of the pipeline as a whole: submitting PDFs containing text with small perturbations (replacing a word with a synonym, etc.) should result in very similar relevance scores. We can do the same with invariants like punctuation and capitalisation, both of which should be removed during data preparation. These tests and the corresponding monitoring facilities should be designed to cover all parts of the pipeline, to be as few as possible (Section 9.4.6) and to be fast enough to allow for live monitoring.

Having such a suite of software tests integrated in our CI/CD and monitoring facilities makes it possible to safely plug in new software and models to upgrade different parts of the pipeline. However, we should measure and log how many resources the upgraded parts use (Section 5.3.6). Firstly, we should ensure that the hardware infrastructure we will draw up in Section 12.3 is sufficient to run them or scale it as appropriate (Section 2.4). Secondly, monitoring facilities should still be able to provide real-time feedback. After all, NLP models are notorious for being resource intensive

(Section 9.2.3)! For the particular application in Lipizzi et al. [195], it is particularly important for inference to have low latency because we envisage that users will expect the documents to be ranked in real time.

12.3 The Infrastructure

How the software implementation of the pipeline should be divided into modules should be apparent: the data processing steps we described in Section 12.2 map well to the general architecture we discussed in Section 5.3. In order to support it, we should perform some capacity planning and estimate its compute, memory and storage needs (Section 2.4).

The pipeline described in Lipizzi et al. [195] is not particularly demanding in terms of computing power. The narrow focus of the "room" on a single type of goods or services means that we can keep our training set small and limit our storage needs as well. We do not have stringent memory requirements either: the word embeddings are limited in size because of the limited number of key terms in the vocabulary. Furthermore, we do not need to load the complete training set into memory to learn them: we can use the documents in smaller batches and learn the embeddings incrementally [172].

Therefore, at a bare minimum, we need:

- a machine learning system for model training, optimised for compute and memory;
- a set of systems with less memory and compute but good network connectivity to distribute the inference load and keep latency low;
- a storage system to hold the PDF documents used for training, the prepared textual data we extract from them and a model repository with the embeddings;

- a separate system hosting the pipeline orchestrator, the CI/CD infrastructure and the server components of logging and monitoring (Section 5.3.6).

We should also take care of assigning sufficient resources to all the environments we use (test, pre-production, production) and of making as similar as possible in their hardware configurations.

The machine learning system dedicated to model training may be a local system: this facilitates experimentation because observability is more limited on remote systems (Section 2.3). Furthermore, we should plan for the future: we should equip it with GPUs or TPUs to be able to explore more complicated NLP models (with an eye towards adopting them and replacing word2vec if they perform better) and to accelerate word2vec to the point where increasing the size of the training set over time becomes a non-issue. It then makes sense for the storage systems holding the raw and prepared data to be local systems as well, and to be placed in the same facility as that performing model training to reduce the overhead of data access in model training. Cold storage (Section 2.1.2) is suitable for raw data (the PDF documents): we need to access them only when working on data ingestion and preparation, not for training. Hot storage may be better for the prepared data, again to limit the overhead of data accesses and increase operational intensity (Section 2.2).

In contrast, the machine learning systems running the inference modules are better placed in geographically-distributed cloud instances if the users are spread over the world, which is definitely the case for U.S. Defense personnel, to reduce latency across the board. We may locate the model repository in the same cloud to facilitate model deployment (Section 5.3.5 and Chapter 7).

Finally, the orchestrator, the CI/CD infrastructure, and the logging and monitoring facilities should be placed on completely separate hardware and network connections to ensure they will be available and accessible regardless of any hardware or software issues affecting the other modules in the pipeline. We should also set them up (or the MLOps platform, if we are using one in their place) in a clustered configuration to avoid single points of failure and strive for maximum scalability and reliability. They will be required to restore the pipeline to a functional state, for instance, by rolling back malfunctioning machine learning models. Keeping the model registry in the cloud makes replicating it it in different geographical regions easier, increasing its availability and reliability in adverse scenarios.

How can we design a backup and disaster recovery strategy? That depends on how we manage our infrastructure and on whether the infrastructure is local, remote or a mix of both. If we can rely on configuration management and we have our infrastructure completely described as-code, it may be preferable to re-create it from scratch and re-run the CI/CD pipeline. Just re-running the CI/CD pipeline may be enough to fix minor issues such as a botched module deployment. For instance, Kubernetes [364] can back up the state of any cluster it manages and restore from a single component to the complete cluster in case of disaster [387]. If our infrastructure is not stored as-code, which may be the case for legacy environments, we can only rely on taking regular snapshots of all systems and restoring them as needed.

If part of our infrastructure is remote, we should keep in mind that cloud providers and third-party services can fail and have downtimes of a day or two. Therefore, it is safer to have a set of geographically-distributed systems with a mix of cloud and local deployments. In the case of inference modules, we can thus ensure that the users or the services that consume the inference outputs can fall back to a functioning system in case of failures (hopefully handling retries and fallbacks transparently).

12.4   The Architecture of the Pipeline

We aim to develop a pipeline that is as close as possible to production grade for the use case presented by Lipizzi et al. [195], while keeping it simple enough that it can serve as a useful illustration of the practices we discussed in Parts II and III. To make it completely reproducible, we use only open-source components, installed and executed as standalone applications or from container images [82]. Furthermore, we choose to manage the whole pipeline with a Git [360] monorepo (Section 6.4) that encloses all the components to configure, provision, start and monitor its execution. Additional documentation on the pipeline architecture and a list of the software prerequisites for our development environment can be found on the README.md file in the repository's root.

We will use as reference architecture the pipeline structure presented in Section 5.3, which outlines at a high level a pipeline enclosed in five architectural modules:

- data ingestion and data preparation (Section 12.4.1);
- data tracking and versioning (Section 12.4.2);
- model training, validation and experiment tracking (Section 12.4.3);
- model packaging (Section 12.4.4);
- CI/CD deployment and inference (Section 12.4.5).

We decided on this design, shown in Figure 12.1, for two reasons:

- Pipelines are rarely managed end-to-end by a single software solution in practice: in the vast majority of cases, they comprise and integrate multiple platforms and components working together.
- Different pieces of software have different strengths and weaknesses and each excels in a specific area: as we

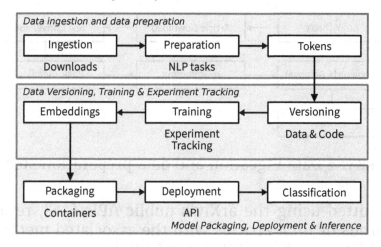

FIGURE 12.1 The architecture of our NLU ML pipeline.

have pointed out in Part III, there is no one-size-fits-all MLOps solution! Using separate solutions for data engineering, model training and experimental tracking, we can illustrate different open-source tools and how to interface them.

12.4.1 Data Ingestion and Data Preparation

For reproducibility, we decided to use a set of freely-accessible documents instead of those originally used in Lipizzi et al. [195]: a corpus of scientific articles belonging to a research topic that is fairly homogeneous but, at the same time, has a large enough number of publications. The corpus we chose comprises the arXiv preprints whose abstract contains the terms "causal inference", "causal network", "counterfactual" or "causal reasoning", and that were submitted between August 1, 2021 and August 31, 2022. The resulting query

```
date_range:from 2021-08-01 to 2022-08-31;abs:"causal inference" OR
  "causal network" OR "counterfactual" OR "causal reasoning"
```

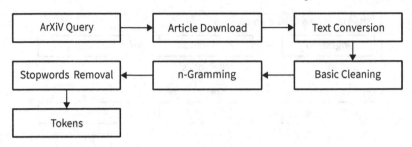

FIGURE 12.2 Data ingestion and data preparation steps.

submitted using the arXiv's public APIs [26], returns a corpus of 1044 articles with the associated metadata, including the HTTP URL of the PDF file.

We implement this part of the pipeline using Apache Airflow [348], which we introduced in Section 10.3. The DAG that represents the data ingestion and data preparation steps is shown in Figure 12.2: each step is implemented as a Python function and called by Airflow using the generic PythonOperator and pythonVirtualenvOperator interfaces. More in detail:

1. *ArXiv Query*: we call the arXiv APIs and process the returned list to extract the PDF URLs.
2. *Article Download*: we download the PDFs returned by the query with a multi-threaded HTTP Python client, respecting the rate limits imposed by arXiv, and we store them in a local filesystem or local object storage (implemented with MinIO [223]).
3. *Text Conversion*: we extract the text in PDF into a plain-text file using one of the many available Python libraries, such as PyPDF2 [99], PdfMiner [320] or Spacy [97]. As before, we process multiple documents in parallel using a thread pool.
4. *Basic Cleaning, n-Gramming, Stopwords Removal*: we preprocess the text files using NLP libraries such NLTK [240], Spacy [97] and Gensim

[292]. In particular, we perform case conversion, punctuation and stopword removal, stemming, lemmatisation and n-gramming.

5. *Tokens*: what is left are tokens[1] suitable for modelling in NLP and NLU applications.

The Python code for the Airflow DAG provides a programmatic view of how the blocks in Figure 12.1 are implemented and linked together.

```Python
with DAG('ingestion', ...) as dag:
    [...]
    get_article_urls = PythonOperator(
        task_id='query_arxiv_archive',
        python_callable=query_arxiv,
        op_kwargs={'query': query}
    )

    download_article = PythonOperator(
        task_id='download_from_arxiv_archive',
        python_callable=download_arxiv,
        op_kwargs={}
    )

    extract_text_from_article = PythonOperator(
        task_id='extract_text',
        python_callable=convert_pdf_to_text
        op_kwargs={},
    )
    [...]
    get_article_urls >> download_article
    download_article >> extract_text_from_article
    [...]
```

The two main challenges we tackle are the scalability of extracting the text from the PDF files and the

---

[1]A sequence of characters grouped to provide a semantic unit for NLP processing.

robustness of the software tests. We achieve scalability with multithreading in the Python code we call from Airflow; we could have achieved similar results at the level of the Airflow DAG using Celery [19] or the Kubernetes [364] executor, or by completely replacing Airflow with Apache Spark [353]. As for cleaning the extracted text, we develop a set of custom methods to perform the basic NLP cleaning tasks, and a custom n-gramming method for detecting the unigrams, bigrams and trigrams identified as the key terms by experts in the domain of causal inference. Both are organised in dedicated submodules and complemented by unit tests. The n-grams list is a static resource file versioned in Git and referenced via environment variables in the pipeline stages.

The output of the DAG is a list of tokens that we will model with word2vec. The tokens, the list of the PDF URLs, the list of n-grams and the metadata that define the arXiv query are stored inside a data tracking and versioning repository backed by DVC [158] to ensure reproducibility and to allow us to track data provenance, as discussed in Section 5.3.3. We can integrate Airflow and DVC with a custom Airflow operator or by calling the dvc commandline client from the Airflow built-in operator BashOperator.

The Airflow DAG is configured to write task logs to stdout, where they are collected by a tool such as Fluentd [359] and forwarded to a logging database such as Elasticsearch [91]. Airflow can also be configured to export task execution metrics to dashboards built by tools such as Grafana [133]. The logs themselves take the form of a JSON object representation of the LogRecord object in the Python Airflow code, which can be passed to the Python logging module.

12.4.2 Data Tracking and Versioning

In addition to ingesting and cleaning the data in a reproducible way, we also want to track all the data sets that are produced by the steps described in Section 12.4.1: the DAG may be scheduled to run daily with different search queries to create additional knowledge domains as described in Lipizzi et al. [195] or to retrain existing word2vec models. Therefore, we choose to version the machine learning code (Section 6.5) together with the text corpus. This allows us to evaluate different NLP frameworks, choices for the parameters of word2vec and sets of n-grams from the domain experts.

As we mentioned in Section 12.4.1, we choose DVC to implement data versioning. DVC can also perform experiment tracking, but we will implement that in Section 12.4.3 with MLflow (which we introduced in Section 10.1 along with DVC). We initialise the Git repository for use by DVC, and we pull the tokens produced by the Airflow DAG from the remote object-storage we stored them in with the command *dvc pull*. This also pulls the corresponding metadata, which are versioned and stored in a YAML .dvc file like that below.

```YAML
outs:
- md5: 853c9693c5aac78162da1c3b46aec63e
  size: 2190841
  path: causal_inference.txt

meta:
  search_query: "causal inference"
  search_start: 1629410400
  search_end: 1672441200
  [...]
```

The md5 attribute represents the hash of content and the path attribute is the path of the file or directory relative to the working directory, which defaults to the file's location. We can then start experimenting using a development flow like the following.

```shell
$ git log --oneline                                              Shell
669a39e (HEAD -> master, tag: v0.0.1) - w2v baseline impl.
[...]
$ dvc remote list # list remote storage configured in DVC
exp_bucket   s3://exp_bucket
$ dvc pull # fetch data from remote storage into the project
A       datasets/causal_inference.txt
A       datasets/causal_inference_small.txt
2 files added
$ nvim src/train-cli.py # tune the training code
$ pipenv run src/train-cli.py --dataset=datasets/causal_inference.txt
...
$ git status -s
 M src/train.py
$ git add src/train-cli.py
$ git commit -m 'Changed word2vec window size to 4'
$ git tag -a 'v0.0.2' -m 'Changed word2vec window size to 4'
```

12.4.3 Training and Experiment Tracking

The tokens we produced in Section 12.4.1 and tracked in Section 12.4.2 are the input for the word2vec implementation in Gensim, available from models.word2vec, together with the list of n-grams provided by the domain experts (the vocabulary variable in the code below). word2vec returns a wv object that stores each embedding (that is, a word vector) in a structure called KeyedVectors that maps the n-grams (the "keys") to vectors. The KeyedVectors can be used to perform operations on the vectors, such as computing their distance or their similarity.

```python
[...]                                                            Python
model = Word2Vec(
    callbacks=[Word2vecCallback()],
    compute_loss=True,
```

```
        vector_size=vector_size,
        min_count=min_count,
        window=window,
        workers=workers)
)

model.build_vocab(
    corpus_iterable=vocabulary,
    progress_per=1,
    trim_rule=_rule
)

model.train(
    sentences,
    total_examples=model.corpus_count,
    epochs=epochs,
    report_delay=1.0,
    compute_loss=True,
    callbacks=[Word2vecCallback()],
)

word_vectors = model.wv
[...]
```

We obtain the tokens by calling the get_url() method
of the DVC Python API [159], which returns the URL of
the storage location of corpus_path for a specific revision
defined in revision of the dataset present in the path.

```
import dvc.api                                          Python
...
corpus_path = dvc.api.get_url(
    path=corpus_path,
    repo=repo_path,
    rev=revision,
    remote=remote
```

```
)
...
```

The corpus is sequentially read, tokenised and fed directly to the `train()` method of word2vec. We set the arguments of the `train()` method [293] using environment variables, as suggested in Section 5.1, to facilitate multiple experimentations with different combinations of:

- *vector_size*: the number of dimensions of the word vectors (default: 100);
- *window*: the maximum distance between the current and predicted word within a sentence (default: 5).
- *min_count*: the minimum frequency for a word to be considered (default: 5).
- *workers*: the number of worker threads to train the model (default: 3).

As for experiment tracking, we implement it using the following MLflow tracking APIs:

- `log_param()`: for tracking the word2vec parameters and the metadata associated with the input tokens, in particular the arXiv query that produced them and the DVC file path and hash they were pulled from;
- `log_metric()`: for logging the dimensions of the embeddings produced by the model;
- `log_artifact()`: for logging the name of a local file or directory, such as those containing the n-grams from the domain experts and the word vectors of the trained model, as an artefact of the experiment.

Here is a short example of how we use these methods in our code.

```python
from mlflow import (log_metric,log_param,log_artifacts,
    create_experiment,start_run,end_run)
[...]
experiment_id = create_experiment(
```

```
    "NLU experiments on causal inference corpus",
    artifact_location=Path.cwd().joinpath("mlruns").as_uri(),
    tags={},
)
start_run(experiment_id=experiment_id)
log_param("query", query)
[...]
log_param("window", window)
log_param("stop_date", stop_data)
[...]
log_metric("wv_size", model.wv.vector_size)
[...]
log_artifact("corpus.txt")
log_artifact("keywords.txt")
log_artifact("vectors.kv")
end_run()
[...]
```

We save the model in MLflow using its `python_function` interface, which supports custom models implemented as generic Python functions. Specifically, we serialise the learned word vectors contained in `model.wv` with the Gensim function `save()`, and we reload them later with the function `KeyedVectors.load()` when the serving model.

12.4.4 Model Packaging

BentoML [37], which we introduced in Section 11.2, can import a serialised Python model or an MLflow model, and it can bind its API to a RESTful endpoint with a minimal use of glue code. Therefore, it is a convenient choice to package and serve the word2vec model. In our case, the classification API that computes the degree of similarity between the PDF document submitted by the user and those used to train the word2vec model (that is, what we call the "room" in Section 12.1) is exposed as a /classify endpoint.

The code snippet below shows the declaration of the service with the API and decorator provided by BentoML. Once the service is running, the API will be available at /classify: it will accept a PDF file as input and return a scalar between 0 and 1. As a future enhancement, we could build an additional /rank API endpoint that accepts a JSON-formatted list of PDF URLs as input, runs calls /classify API for each of them and returns a sorted list of documents with the associated ranking and similarities.

```python
from __future__ import annotations                          Python

import io
from typing import Any
import typing

import numpy as np

import bentoml
from bentoml.io import File
from bentoml.io import JSON

nlu_runner = bentoml.picklable_model.get("nlu_exp:v0.0.2).to_runner()
svc = bentoml.Service("pdf_classifier", runners=[nlu_runner])

@svc.api(input=File(), output=JSON())
def classify(input_pdf: io.BytesIO[Any]) -> typing.List[float]:
    return nlu_runner.classify.run(input_pdf)
```

12.4.5 Deployment and Inference

One advantage of using containers to deploy and serve models is that they can be deployed locally using Docker or in a target (possibly remote) environment using Kubernetes (Section 7.1.4). This is an important point in our use case: as discussed in Section 12.3, our pipeline runs on a combination of local and remote systems. Therefore, we use the bentoml containerize command to build a container image with all the requirements needed to run the inference API we defined in Section 12.4.4: the output is a Docker container with a stateless RESTful API server implemented in Python. The commands for building the container are shown below.

```
$ bentoml containerise nlu_exp:v0.0.2                        Shell
$ docker run -d --rm -p 3000:3000 nlu_exp:v0.0.2
```

After starting the container, the API server is reachable at http://127.0.0.1:3000. The URL http://127.0.0.1:3000 /classify serves the API from Section 12.4.4 and http://127.0.0.1:3000/ displays a web page with the dynamically-generated OpenAPI documentation [326] (Figure 12.3). We also make available additional liveness and readiness APIs to support deployment on Kubernetes,

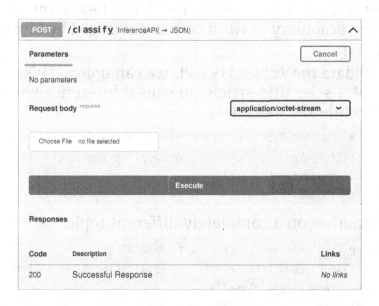

FIGURE 12.3 The OpenAPI specification generated by BentoML.

as well as a /metrics endpoint that returns the service metrics in Prometheus format [275].

The RESTful interface is designed to be used program-matically: we can access it using tools like curl or API testing tools like Postman [386]. We can also query it in our continuous integration setup to run integration tests and verify that the build process successfully created the container image. However, the RESTful interface can also serve as a backend to build web applications that consume the API outputs and display them through dash-boards (using the tools we discussed in Section 11.3) or simple web interfaces (using libraries such as React [211] or frameworks such as Vue.js [419]; or libraries for UI development in Python such as Gradio [1] and Streamlit [333]). They are useful to domain experts to inspect the inference outputs and validate them and the model that generates them as humans-in-the loop (Sections 5.3.4 and 5.3.6). In particular, they make it possible for domain experts to iteratively refine the list of key terms we use as the vocabulary of word2vec as envisaged by Lipizzi et al. [195].

To validate the /classify API, we can upload (POST) the PDF of a scientific article on causal inference with the command-line tool curl,

```
$ curl -H "Content-Type: multipart/form-data" \                      Shell
    -F 'fileobj=@good-article.pdf;type=application/octet-stream' \
    http://remote:3000/classify
{"value":0.8203434225167339}%
```

and another on a completely different topic.

```
$ curl -H "Content-Type: multipart/form-data" \                      Shell
    -F 'fileobj=@bad-article.pdf;type=application/octet-stream' \
    http://remote:3000/classify
{"value":0.24675693999330117}%
```

As we can see from the relevance scores, the "/classify" API responds correctly for both relevant and unrelated

documents (Section 9.4.6). The underlying classify()
method computes the cosine distance between the
KeyedVectors, returns the degree of similarity as a float,
and logs the PDF metadata and the relevance to a remote
logging database via Fluentd.

```Python
[...]
# load serialised KeyedVectors from the `knowledge_ww_fp` path
knowledge_wv = KeyedVectors.load(knowledge_ww_fp, mmap="r")
# get the KeyedVectors pairs that match the
# vocabulary word (the keyword list from the expert)
knowledge_v = get_word2vec_vectors(
        word_vectors=knowledge_wv,
        vocabulary=vocab
)
# train on the fly a word2vec model on
# the PDF converted into text
model = word2vec(text, vocab)
document_v = get_word2vec_vectors(
    word_vectors=model.wv,
    vocabulary=vocab
)
[...]
dist = 1 - distance.cosine(document_v.mean(0), knowledge_v.mean(0))
[...]
logger.warning("Classify request with distance %f for %s",
    dist, metadata)
[...]
return dist
```

The Docker image that serves the APIs can be
automatically rebuilt using tools like Jenkins [164],
GitLab CI or GitHub Actions each time we release a new
model. We can deploy it to a container service or to an
orchestrator by applying one of the techniques discussed

in Section 7.2. Thanks to its stateless composition, the container can scale horizontally if necessary (we just deploy more instances of it) so we can handle increasing loads over time.

Bibliography

[1] Abid A, Abdalla A, Ali A, Khan D, Alfozan A, Zou J (2022). *Gradio: Hassle-Free Sharing and Testing of ML Models in the Wild.* URL https://www.gradio.app/docs/.

[2] Aggarwal CC (2018). *Machine Learning for Text.* Springer.

[3] Alam S, Bălan L, Chan NL, Comym G, Dada Y, Danov I, Hoang L, Kanchwala R, Klein J, Milne A, Schwarzmann J, Theisen M, Wong S (2022). *Kedro.* URL https://github.com/kedro-org/kedro.

[4] Alnæs MS, Project Jupyter (2022). *nbdime – Diffing and Merging of Jupyter Notebooks.* URL https://nbdime.readthedocs.io.

[5] Alquraan A, Takruri H, Alfatafta M, Al-Kiswany S (2018). "An Analysis of Network-Partitioning Failures in Cloud Systems." In *13th USENIX Symposium on Operating Systems Design and Implementation (OSDI 18)*, pp. 51–68.

[6] Altair (2022). *Altair: Declarative Visualization in Python.* URL https://altair-viz.github.io/.

[7] Amazon (2021). *Dynamic A/B Testing for Machine Learning Models with Amazon SageMaker MLOps Projects.* URL https://aws.amazon.com/blogs/machine-learning/dynamic-a-b-testing-for-machine-learning-models-with-amazon-sagemaker-mlops-projects/.

[8] Amazon (2022). *Amazon Redshift Documentation.* URL https://docs.aws.amazon.com/redshift/index.html.

[9] Amazon (2022). *Amazon SageMaker Examples.* URL https://sagemaker-examples.readthedocs.io/en/latest/sagemaker_model_monitor/index.html.

[10] Amazon (2022). *AWS Cloud9 Documentation.* URL https://docs.aws.amazon.com/cloud9.

[11] Amazon (2022). *Machine Learning: Amazon Sagemaker.* URL https://aws.amazon.com/sagemaker/.

[12] Amazon Web Services (2022). *Amazon Elastic Kubernetes Service Documentation.* URL https://docs.aws.amazon.com/eks.

[13] Amazon Web Services (2022). *Amazon Machine Images (AMI).* URL https://docs.aws.amazon.com/AWSEC2/latest/UserGuide/AMIs.html.

[14] Amazon Web Services (2022). *AWS Trainium.* URL https://aws.amazon.com/machine-learning/trainium/.

[15] Anaconda (2022). *Conda for Data Scientists.* URL https://docs.conda.io/projects/conda/en/latest/user-guide/concepts/data-science.html.

[16] Anaconda (2022). *Package, Dependency and Environment Management for Any Language.* URL https://docs.conda.io.

[17] Anderson E, Bai Z, Bishof C, Blackford S, Demmel J, Dongarra J, Du Croz J, Greenbaum A, Hammarling S, McKenney A, Sorensen D (1999). *LAPACK Users' Guide.* 3rd edition. SIAM.

[18] Ansible Project (2022). *Ansible Documentation.* URL https://docs.ansible.com/ansible/latest/index.html.

[19] Apache Software Foundation (2022). *Celery Executor.* URL https://airflow.apache.org/docs/apache-airflow/stable/executor/celery.html.

[20] Apache Software Foundation (2022). *Impala Documentation.* URL https://impala.apache.org/impala-docs.html.

[21] Apple (2022). *TensorFlow 2 Conversion.* URL https://coremltools.readme.io/docs/tensorflow-2.

[22] Aquasecurity (2022). *Trivy Documentation.* URL https://aquasecurity.github.io/trivy/.

[23] Argo Project (2022). *Argo Workflow Documentation.* URL https://argoproj.github.io/argo-workflows.

[24] Arisholm E, Gallis H, Dybå T, Sjøberg DIK (2007). "Evaluating Pair Programming with Respect to System Complexity and Programmer Expertise." *IEEE Transactions on Software Engineering,* **33**(2), 5–86.

[25] Arpteg A, Brinne B, Crnkovic-Friis L, Bosch J (2018). "Software Engineering Challenges of Deep Learning." In *Euromicro Conference on Software Engineering and Advanced Applications,* pp. 50–59. IEEE.

[26] ArXiv (2022). *arXiv API Access.* URL https://arxiv.org/help/api.

[27] Atom (2022). *A hackable text editor for the 21st Century.* URL https://atom.io/.

[28] Ayer A (2022). *git-crypt: Transparent File Encryption in Git.* URL https://github.com/AGWA/git-crypt.

[29] Batchelder N, et al (2022). *A Static Type Analyzer for Python Code.* URL https://google.github.io/pytype.

[30] Bates D, Maechler M (2021). *Matrix: Sparse and Dense Matrix Classes and Methods.* URL https://cran.r-project.org/web/packages/Matrix/.

[31] BBC (2018). *Amazon Scrapped 'Sexist AI' Tool.* URL https://www.bbc.com/news/technology-45809919.

[32] BBC (2021). *Facebook Apology as AI Labels Black Men 'Primates'.* URL https://www.bbc.com/news/technology-58462511.

[33] BBC (2021). *Twitter Finds Racial Bias in Image-Cropping AI.* URL https://www.bbc.com/news/technology-57192898.

[34] Beam AL, Manrai AK, Ghassemi M (2020). "Challenges to the Reproducibility of Machine Learning Models in Health Care." *Journal of the American Medical Association,* **323**(4), 305–306.

[35] Beck K (2002). *Test-Driven Development by Example.* Addison-Wesley.

[36] Beck K, Beedle M, Van Bennekum A, Cockburn A, Cunningham W, Fowler M, Grenning J, Highsmith J, Hunt A, Jeffries R, Kern J (2001). *The Agile Manifesto.* URL https://www.agilealliance.org/wp-content/uploads/2019/09/agile-manifesto-download-2019.pdf.

[37] BentoML (2022). *Unified Model Serving Framework.* URL https://docs.bentoml.org/en/latest/.

[38] Bezanson J, Karpinski S, Shah VB, et al (2022). *Style Guide: The Julia Language.* URL https://docs.julialang.org/en/v1/manual/style-guide/index.html.

[39] Bhupinder K, Dugré M, Hanna A, Glatard T (2021). "An Analysis of Security Vulnerabilities in Container Images for Scientific Data Analysis." *GigaScience,* **10**(6), giab025.

[40] Bishop CM (1995). "Training with Noise is Equivalent to Tikhonov Regularization." *Neural Computation*, **7**(1), 108–116.

[41] Blackford LS, Demmel J, Dongarra J, Duff I, Hammarling S, Henry G, Heroux, Kaufman L, Lumsdaine A, Petitet A, Pozo R, Remington K, Whaley RC (2002). "An Updated Set of Basic Linear Algebra Subprograms (BLAS)." *ACM Transactions on Mathematical Software*, **28**(2), 135–151.

[42] Blagotic A, Valle-Jones D, Breen J, Lundborg J, White JM, Bode J, White K, Mueller K, Redaelli M, Lorang N, Schalk P, Schneider D, Hepp G, Jamile Z (2021). *ProjectTemplate: Automates the Creation of New Statistical Analysis Projects.* URL https://cran.r-project.org/web/packages/ProjectTemplate/.

[43] Blei DM, Kucukelbir A, McAuliffe JD (2017). "Variational Inference: A Review for Statisticians." *Journal of American Statistical Association*, **112**(518), 859–877.

[44] Blischak JD, Carbonetto P, Stephens M (2022). *workflowr: A Framework for Reproducible and Collaborative Data Science.* URL https://cran.r-project.org/web/packages/workflowr.

[45] Bogner J, Verdecchia R, Gerostathopoulos I (2021). "Characterizing Technical Debt and Antipatterns in AI-Based Systems: A Systematic Mapping Study." In *2021 IEEE/ACM International Conference on Technical Debt (TechDebt)*, pp. 64–73.

[46] Bokeh (2022). *Bokeh Documentation.* URL https://docs.bokeh.org/en/latest/.

[47] Bonawitz K, Eichner H, Grieskamp W, Huba D, Ingerman A, Ivanov V, Kiddon C, Konečný J, Mazzocchi S, McMahan HB, Van Overveldt T, Petrou D, Ramage D, Roselander J (2019). "Towards Federated Learning at Scale: System Design." In *Proceedings of Machine Learning and Systems*, pp. 374–388.

[48] Braiek HB, Khomh F (2020). "On Testing Machine Learning Programs." *Journal of Systems and Software*, **164**, 110542.

[49] Brandl G, the Sphinx Team (2022). *Sphinx: Python Documentation Generator.* URL https://www.sphinx-doc.org/en/master/.

[50] Brass P (2008). *Advanced Data Structures.* Cambridge University Press.

[51] Breck E, Cai S, Nielsen E, , Salib M, Sculley D (2017). "The ML Test Score: A Rubric for ML Production Readiness and Technical Debt Reduction." In *IEEE International Conference on Big Data*, pp. 1123–1132.

[52] Breiman L (1996). *Out-of-Bag Estimation.* URL https://www.stat.berkeley.edu/pub/users/breiman/OOBestimation.pdf.

[53] Breiman L (2001). "Random Forests." *Machine Learning*, **45**(1), 5–32.

[54] Breiman L (2001). "Statistical Modeling: The Two Cultures." *Statistical Science*, **16**(3), 199–231.

[55] Callon R (1996). *The Twelve Networking Truths.* URL https://rfc-editor.org/rfc/rfc1925.txt.

[56] Canonical (2022). *Cloud-Init Documentation.* URL https://cloudinit.readthedocs.io/en/latest.

[57] Canonical (2022). *MicroK8s Documentation.* URL https://microk8s.io/docs.

[58] Carpenter B, Gelman A, Hoffman MD, Lee D, Goodrich B, Betancourt M, Brubaker M, Guo J, Li P, Riddell A (2017). "Stan: A Probabilistic Programming Language." *Journal of Statistical Software*, **76**(1), 1–32.

[59] Cass S (2019). "Taking AI to the Edge: Google's TPU Now Comes in a Maker-Friendly Package." *IEEE Spectrum*, **56**(5), 16–17.

[60] Castillo E, Gutiérrez JM, Hadi AS (1997). *Expert Systems and Probabilistic Network Models.* Springer.

[61] Chang AC, Li P (2015). "Is Economics Research Replicable? Sixty Published Papers from Thirteen Journals Say 'Usually Not'." In *Federal Reserve Board Finance and Economics Discussion Paper*, p. 083.

[62] Chang W, Cheng J, Allaire JJ, Sievert C, Schloerke B, Xie Y, Allen J, McPherson J, Dipert A, Borges B (2022). *shiny: Web Application Framework for R.* URL https://cran.r-project.org/web/packages/shiny.

[63] Cheney J, Chiticariu L, Tan WC (209). "Provenance in Databases: Why, How and Where." *Foundations and Trends in Databases*, **1**(4), 379–474.

[64] Clements P, Bachmann F, Bass L, Garlan D, Ivers J, Little R, Merson P, Nord R, Stafford J (2011). *Documenting Software Architectures: Views and Beyond.* 2nd edition. Addison-Wesley.

[65] Cloudera (2022). *Cloudera: The Hybrid Data Company.* URL https://www.cloudera.com/.

[66] Cohen AGV, Pavlick E, Tellex S (2019). *OpenGPT-2: We Replicated GPT-2 Because You Can Too.* URL https://blog.usejournal.com/opengpt-2-we-replicated-gpt-2-because-you-can-too-45e34e6d36dc.

[67] Comet (2022). *Comet Documentation.* URL https://www.comet.com/docs/v2.

[68] Cormen TH (2013). *Algorithms Unlocked.* The MIT Press.

[69] Cortes-Ortuno D, Laslett O, Kluyver T, Fauske V, Albert M, MinRK, Hovorka O, Fangohr H (2022). *IPython Notebook Validation for py.test: Documentation.* URL https://nbval.readthedocs.io.

[70] CRAN Team (2022). *The Comprehensive R Archive Network.* URL https://cran.r-project.org/.

[71] Crook J, Banasik J (2004). "Does Reject Inference Really Improve the Performance of Application Scoring Models?" *Journal of Banking and Finance*, **28**, 857–874.

[72] Crosley T (2022). *A Python Utility and Library to Sort Imports.* URL https://pycqa.github.io/isort/.

[73] Cunningham W (1992). "The WyCash Portfolio Management System." In *Addendum to the Proceedings of ACM Object-Oriented Programming, Systems, Languages & Applications Conference*, pp. 29–30.

[74] Cunningham W (2011). *Ward Explains the Debt Metaphor.* URL https://wiki.c2.com/?WardExplainsDebtMetaphor.

[75] DagsHub (2022). *Welcome to the DagsHub Docs.* URL https://dagshub.com/docs/.

[76] Databricks (2022). *Databricks Documentation.* URL https://docs.databricks.com/applications/machine-learning/index.html.

[77] de Lima Salge CA, Berente N (2016). "Pair Programming vs. Solo Programming: What Do We Know After 15 Years of Research?" In *Proceedings of the Annual Hawaii International Conference on System Sciences*, pp. 5398–5406.

[78] Devlin J, Chang MW, Lee K, Toutanova K (2019). "BERT: Pre-training of Deep Bidirectional Transformers for Language Understanding." In *Proceedings of the Annual Conference of the North American Chapter of the Association for Computational Linguistics (NNACL-HLT)*, pp. 4171–4186.

[79] Dimakopoulou M, Zhou Z, Athey S, Imbens G (2018). *Estimation Considerations in Contextual Bandits.* URL https://arxiv.org/abs/1711.07077.

[80] Dimakopoulou M, Zhou Z, Athey S, Imbens G (2019). "Balanced Linear Contextual Bandits." In *Proceedings of the AAAI Conference on Artificial Intelligence*, pp. 3445–3453.

[81] DMTF (2022). *Open Virtualization Format.* URL https://www.dmtf.org/standards/ovf.

[82] Docker (2022). *Docker.* URL https://www.docker.com/.

[83] Docker (2022). *Docker Registry HTTP API V2 Documentation.* URL https://docs.docker.com/registry/spec/api/.

[84] Docker (2022). *Overview of Docker Compose.* URL https://docs.docker.com/compose.

[85] Dusserre E, Padró M (2017). "Bigger Does Not Mean Better! We Prefer Specificity." In *Proceedings of the 12th International Conference on Computational Semantics*, pp. 1–6.

[86] Duvall PM, Matyas S, Glover A (2007). *Continuous Integration: Improving Software Quality and Reducing Risk.* Addison-Wesley.

[87] Eclipse Che (2022). *Run your favorite IDE on Kubernetes.* URL https://www.eclipse.org/che/technology/.

[88] Eclipse Foundation (2022). *Desktop IDEs.* URL https://www.eclipse.org/ide/.

[89] Eclipse Foundation (2022). *Theia: Cloud & Desktop IDE.* URL https://theia-ide.org/docs/.

[90] Edmundson A (2021). *The Rise (and Lessons Learned) of ML Models to Personalize Content on Home.* URL https://engineering.atspotify.com/2021/11/the-rise-and-lessons-learned-of-ml-models-to-personalize-content-on-home-part-i/, https://engineering.atspotify.com/2021/11/the-rise-and-lessons-learned-of-ml-models-to-personalize-content-on-home-part-ii/.

[91] Elasticsearch (2022). *Free and Open Search: The Creators of Elasticsearch, ELK & Kibana.* URL https://www.elastic.co/.

[92] Elementl (2022). *Dagster Documentation.* URL https://docs.dagster.io.

[93] Espe L, Jindal A, Podolskiy V, Gerndt M (2020). "Performance Evaluation of Container Runtimes." In *Proceedings of the 10th International Conference on Cloud Computing and Services Science*, pp. 273–281.

[94] Espeholt L, Soyer H, Munos R, Simonyan K, Mnih V, Ward T, Doron Y, Firoiu V, Harley T, Dunning I, Legg S, Kavukcuoglu K (2018). "IMPALA: Scalable Distributed Deep-RL with Importance Weighted Actor-Learner Architectures." In *Proceedings of the 35th International Conference on Machine Learning (ICML)*, pp. 1407–1416.

[95] ETF OAuth Working Group (2022). *OAuth 2.0.* URL https://oauth.net/2/.

[96] Evans E (2003). *Domain-Driven Design: Tackling Complexity in the Heart of Software.* Addison-Wesley.

[97] Explosion (2021). *Spacy: Industrial-Strength Natural Language Processing.* URL https://spacy.io/.

[98] Feast Authors (2022). *Feast Documentation.* URL https://docs.feast.dev/.

[99] Fenniak M (2022). *PyPDF2 Documentation.* URL https://pypdf2.readthedocs.io/en/latest/.

[100] Fernandez A, Garcia S, Herrera F, Chawla NV (2018). "SMOTE for Learning from Imbalanced Data: Progress and Challenges, Marking the 15-Year Anniversary." *Journal of Artificial Intelligence Research*, **61**, 863–905.

[101] Firke S, Denney B, Haid C, Knight R, Grosser M, Zadra J (2022). *janitor: Simple Tools for Examining and Cleaning Dirty Data.* URL https://cran.r-project.org/web/packages/janitor.

[102] Formagrid (2022). *Airtable Is a Modern Spreadsheet Platform with Database Functionalities.* URL https://airtable.com.

[103] Fortin P, Fleury A, Lemaire F, Monagan M (2021). "High-Performance SIMD Modular Arithmetic for Polynomial Evaluation." *Concurrency and Computation: Practice and Experience*, **33**(16), e6270.

[104] Fowler M (2003). *UML Distilled.* 3rd edition. Addison-Wesley.

[105] Fowler M (2018). *Refactoring: Improving the Design of Existing Code.* 2nd edition. Addison-Wesley.

[106] Galassi M, Davies J, Theiler J, Gough B, Jungman G, Alken P, Booth M, Rossi F, Ulerich R (2021). *GNU Scientific Library.* URL https://www.gnu.org/software/gsl/doc/latex/gsl-ref.pdf.

[107] Gama J, Žliobaitè I, Bifet A, Pechenizkiy M, Bouchachia A (2014). "A Survey on Concept Drift Adaptation." *ACM Computing Surveys*, **46**(4), 44.

[108] Ganiev A, Chapin C, Andrade A, Liu C (2021). "An Architecture for Accelerated Large-Scale Inference of Transformer-Based Language Models." In *Proceedings of the 2021 Conference of the North American Chapter of the Association for Computational Linguistics*, pp. 163–169.

[109] Gelman A, Carlin B, Stern HS, Dunson DB, Vehtari A (2013). *Bayesian Data Analysis.* 3rd edition. CRC Press.

[110] Ghahramani Z (2015). "Probabilistic Machine Learning and Artificial Intelligence." *Nature*, **521**, 452–459.

[111] GitHub (2022). *GitHub Codespaces.* URL https://github.com/features/codespaces.

[112] GitHub (2022). *Storing Workflow Data as Artifacts.* URL https://docs.github.com/en/actions/using-workflows/storing-workflow-data-as-artifacts.

[113] GitHub (2022). *Working with the Container Registry.* URL https://docs.github.com/en/packages/working-with-a-github-packages-registry/working-with-the-container-registry.

[114] GitLab (2022). *GitLab Artifacts.* URL https://docs.gitlab.com/ee/ci/pipelines/job_artifacts.html, https://docs.gitlab.com/ee/ci/pipelines/pipeline_artifacts.html.

[115] GitLab (2022). *GitLab Container Registry.* URL https://docs.gitlab.com/ee/user/packages/container_registry/.

[116] Gitlab (2022). *GitLab Runner Documentation.* URL https://docs.gitlab.com/runner/.

[117] GitLab (2022). *Group Direction: MLOps.* URL https://about.gitlab.com/direction/modelops/mlops/.

[118] Gitlab (2022). *What Is GitOps?* URL https://about.gitlab.com/topics/gitops.

[119] Gitpod (2022). *Gitpod: Always Ready to Code.* URL https://www.gitpod.io.

[120] GNU Project (2022). *GNU EMacs.* URL https://www.gnu.org/software/emacs/.

[121] Gong M, Xie Y, Pan K, Feng K (2020). "A Survey on Differentially Private Machine Learning." *IEEE Computational Intelligence Magazine*, **15**(2), 49–64.

[122] Goodfellow I, Bengio Y, Courville A (2016). *Deep Learning.* MIT Press.

[123] Goodfellow I, Pouget-Abadie J, Mirza M, Xu B, Warde-Farley D, Ozair S, Courville A, Bengio Y (2014). "Generative Adversarial Nets." In *Advances in Neural Information Processing Systems (NIPS)*, pp. 2672–2680.

[124] Goodger D, van Rossum G (2022). *PEP 257: Docstring Conventions.* URL https://peps.python.org/pep-0257/#what-is-a-docstring].

[125] Google (2022). *BigQuery Documentation.* URL https://cloud.google.com/bigquery/docs.

[126] Google (2022). *Deep Learning Containers.* URL https://cloud.google.com/deep-learning-containers.

[127] Google (2022). *Google Kubernetes Engine.* URL https://cloud.google.com/kubernetes-engine/docs.

[128] Google (2022). *Google Python Style Guide.* URL https://google.github.io/styleguide/pyguide.html.

[129] Google (2022). *repo: The Multiple Git Repository Tool.* URL https://github.com/GerritCodeReview/git-repo.

[130] Google (2022). *Vertex AI Documentation.* URL https://cloud.google.com/vertex-ai/docs.

[131] Google (2022). *Welcome to Colab!* URL https://colab.research.google.com.

[132] Grafana Labs (2022). *Grafana Loki Documentation.* URL https://grafana.com/docs/loki/latest/.

[133] GrafanaLabs (2022). *Grafana: The Open Observability Platform.* URL https://grafana.com/.

[134] Greenfeld AR (2022). *Cookiecutter Data Science.* URL https://drivendata.github.io/cookiecutter-data-science/.

[135] Gregg B (2021). *Systems Performance: Enterprise and the Cloud.* 2nd edition. Addison-Wesley.

[136] Grotov K, Titov S, Sotnikov V, Golubev Y, Bryksin T (2022). "A Large-Scale Comparison of Python Code in Jupyter Notebooks and Scripts." In *Proceedings of the 19th Working Conference on Mining Software Repositories*, pp. 1–12.

[137] Groves RM, Fowler FJ, Couper MP, Lepkowski JM, Singer E, Tourangeau R (2009). *Survey Methodology.* Wiley.

[138] Hammant P (2020). *Trunk Based Development.* URL https://trunkbaseddevelopment.com/.

[139] Hao J, anang TJ, Kim K (2021). "An Empirical Analysis of VM Startup Times in Public IaaS Clouds: An Extended Report." In *Proceedings of the 14th IEEE International Conference on Cloud Computing*, pp. 398–403.

[140] Harbor (2022). *Harbor Documentation.* URL https://goharbor.io/docs/.

[141] Harris CR, Millman KJ, van der Walt SJ, Gommers R, Virtanen P, Cournapeau D, Wieser E, Taylor J, Berg S, Smith NJ, Kern R, Picus M, Hoyer S, van Kerkwijk MH, Brett M, Haldane A, Fernández del Río J, Wiebe M, Peterson P, Gérard-Marchant P, Sheppard K, Reddy T, Weckesser W, Abbasi H, Gohlke C, Oliphant TE (2020). "Array Programming with NumPy." *Nature*, **585**(7285), 357–362.

[142] Harvard Business Review (2012). *Data Scientist: The Sexiest Job of the 21st Century.* URL https://hbr.org/2012/10/data-scientist-the-sexiest-job-of-the-21st-century.

[143] HashiCorp (2022). *Packer Documentation.* URL https://www.packer.io/docs.

[144] HashiCorp (2022). *Terraform Documentation.* URL https://www.terraform.io/docs.

[145] HashiCorp (2022). *Terraform Registry.* URL https://registry.terraform.io.

[146] HashiCorp (2022). *Vagrant Documentation.* URL https://www.vagrantup.com/docs.

[147] Hastie T, Tibshirani R, Friedman J (2009). *The Elements of Statistical Learning: Data Mining, Inference, and Prediction.* 2nd edition. Springer.

[148] Hazelwood K, Bird S, Brooks D, Chintala S, Diril U, Dzhulgakov D, Fawzy M, Jia B, Jia Y, Kalro A, Law J, Lee K, Lu J, Noordhuis P, Smelyanskiy M, Xiong L, Wang X (2018). "Applied Machine Learning at Facebook: A Datacenter Infrastructure Perspective." In *Proceedings of the IEEE International Symposium on High Performance Computer Architecture (HPCA)*, pp. 620–629.

[149] He X, Zhao K, Chu X (2021). "AutoML: A Survey of the State-of-the-Art." *Knowledge-Based Systems*, **212**, 106622.

[150] Hester J, Angly F, Hyde R, Chirico M, Ren K, Rosenstock A (2022). *A Linter for R Code.* URL https://cran.r-project.org/web/packages/lintr.

[151] Holoviz (2022). *Panel User Guide.* URL https://panel.holoviz.org/user_guide/index.html.

[152] Hopsworks (2022). *Hopsworks Documentation.* URL https://docs.hopsworks.a.

[153] Humble J, Farley D (2011). *Continuous Delivery.* Addison Wesley.

[154] Hunt E (2016). *Tay, Microsoft's AI Chatbot, Gets a Crash Course in Racism from Twitter.* URL https://www.theguardian.com/technology/2016/mar/24/tay-microsofts-ai-chatbot-gets-a-crash-course-in-racism-from-twitter.

[155] Hunter JD (2022). *Matplotlib API Reference.* URL https://matplotlib.org/stable/api/index.

[156] Intel (2021). *Intel oneAPI Math Kernel Library.* URL https://software.intel.com/content/www/us/en/develop/tools/oneapi/components/onemkl.html.

[157] Iterative (2022). *CML Documentation.* URL https://cml.dev/doc.

[158] Iterative (2022). *DVC: Data Version Control. Git for Data & Models.* URL https://github.com/iterative/dvc.

[159] Iterative (2022). *DVC Python API.* URL https://dvc.org/doc/api-reference.

[160] Iterative (2022). *MLEM Documentation.* URL https://mlem.ai/doc.

[161] Jacek C, Greiler M, Bird C, Panjer L, Coatta T (2018). "CodeFlow: Improving the Code Review Process at Microsoft." *ACM Queue,* **6**(5), 1–20.

[162] Jain P, Mo X, Jain A, Subbaraj H, Durrani R, Tumanov A, Gonzalez J, Stoica I (2018). "Dynamic Space–Time Scheduling for GPU Inference." In *Workshop on Systems for ML and Open Source Software, NeurIPS 2018,* pp. 1–9.

[163] Jenkins (2022). *A Command Line Tool to Run Jenkinsfile as a Function.* URL https://github.com/jenkinsci/jenkinsfile-runner.

[164] Jenkins (2022). *Jenkins User Documentation.* URL https://www.jenkins.io/doc/.

[165] JetBrains (2022). *IntelliJ IDEA.* URL https://www.jetbrains.com/idea/.

[166] JetBrains (2022). *PyCharm.* URL https://www.jetbrains.com/pycharm/.

[167] Jouppi NP, Yoon DH, Kurian G, Li S, Patil N, Laudon J, Young C, Patterson D (2020). "A Domain–Specific Supercomputer for Training Deep Neural Networks." *Communications of the ACM,* **63**(7), 67–78.

[168] Jouppi NP, Young C, Patil N, Patterson D (2018). "A Domain–Specific Architexture for Deep Neural Networks." *Communications of the ACM,* **61**(9), 50–59.

[169] Julia VS Code (2022). *An Implementation of the Microsoft Language Server Protocol for the Julia Language.* URL https://juliapackages.com/p/languageserver.

[170] Julia VS Code (2022). *Julia for Visual Studio Code.* URL https://www.julia-vscode.org.

[171] JuliaLang (2022). *Pkg: Package Manager for the Julia Programming Language.* URL https://pkgdocs.julialang.org/v1/.

[172] Kaji N, Kobayashi H (2017). "Incremental Skip-gram Model with Negative Sampling." In *Proceedings of the 2017 Conference on Empirical Methods in Natural Language Processing*, pp. 363–371.

[173] Kalnytskyi I (2022). *Poetry Documentation*. URL https://python-poetry.org/docs.

[174] Kalnytskyi I (2022). *sphinxcontrib-openapi Is a Sphinx Extension to Generate APIs Docs from OpenAPI*. URL https://sphinxcontrib-openapi.readthedocs.io.

[175] Kalnytskyi I (2022). *The Sphinx Extension that Renders OpenAPI Specs Using ReDoc.* URL https://sphinxcontrib-redoc.readthedocs.io/en/stable.

[176] Kanagawa M, Hennig P, Sejdinovic D, Sriperumbudur BK (2018). *Gaussian Processes and Kernel Methods: A Review on Connections and Equivalences*. URL https://arxiv.org/abs/1807.02582.

[177] Kang S, Jin R, Deng X, Kenett RS (2021). "Challenges of Modeling and Analysis in Cybermanufacturing: A Review from a Machine Learning and Computation Perspective." *Journal of Intelligent Manufacturing*, **Online first**.

[178] Katal A, Wazid M, Goudar RH (2013). "Big Data: Issues, Challenges, Tools and Good Practices." In *Proceedings of the International Conference on Contemporary Computing*, pp. 404–409.

[179] Kenett RS, Redman TC (2019). *The Real Work of Data Science*. Wiley.

[180] Kernigham BW, Pike R (1999). *The Practice of Programming*. Addison-Wesley.

[181] Khan WZ, Ahmed E, Hakak S, Yaqoob I, Ahmed A (2019). "Edge Computing: A Survey." *Future Generation Computer Systems*, **97**, 219–235.

[182] Kibirige H (2022). *Plotnine API Reference*. URL https://plotnine.readthedocs.io/en/stable/api.html.

[183] Knuth DE (1976). "Big Omicron and Big Omega and Big Theta." *ACM Sigact News*, **8**(2), 18–24.

[184] Knuth DE (1997). *The Art of Computer Programming, Volume 1: Fundamental Algorithms*. 3rd edition. Addison-Wesley.

[185] Krämer S (2022). *Julia Autodoc*. URL https://bastikr.github.io/sphinx-julia/juliaautodoc.html#julia-autodoc].

[186] Kriasoft (2016). *Folder Structure Conventions*. URL https://github.com/kriasoft/Folder-Structure-Conventions.

[187] Kuhn DR, Kacker RN, Lei Y (2013). *Introduction to Combinatorial Testing*. CRC Press.

[188] Kuhn M, Johnson K (2013). *Applied Predictive Modeling*. Springer.

[189] Lai R, Ren K (2022). *An Implementation of the Language Server Protocol for R*. URL https://cran.r-project.org/web/packages/languageserver.

[190] Langa Ł, et al (2022). *Black: The Uncompromising Code Formatter*. URL https://black.readthedocs.io/en/stable/.

[191] Li J, Chen X, Hovy E, Jurafsky D (2016). "Visualizing and Understanding Neural Models in NLP." In *Proceedings of the 2016 Conference of the North American Chapter of the Association for Computational Linguistics: Human Language Technologies*, pp. 681–691. Association for Computational Linguistics.

[192] Li Q, Wen Z, Wu Z, Hu S, Wang N, Li Y, Liu X, He B (2021). "A Survey on Federated Learning Systems: Vision, Hype and Reality for Data Privacy and Protection." *IEEE Transactions on Knowledge and Data Engineering*, **Advance publication**.

[193] Linardatos P, Papastefanopoulos V, Kotsiantis S (2021). "Explainable AI: A Review of Machine Learning Interpretability Methods." *Entropy*, 23(1), 18.

[194] Linux Kernel Organization (2022). *The Linux Kernel Archives*. URL https://kernel.org/.

[195] Lipizzi C, Behrooz H, Dressman M, Vishwakumar AG, Batra K (2022). "Acquisition Research: Creating Synergy for Informed Change." In *Proceedings of the 19th Annual Acquisition Research Symposium*, pp. 242–255.

[196] Lipizzi C, Borrelli D, de Oliveira Capela F (2021). *A Computational Model Implementing Subjectivity with the*

'*Room Theory': The case of Detecting Emotion from Text.* URL https://arxiv.org/abs/2005.06059.

[197] Logilab and PyCQA and contributors (2022). *Pylint is a Static Code Analyser for Python 2 or 3.* URL https://pylint.pycqa.org/en/latest/.

[198] Lohr SL (2021). *Sampling: Design and Analysis.* 3rd edition. CRC Press.

[199] Lopes CV (2020). *Exercises in Programming Style.* CRC Press.

[200] Loria S, et al (2022). *A Pluggable API Specification Generator.* URL https://apispec.readthedocs.io/en/latest.

[201] Lundberg SM, Lee SI (2017). "A Unified Approach to Interpreting Model Predictions." In *Advances in Neural Information Processing Systems (NIPS)*, pp. 4765–4774.

[202] Lyttle I, Jeppson H, Altair Developers (2022). *altair: Interface to Altair.* URL https://cran.r-project.org/web/packages/altair.

[203] Manohar A (2022). *asdf Documentation.* URL https://asdf-vm.com/guide/getting-started.html.

[204] Marin JM, Robert CP (2014). *Bayesian Essentials with R.* 2nd edition. Springer.

[205] Martin RC (2008). *Clean Code.* Prentice Hall.

[206] McConnell S (2004). *Code Complete.* 2nd edition. Microsoft Press.

[207] McKinney W (2017). *Python for Data Analysis.* 2nd edition. O'Reilly.

[208] Mehrabi N, Morstatter F, Saxena N, Lerman K, Galstyan A (2021). "A Survey on Bias and Fairness in Machine Learning." *ACM Computing Surveys*, **54**(6), 115.

[209] Melançon G, Dutour I, Bousquet-Mélou M (2001). "Random Generation of Directed Acyclic Graphs." *Electronic Notes in Discrete Mathematics*, **10**, 202–207.

[210] Meta Platforms (2022). *A Performant Type-Checker for Python 3.* URL https://pyre-check.org.

[211] Meta Platforms (2022). *React: A JavaScript Library for Building User Interfaces.* URL https://reactjs.org/.

[212] Microsoft (2022). *A performant, Feature-Rich Language Server for Python in VS Code.* URL https : / / marketplace.visualstudio.com / items?itemName = ms - python.vscode - pylance.

[213] Microsoft (2022). *Azure Kubernetes Service (AKS).* URL https://docs.microsoft.com/en-gb/azure/aks.

[214] Microsoft (2022). *Azure Machine Learning.* URL https://azure.microsoft.com/en-us/services/machine-learning/.

[215] Microsoft (2022). *Code editing. Redefined.* URL https://code.visualstudio.com/.

[216] Microsoft (2022). *Data Visualization: Microsoft PowerBI.* URL https://powerbi.microsoft.com/.

[217] Microsoft (2022). *Language Server Protocol.* URL https://microsoft.github.io/language-server-protocol.

[218] Microsoft (2022). *Shadow Testing.* URL https : // microsoft.github.io / code - with - engineering - playbook / automated - testing/shadow-testing/.

[219] Microsoft (2022). *Virtualization Documentation.* URL https://docs.microsoft.com/en-us/virtualization/.

[220] Microsoft (2022). *Visual Studio Code: Code Editing, Redefined.* URL https://code.visualstudio.com/.

[221] Microsoft (2022). *VS Code in the Web.* URL https://vscode.dev.

[222] Microsoft Research Cambridge (2022). *Project InnerEye– Democratizing Medical Imaging AI.* URL https : // www.microsoft.com/en-us/research/project/medical-image-analysis/, https : / / www.microsoft.com / en - us / research / video / five - minute - overview-innereye-research-project/.

[223] MinIO (2022). *MinIO Documentation.* URL https:// docs.min.io/docs.

[224] Miłkowski M, Hensel WM, Hohol M (2018). "Replicability or Reproducibility? On the Replication Crisis in Computational Neuroscience and Sharing Only Relevant Detail." *Journal of Computational Neuroscience*, **45**, 163–172.

[225] Montgomery DC (20). *Design and Analysis of Experiments.* 10th edition. Wiley.

[226] Mood C (2010). "Logistic Regression: Why We Cannot Do What We Think We Can Do, and What We Can Do About It." *European Sociological Review*, **26**(1), 67–82.

[227] Mujtaba H (2018). *Samsung Powers NVIDIA Quadro RTX Graphics Cards With 16Gb GDDR6 Memory.* URL https://wccftech.com/nvidia-quadro-rtx-turing-gpu-samsung-gddr6-memory/.

[228] Müller K, Walthert L (2022). *Non-Invasive Pretty Printing of R Code.* URL https://cran.r-project.org/web/packages/styler.

[229] Müller K, Walthert L (2022). *Third-Party Integrations.* URL https://styler.r-lib.org/articles/third-party-integrations.html.

[230] Muth C, Oravecz Z, Gabry J (2018). "User-Friendly Bayesian Regression Modeling: A Tutorial with rstanarm and shinystan." *The Quantitative Methods for Psychology*, **14**(2), 99–119.

[231] Myers GJ, Badgett T, Sandler C (2012). *The Art of Software Testing.* 3rd edition. Wiley.

[232] Narayanan A, Shmatikov V (2008). "Robust De-Anonymization of Large Sparse Datasets." In *Proceedings of the IEEE Symposium on Security and Privacy*, pp. 111–125.

[233] Natekin A, Knoll A (2013). "Gradient Boosting Machines, a Tutorial." *Frontiers in Neurorobotics*, **7**(21), 1–21.

[234] Nature (2016). "Reality Check on Reproducibility." *Nature*, **533**(437).

[235] nbQA Team (2022). *Run isort, pyupgrade, mypy, pylint, flake8, and More on Jupyter Notebooks.* URL https://github.com/nbQA-dev/nbQA.

[236] Nektos (2022). *Run Your GitHub Actions Locally.* URL https://github.com/nektos/act.

[237] Neovim (2022). *Hyperextensible Vim-Based Text Editor.* URL https://neovim.io/.

[238] Neptune Labs (2022). *Neptune Documentation.* URL https://docs.neptune.ai/.

[239] Newman S (2021). *Building Microservices: Designing Fine-Grained Systems.* O'Reilly.

[240] NLTK Team (2021). *NLTK: A Natural Language Toolkit.* URL https://www.nltk.org/.

[241] Nteract Team (2022). *Papermill Is a Tool for Parameterizing and Executing Jupyter Notebooks.* URL https://papermill.readthedocs.io.

[242] Nteract Team (2022). *Testbook.* URL https://testbook.readthedocs.io/en/latest/.

[243] Nvidia (2018). *Nvidia Turing GPU Architecture: Graphics Reinvented.* URL https://images.nvidia.com/aem-dam/en-zz/Solutions/design-visualization/technologies/turing-architecture/NVIDIA-Turing-Architecture-Whitepaper.pdf.

[244] Nvidia (2021). *CUDA Toolkit Documentation.* URL https://docs.nvidia.com/cuda/.

[245] Oanda (2018). *A C++ Fixed Point Math Library Suitable for Financial Applications.* URL https://github.com/oanda/libfixed.

[246] Odena A, Olsson C, Andersen D, Goodfellow I (2019). "TensorFuzz: Debugging Neural Networks with Coverage-Guided Fuzzing." *Proceedings of Machine Learning Research (ICML 2018)*, **97**, 4901–4911.

[247] ONNX (2021). *Open Neural Network Exchange.* URL https://github.com/onnx/onnx.

[248] Open Container Initiative (2022). *Open Container Initiative.* URL https://opencontainers.org/.

[249] Open Virtualization Alliance (2022). *Documents.* URL https://www.linux-kvm.org/page/Documents.

[250] Openrefine (2022). *A Free, Open Source, Powerful Tool for Working with Messy Data.* URL https://openrefine.org.

[251] Oracle (2022). *Oracle VM Virtualbox.* URL https://www.virtualbox.org/.

[252] Ousterhout J (2018). *A Philosophy of Software Design.* Yaknyam Press.

[253] Overton ML (2001). *Numerical Computing with IEEE Floating Point Arithmetic.* SIAM.

[254] Pachyderm (2022). *Data-Centric Pipelines and Data Versioning.* URL https://docs.pachyderm.com/latest.

[255] PagerDuty (2022). *PagerDuty: Uptime Is Money.* URL https://www.pagerduty.com/.

[256] Palantir (2022). *Python Language Server.* URL https://github.com/palantir/python-language-server.

[257] Pallets Team (2022). *Flask Documentation.* URL https://flask.palletsprojects.com/en/latest.

[258] Papernot N, McDaniel P, Sinha A, Wellman MP (2018). "SoK: Security and Privacy in Machine Learning." In *Proceedings of the IEEE European Symposium on Security and Privacy,* pp. 399–414.

[259] Paszke A, Gross S, Massa F, Lerer A, Bradbury J, Chanan G, Killeen T, Lin Z, Gimelshein N, Antiga L, Desmaison A, Kopf A, Yang E, DeVito Z, Raison M, Tejani A, Chilamkurthy S, Steiner B, Fang L, Bai J, Chintala S (2019). "PyTorch: An Imperative Style, High-Performance Deep Learning Library." In *Advances in Neural Information Processing Systems (NIPS),* volume 32, pp. 8026–8037.

[260] Pennington J, Socher R, Manning C (2014). "Glove: Global Vectors for Word Representation." In *Proceedings of the 2014 Conference on Empirical Methods in Natural Language Processing (EMNLP),* pp. 1532–1543.

[261] Pineau J, Vincent-Lamarre P, Sinha K, Larivière V, Beygelzimer A, d'Alché-Buc F, Fox E, Larochelle H (2021). "Improving Reproducibility in Machine Learning Research (A Report from the NeurIPS 2019 Reproducibility Program)." *Journal of Machine Learning Research,* **22**, 1–20.

[262] Plotly (2022). *Analytical Web Apps for Python, R, Julia, and Jupyter. No JavaScript Required.* URL https://github.com/plotly/dash.

[263] Plotly (2022). *Dash Python User Guide.* URL https://dash.plotly.com/.

[264] Plotly (2022). *Plotly Open Source Graphing Library for Python.* URL https://plotly.com/python/.

[265] Polyaxon (2022). *Polyaxon Documentation.* URL https://github.com/polyaxon/polyaxon.

[266] Popejoy A, Fullerton SM (2016). "Genomics Is Failing on Diversity." *Nature,* **538**, 161–164.

[267] Popescu M (2019). *Pair Programming Explained.* URL https://shopify.engineering/pair-programming-explained.

[268] Poseidon Laboratories (2022). *Typhoon Documentation.* URL https://typhoon.psdn.io/#documentation.

[269] Potvin R, Levenberg J (2016). "Why Google Stores Billions of Lines of Code in a Single Repository." *Communications of the ACM,* **59**(7), 78–87.

[270] Prefect (2022). *Prefect 2.0 Documentation.* URL https://docs.prefect.io.

[271] Preston-Werner T (2022). *Semantic Versioning.* URL https://semver.org/.

[272] Prinz F, Schlange T, Asadullah K (2011). "Believe It or Not: How Much Can We Rely on Published Data on Potential Drug Targets?" *Nature Reviews Drug Discovery,* **10**, 712.

[273] Progress Software (2022). *Chef Documentation.* URL https://docs.chef.io.

[274] Project Jupyter (2022). *Jupyter.* URL https://jupyter.org/.

[275] Prometheus Authors, The Linux Foundation (2022). *Prometheus: Monitoring System and Time Series Databases.* URL https://prometheus.io/.

[276] Puppet (2022). *Puppet Documentation.* URL https://puppet.com/docs.

[277] Pyright (2022). *Static Type Checker for Python.* URL https://github.com/microsoft/pyright.

[278] Python Packaging Authority (2022). *Building and Distributing Packages with Setuptools.* URL https://setuptools.pypa.io/en/latest/userguide/index.html.

[279] Python Packaging Authority (PyPA) (2022). *Virtualenv Documentation.* URL https://virtualenv.pypa.io/en/latest/.

[280] Python Software Foundation (2022). *PyPI: The Python Package Index.* URL https://pypi.org/.

[281] Python Software Foundation (2022). *Test Interactive Python Examples.* URL https://docs.python.org/3/library/doctest.html.

[282] Python Software Foundation (2022). *unittest: Unit Testing Framework.* URL https://docs.python.org/3/library/unittest.html.

[283] QS Quacquarelli Symonds (2022). *QS World University Rankings.* URL https://www.topuniversities.com/qs-world-university-rankings.

[284] Quest K (2022). *Standard Go Project Layout.* URL https://github.com/golang-standards/project-layout.

[285] Radford A, Wu J, Child R, Luan D, Amodei D, Sutskever I (2019). *Language Models Are Unsupervised Multitask Learners.* URL https://openai.com/blog/better-language-models/.

[286] Ramírez S (2022). *FastAPI Framework, High Performance, Easy to Learn, Fast to Code, Ready for Production.* URL https://fastapi.tiangolo.com.

[287] Ranganathan P, Pramesh CS, Aggarwal R (2017). "Common Pitfalls in Statistical Analysis: Logistic Regression." *Perspectives in Clinical Research*, **8**(3), 148–151.

[288] Rasmussen CE, Williams CKI (2006). *Gaussian Processes for Machine Learning.* MIT Press.

[289] Rathgeber F (2022). *Strip Output from Jupyter and IPython Notebooks.* URL https://github.com/kynan/nbstripout.

[290] Read the Docs (2022). *Read the Docs: Documentation Simplified.* URL https://docs.readthedocs.io.

[291] REditorSupport (2022). *R in Visual Studio Code.* URL https://marketplace.visualstudio.com/items?itemName=REditorSupport.r.

[292] Řehůřek R, Sojka P (2022). *Gensim Documentation.* URL https://radimrehurek.com/gensim/auto_examples/index.html.

[293] Řehůřek R, Sojka P (2022). *Gensim Documentation.* URL https://radimrehurek.com/gensim/models/word2vec.html.

[294] Reitz K, Python Packaging Authority (PyPA) (2022). *Pipenv: Python Dev Workflow for Humans.* URL https://pipenv.pypa.io.

[295] Reuther A, Michaleas P, Jones M, Gadepally V, Samsi S, Kepner J (2020). "Survey of Machine Learning Accelerators." In *Proceedings of the 2020 IEEE High Performance Extreme Computing Conference (HPEC)*, pp. 1–12.

[296] Ribeiro MT, Singh S, Guestrin C (2016). "Why Should I Trust You? Explaining the Predictions of Any Classifier." In *Proceedings of the 22nd ACM SIGKDD International Conference on Knowledge Discovery and Data Mining*, pp. 1135–1144. ACM.

[297] Rice L (2020). *Container Security: Fundamental Technology Concepts that Protect Containerized Applications.* O'Reilly.

[298] Rigby P, Bird C (2013). "Convergent Contemporary Software Peer Review Practices." In *Proceedings of the 9th Joint Meeting of the European Software Engineering Conference and the ACM SIGSOFT Symposium on the Foundations of Software Engineering*, pp. 202–212.

[299] Rong X (2014). "Word2vec Parameter Learning Explained." *arXiv preprint arXiv:1411.2738*.

[300] Royce WW (1987). "Managing the Development of Large Software Systems: Concepts and Techniques." In *Proceedings of the 9th International Conference on Software Engineering*, pp. 328–338.

[301] RStudio (2022). *Open Source and Enterprise-Ready Professional Software for Data Science.* URL https://www.rstudio.com.

[302] RStudio (2022). *RStudio Server.* URL https://www.rstudio.com/products/rstudio/#rstudio-server.

[303] Rump SM (2020). "Addendum to 'On Recurrences Converging to the Wrong Limit in Finite Precision'." *Electronic Transactions on Numerical Analysis*, **52**, 571–575.

[304] Rump SM (2020). "On Recurrences Converging to the Wrong Limit in Finite Precision." *Electronic Transactions on Numerical Analysis*, **52**, 358–369.

[305] Russell SJ, Norvig P (2009). *Artificial Intelligence: A Modern Approach.* 3rd edition. Prentice Hall.

[306] Sadowski C, Söderberg E, Church L, Sipko M, Bacchelli A (2018). "Modern Code Review: A Case Study at Google."

In *Proceedings of the 40th International Conference on Software Engineering: Software Engineering in Practice*, pp. 181–190.

[307] Saltz JS, Shamshurin I (2017). "Does Pair Programming Work in a Data Science Context? An Initial Case Study." In *Proceedings of the IEEE International Conference on Big Data*, pp. 2348–2354.

[308] Santner TJ, Williams BJ, Notz EI (2018). *The Design and Analysis of Computer Experiments*. 2nd edition. Springer.

[309] Satyanarayan A, Moritz D, Wongsuphasawat K, Heer J (2022). *A High-Level Grammar of Interactive Graphics*. URL https://vega.github.io/vega-lite/docs/.

[310] Schubert E, Sander J, Ester M, Kriegel HP, Xu X (2017). "DBSCAN Revisited, Revisited: Why and How You Should (Still) Use DBSCAN." *ACM Transactions on Database Systems*, 42(3), 19.

[311] Scikit-learn Developers (2022). *Scikit-learn: Machine Learning in Python*. URL https://scikit-learn.org/.

[312] Sculley D, Holt G, Golovin D, Davydov E, Phillips T, Ebner D, Chaudhary V, Young M (2014). "Machine Learning: The High Interest Credit Card of Technical Debt." In *SE4ML: Software Engineering for Machine Learning (NIPS 2014 Workshop)*.

[313] Sculley D, Holt G, Golovin D, Davydov E, Phillips T, Ebner D, Chaudhary V, Young M, Crespo JF, Dennison D (2015). "Hidden Technical Debt in Machine Learning Systems." In *Proceedings of the 28th International Conference on Neural Information Processing Systems (NIPS)*, volume 2, pp. 2503–2511.

[314] Scutari M, Denis JB (2021). *Bayesian Networks with Examples in R*. 2nd edition. Chapman & Hall.

[315] Seldon Technologies (2022). *Seldon Core*. URL https://docs.seldon.io/projects/seldon-core/en/latest/.

[316] Services AW (2022). *AWS Deep Learning Containers*. URL https://aws.amazon.com/en/machine-learning/containers/.

[317] Seven D (2014). *Knightmare: A DevOps Cautionary Tale*. URL https://dougseven.com/2014/04/17/knightmare-a-devops-cautionary-tale/.

[318] Shelton K (2017). *The Value of Search Results Rankings.* URL https://www.forbes.com/sites/forbesagencycouncil/2017/10/30/the-value-of-search-results-rankings/.

[319] Sherman E (2022). *What Zillow's Failed Algorithm Means for the Future of Data Science.* URL https://fortune.com/education/business/articles/2022/02/01/what-zillows-failed-algorithm-means-for-the-future-of-data-science/.

[320] Shinyama Y, Guglielmetti P, Marsman P (2022). *Pdfminer.six's Documentation.* URL https://pdfminersix.readthedocs.io/en/latest/.

[321] Shiraishi M, Washizaki H, Fukazawa Y, Yoder J (2019). "Mob Programming: A Systematic Literature Review." In *Proceedings of the IEEE 43rd Annual Computer Software and Applications Conference*, pp. 616–621.

[322] SIGHUP (2022). *Kubernetes Fury Distribution.* URL https://docs.kubernetesfury.com/docs/distribution/.

[323] Silverlake Software (2022). *Velocity: The Documentation and Docset Viewer for Windows.* URL https://velocity.silverlakesoftware.com/.

[324] Simmons AJ, Barnett S, Rivera-Villicana J, Bajaj A, Vasa R (2020). "A Large-Scale Comparative Analysis of Coding Standard Conformance in Open-Source Data Science Projects." In *Proceedings of the 14th ACM / IEEE International Symposium on Empirical Software Engineering and Measurement (ESEM)*, pp. 1–11.

[325] Simonyan K, Vedaldi A, Zisserman A (2014). "Deep Inside Convolutional Networks: Visualising Image Classification Models and Saliency Maps." In *Proceedings of the 2nd International Conference on Learning Representations (ICLR), Workshop Track.*

[326] SmartBear Software (2021). *OpenAPI Specification.* URL https://swagger.io/specification/.

[327] Snowflake (2022). *Snowflake Documentation.* URL https://docs.snowflake.com.

[328] Sonatype (2022). *Nexus Repository Manager.* URL https://www.sonatype.com/products/nexus-repository.

[329] Spotify (2022). *Luigi Documentation.* URL https://luigi.readthedocs.io/en/stable/.

[330] Spotify (2022). *Spotify Engineering Blog.* URL https://engineering.atspotify.com/.

[331] Stapleton Cordasco I (2022). *Flake8: Your Tool for Style Guide Enforcement.* URL https://flake8.pycqa.org/en/latest/.

[332] Stevens JR (2017). "Replicability and Reproducibility in Comparative Psychology." *Frontiers in Psychology,* **8**, 862.

[333] Streamlit (2022). *Streamlit Documentation.* URL https://docs.streamlit.io/.

[334] Superconductive (2022). *Great Expectations.* URL https://docs.greatexpectations.io/docs.

[335] Swoboda S (2021). *Connecting with Mob Programming.* URL https://shopify.engineering/mob-programming.

[336] Tableau (2022). *Execute Python Code on The Fly and Display Results in Tableau Visualizations.* URL https://tableau.github.io/TabPy.

[337] Tableau Software (2022). *Tableau.* URL https://www.tableau.com/.

[338] Tabuchi A, Kasagi A, Yamazaki M, Honda T, Miwa M, Shiraishi T, Kosaki M, Fukumoto N, Tabaru T, Ike A, Nakashima K (2019). "Extremely Accelerated Deep Learning: ResNet-50 Training in 70.4 Seconds." Poster at SC19., URL https://sc19.supercomputing.org/proceedings/tech_poster/poster_files/rpost203s2-file3.pdf.

[339] Tang Y, Khatchadouriant R, Bagherzadeh M, Singh R, Stewart A, Raja A (2021). "An Empirical Study of Refactorings and Technical Debt in Machine Learning Systems." In *Proceedings of the 2021 IEEE/ACM 43rd International Conference on Software Engineering,* pp. 238–250.

[340] Tatman R, VanderPlas J, Dane S (2018). "A Practical Taxonomy of Reproducibility for Machine Learning Research." In *Proceedings of 2nd the Reproducibility in Machine Learning Workshop at ICML 2018.*

[341] TensorFlow (2021). *TensorFlow.* URL https://www.tensorflow.org/overview/.

[342] TensorFlow (2021). *TensorFlow Extended (TFX).* URL https://www.tensorflow.org/tfx/.

[343] Tensorflow (2021). *XLA: Optimizing Compiler for Machine Learning*. URL https://www.tensorflow.org/xla.

[344] TensorFlow (2022). *ML Metadata*. URL https://www.tensorflow.org/tfx/guide/mlmd.

[345] TensorFlow (2022). *Serving Models*. URL https://www.tensorflow.org/tfx/guide/serving.

[346] TensorFlow (2022). *TensorBoard: TensorFlow's Visualization Toolkit*. URL https://www.tensorflow.org/tensorboard.

[347] TensorFlow (2022). *The TFX User Guide*. URL https://www.tensorflow.org/tfx/guide.

[348] The Apache Software Foundation (2022). *Airflow Documentation*. URL https://airflow.apache.org/docs/.

[349] The Apache Software Foundation (2022). *Apache Beam Documentation*. URL https://beam.apache.org/documentation/.

[350] The Apache Software Foundation (2022). *Apache Hadoop*. URL https://hadoop.apache.org/.

[351] The Apache Software Foundation (2022). *Apache Hive Documentation*. URL https://cwiki.apache.org/confluence/display/Hive.

[352] The Apache Software Foundation (2022). *Apache Pig Documentation*. URL https://pig.apache.org/docs/latest.

[353] The Apache Software Foundation (2022). *Apache Spark Documentation*. URL https://spark.apache.org/docs/latest.

[354] The Containers Organization (2022). *podman*. URL https://podman.io.

[355] The Delta Lake Project Authors (2022). *Delta Lake Documentation*. URL https://docs.delta.io.

[356] The Delta Lake Project Authors (2022). *Zeal Is an Offline Documentation Browser for Software Developers*. URL https://zealdocs.org.

[357] The Economist (2017). *The World's Most Valuable Resource Is No Longer Oil, but Data*. URL https://www.economist.com/leaders/2017/05/06/the-worlds-most-valuable-resource-is-no-longer-oil-but-data.

[358] The Economist (2020). *An Understanding of AI's Limitations Is Starting to Sink In*. URL https://www.economist.com/technology-quarterly/2020/06/11/an-understanding-of-ais-limitations-is-starting-to-sink-in.

[359] The Fluentd Project (2022). *Fluentd: Open Source Data Collector.* URL https://www.fluentd.org/.

[360] The Git Development Team (2022). *Git Source Code Mirror.* URL https://github.com/git/git.

[361] The Hadolint Project (2022). *Hadolint: Haskell Dockerfile Linter Documentation.* URL https://github.com/hadolint/hadolint.

[362] The KServe Authors (2022). *KServe Control Plane.* URL https://kserve.github.io/website/latest/modelserving/control_plane.

[363] The Kubeflow Authors (2022). *All of Kubeflow documentation.* URL https://www.kubeflow.org/docs/.

[364] The Kubernetes Authors (2022). *Kubernetes.* URL https://kubernetes.io/.

[365] The Kubernetes Authors (2022). *Kubernetes Documentation: Schedule GPUs.* URL https://kubernetes.io/docs/tasks/manage-gpus/scheduling-gpus/.

[366] The Kubernetes Authors (2022). *minikube.* URL https://minikube.sigs.k8s.io/docs.

[367] The mypy Project (2014). *mypy: Optional Static Typing for Python.* URL http://mypy-lang.org/.

[368] The Register (2020). *Twilio: Someone Waltzed into Our Unsecured AWS S3 Silo, Added Dodgy Code to Our JavaScript SDK for Customers.* URL https://www.theregister.com/2020/07/21/twilio_javascript_sdk_code_injection.

[369] Thomas D, Hunt A (2019). *The Pragmatic Programmer: Your Journey to Mastery.* Anniversary edition. Addison-Wesley.

[370] Tian Y, Zhang Y, Stol KJ, Jiang L, Liu H (2022). "What Makes a Good Commit Message?" In *Proceedings of the 44th International Conference on Software Engineering*, pp. 1–13.

[371] Tornhill A, Borg M (2022). "Code Red: The Business Impact of Code Quality: A Quantitative Study of 39 Proprietary Production Codebases." In *Proceedings of International Conference on Technical Debt*, pp. 1–10.

[372] Toro AL (2020). *Great Code Reviews–The Superpower Your Team Needs.* URL https://shopify.engineering/great-code-reviews.

[373] Tremel E (2017). *Deployment Strategies on Kubernetes.* URL https://www.cncf.io/wp-content/uploads/2020/08/CNCF-Presentation-Template-K8s-Deployment.pdf.

[374] Trifacta (2022). *Profile, Prepare, and Pipeline Data for Analytics and Machine Learning.* URL https://www.trifacta.com.

[375] Tsay RS (2010). *Analysis of Financial Time Series.* 3rd edition. Wiley.

[376] Uber (2022). *Piranha: A Tool for Refactoring Code Related to Feature Flag APIs.* URL https://github.com/uber/piranha.

[377] Uber Technologies (2022). *Uber Engineering Blog.* URL https://eng.uber.com/.

[378] Unicode (2021). *Unicode Technical Documentation.* URL https://www.unicode.org/main.html.

[379] Ushey K, Allaire J, Tang Y (2022). *reticulate: Interface to Python.* URL https://cran.r-project.org/web/packages/reticulate.

[380] Ushey K, McPherson J, Cheng J, Atkins A, Allaire J, Allen T (2022). *Packrat: Reproducible Package Management for R.* URL https://rstudio.github.io/packrat/.

[381] van der Schaar M, Alaa AM, Floto A, Gimson A, Scholtes S, Wood A, McKinney E, Jarrett D, Liò P, Ercole A (2021). "How Artificial Intelligence and Machine Learning Can Help Healthcare Systems Respond to COVID–19." *Machine Learning*, **110**, 1–14.

[382] van Heesch D (2022). *Doxygen.* URL https://www.doxygen.nl/index.html.

[383] van Oort B, Cruz L, Aniche M, van Deursen A (2021). "The Prevalence of Code Smells in Machine Learning Projects." In *Proceedings of the 2021 IEEE/ACM 1st Workshop on AI Engineering: Software Engineering for AI,* pp. 35–42.

[384] van Rossum G, Warsaw B, Coghlan N (2001). *PEP 8: Style Guide for Python Code.* URL https://peps.python.org/pep-0008/.

[385] van Vliet H (2008). *Software Engineering: Principles and Practice.* Wiley.

[386] Velero Authors (2022). *Postman Documentation.* URL https://learning.postman.com/docs.

[387] Velero Authors (2022). *Velero Documentation.* URL https://velero.io/docs.

[388] Virtanen P, Gommers R, Oliphant TE, Haberland M, Reddy T, Cournapeau D, Burovski E, Peterson P, Weckesser W, Bright J, van der Walt SJ, Brett M, Wilson J, Millman KJ, Mayorov N, Nelson ARJ, Jones E, Kern R, Larson E, Carey CJ, Polat I, Feng Y, Moore EW, VanderPlas J, Laxalde D, Perktold J, Cimrman R, Henriksen I, Quintero EA, Harris CR, Archibald AM, Ribeiro AH, Pedregosa F, van Mulbregt P, SciPy 10 Contributors (2020). "SciPy 1.0: Fundamental Algorithms for Scientific Computing in Python." *Nature Methods*, **17**, 261–272.

[389] VmWare (2022). *VMware vSphere Documentation.* URL https://docs.vmware.com/en/VMware-vSphere/index.html.

[390] VMware (2022). *VMware Workstation Pro.* URL https://www.vmware.com/products/workstation-pro.html.

[391] Voilà Dashboards (2022). *From Notebooks to Standalone Web Applications and Dashboards.* URL https://voila.readthedocs.io/en/stable.

[392] Volkov V, Demmel JW (2008). "Benchmarking GPUs to Tune Dense Linear Algebra." In *Proceedings of the 2008 ACM/IEEE Conference on Supercomputing*, pp. 1–11.

[393] Voulodimos A, Doulamis N, Doulamis A, Protopapadakis E (2018). "Deep Learning for Computer Vision: A Brief Review." *Computational Intelligence and Neuroscience*, **2018**(7068349), 1–13.

[394] VPNOverview (2022). *Fintech App Switch Leaks Users' Transactions, Personal IDs.* URL https://vpnoverview.com/news/fintech-app-switch-leaks-users-transactions-personal-ids.

[395] Walters M, Lee Scott P (2021). *meta-git: Manage Your Meta Repo and Child Git Repositories.* URL https://www.npmjs.com/package/meta-git.

[396] Waskom M (2022). *Seaborn: Statistical Data Visualization.* URL https://seaborn.pydata.org/.

[397] Weights & Biases (2022). *Weights & Biases Documentation.* URL https://docs.wandb.ai/.

[398] Weisberg S (2014). *Applied Linear Regression.* 4th edition. Wiley.

[399] Wickham H (2022). *ggplot2: Elegant Graphics for Data Analysis.* URL https://cran.r-project.org/web/packages/ggplot2.

[400] Wickham H (2022). *The tidyverse Style Guide.* URL https://style.tidyverse.org/.

[401] Wickham H, Danenberg P, Csárdi G, Eugster M, RStudio (2022). *roxygen2: In-Line Documentation for R.*

[402] Wickham H, François R, LHenry, Müller K (2022). *A Fast, Consistent Tool for Working with Data Frame Like Objects, Both in Memory and Out of Memory.* URL https://cloud.r-project.org/web/packages/dplyr.

[403] Wickham H, Girlich M, RStudio (2022). *tidyr: Tidy Messy Data.* URL https://cloud.r-project.org/web/packages/tidyr.

[404] Wickham H, RStudio, R Core Team (2022). *Unit Testing for R.* URL https://cloud.r-project.org/web/packages/testthat.

[405] Widgren S, et al (2022). *git2r: Provides Access to Git Repositories.* URL https://cran.r-project.org/web/packages/git2r/index.html.

[406] Wiggins A (2017). *The Twelve Factor App.* URL https://12factor.net.

[407] Wikipedia (2021). *Cholesky Decomposition.* URL https://en.wikipedia.org/wiki/Cholesky_decomposition.

[408] Wikipedia (2021). *Matrix Multiplication Algorithm.* URL https://en.wikipedia.org/wiki/Matrix_multiplication_algorithm.

[409] Wikipedia (2021). *QR Decomposition.* URL https://en.wikipedia.org/wiki/QR_decomposition.

[410] Wilkinson L (2005). *The Grammar of Graphics.* 2nd edition. Springer.

[411] Williams L, Kessler RR, Cunningham W (2000). "Strengthening the Case for Pair Programming." *IEEE Software,* **17**(4), 19–25.

[412] Williams-Young DB, Li X (2019). *On the Efficacy and High-Performance Implementation of Quaternion Matrix Multiplication.* URL https://arxiv.org/abs/1903.05575.

[413] Wu X, Xiao L, Sun Y, Zhang J, Ma T, He L (2022). "A Survey of Human-in-the-Loop for Machine Learning." *Future Generation Computer Systems*, **135**, 364–381.

[414] Xie Y (2015). *Dynamic Documents with R and knitr.* 2nd edition. CRC Press.

[415] Xie Y, Allaire JJ, Grolemund G (2022). *R Markdown: The Definitive Guide.* URL https://bookdown.org/yihui/rmarkdown/.

[416] Xin D, Ma L, Liu J, Song S, Parameswaran A (2018). "Accelerating Human-in-the-Loop Machine Learning: Challenges and Opportunities." In *Proceedings of the Second Workshop on Data Management for End-to-End Machine Learning*, pp. 1–4.

[417] Yamashita Y, Stephenson S, et al (2022). *pyenv: Simple Python Version Management.* URL https://github.com/pyenv/pyenv.

[418] Yang Z, Dai Z, Yang Y, Carbonell J, Salakhutdinov RR, Le QV (2019). "XLNet: Generalized Autoregressive Pretraining for Language Understanding." In *Advances in Neural Information Processing Systems (NeurIPS)*, pp. 5753–5763.

[419] You E (2022). *Vue.js: The Progressive JavaScript Framework.* URL https://vuejs.org/.

[420] Zaharia M, The Linux Foundation (2022). *MLflow Documentation.* URL https://www.mlflow.org/docs/latest/index.html.

[421] Zellers R, Holtzman A, Rashkin H, Bisk Y, Farhadi A, Roesner F, Choi Y (2019). "Defending against Neural Fake News." In *Advances in Neural Information Processing Systems (NeurIPS)*, pp. 9054–9065.

[422] Zelvenskiy S, Harisinghani G, Yu T, Ng E, Wei R (2022). *Project Radar: Intelligent Early-Fraud Detection.* URL https://eng.uber.com/project-radar-intelligent-early-fraud-detection/.

[423] Zhang H, Cruz L, van Deursen A (2022). "Code Smells for Machine Learning Applications." In *Proceedings of the 1st International Conference on AI Engineering: Software Engineering for AI*, pp. 1–12.

[424] Zhang JM, Harman M, Ma L, Liu Y (2020). "Machine Learning Testing: Survey, Landscapes and Horizons." *IEEE Transactions on Software Engineering*, **48**(1), 1–36.

[425] Zheng A (2015). *Evaluating Machine Learning Models*. O'Reilly.

Index

API, 105–106, 122, 125, 138,
        142, 176, 182–183
    documentation, 136, 141,
        189–199, 206,
        260–261
    liveness, 178, 300
    readiness, 124, 127, 178,
        300
architecture design, 114–115
architecture documentation,
        104, 199–204

baseline implementation,
        115–116

CI
    continuous delivery, 301
    continuous deployment,
        301
    continuous integration,
        301
CI/CD, 107–109, 140
    continuous delivery,
        107–109, 120
    continuous deployment,
        107–109, 121, 143, 172,
        176–177
    continuous integration,
        97, 107–108, 143, 146,
        151, 239
    MLOps, 108–109, 143
cloud instances, 28–29, 33,
        91, 124, 166–167,

        176–177, 179–180, 222,
        239, 253, 264–265,
        286–287
code editors, 251–254, 257
code review, 66, 107, 108, 116,
        137, 146–150, 189
    mob programming,
        148–150
    pair programming, see
        mob programming
    tool-based, 148–150
coding
    standards, 137, 259–260
    styles, 136–137, 260
comments, 106, 135, 145–146,
        148, 149, 156–157,
        186–189
computational complexity,
        66–68, 116, 194,
        225–226
configuration management,
        see experiment
        tracking
containers, 121, 122, 140,
        167–171, 176–177, 253,
        257–258, 265–266,
        298–299
    Docker, 121, 167–171, 253,
        257
    continuous integration,
        258–260

correction cascade, *see*
    entanglement, models

data
    as code, 95–98
    collection, 112–114, 215
    drift, 99–101, 119, 123, 127,
        202, 218–219, 228
    dynamic, 202
    locality, 25, 27, 29, 117
    offline, 97, 119, 230–232
    online, 97, 119, 231–232
    provenance, 101, 112–113,
        117, 118, 292
    visualisation, 117, 127–128,
        248–250, 271–273
data structures, 48–49
    data frames, 51–53
    lists, 50
    matrices, 53
        dense, 53–55
        sparse, 55–56, 80–84,
        86
    vectors, 49–51
delivery
    continuous, *see* CI/CD,
        continuous delivery
    progressive, 172
dependencies
    untracked, 100–103, 106,
        181
    untrusted, 99–101
    vendored, *see*
        dependencies,
        untracked
deployment
    pattern
        A/B testing, 119, 175, 231
        blue-green, 173
        canary, 119, 173
        destroy and re-create,
            175
        rolling, ramped, 175
        shadow, 175
    pattern, strategy, 105, 172,
        267

entanglement
    features, 102, 215–219
    models, 102–103, 217, 222
experiment tracking, 97–98,
        104, 108, 109, 118, 121,
        140, 144, 164, 169, 171,
        176–177, 181–183, 229,
        239, 250, 264–265,
        269–271, 293–297
explainability, 98, 113, 127,
        219–220, 227

fairness, 114, 127, 227
feature flags, 104, 144, 176
feedback loops, 102–103, 222

IDEs, 140, 248, 251–253, 257

machine learning
    pipeline, *see* pipeline
machine learning system, 13
    CPU, 15–17, 58–59, 91,
        165–167
    GPU, TPU, 15, 17–20,
        26–27, 31–32, 58–59,
        91, 171, 216, 238–239
    processor memory, 20–25
    RAM, 23–25, 28, 66
    remote, *see* cloud
        instances
    storage, 24–25
mathematics vs code,
        134–135, 152–153,
        237–239, 243

mission statement, 111, 206–209, 278

notebooks, 137–138, 141, 196, 248, 251, 254–256, 267, 268, 270, 272

observability, 33, 125–126, 131, 137, 177
orchestrator, 102, 111, 167, 171, 265–266, 269–270

packaging
    containers, *see* container
    language packages, 164–165
    model artefacts, 164
    virtual machines, 165–167, 176–177
parallel computing, 16–18, 20, 26–27, 31–33, 50–51, 53, 119, 172, 222, 225, 238, 290
pipeline, 108–109, 172, 176, 202–204
    data ingestion, 109, 116–117, 123, 127, 289–291
    data preparation, 117–118, 123, 127, 248, 290–292
    inference, 31–32, 122–123, 125, 127, 172–173, 178, 298–300
    logging, 33, 109, 124–126, 177, 226, 292
    model evaluation, 119–120
    model training, 31–32, 109, 118–119, 123, 127, 294–296
    model validation, 119–120
    modules, 109, 140–141

monitoring, 109, 123–124, 177–178, 218, 225, 231, 280
reporting, 126–128, 272–273, 300
serving, 109, 122, 123, 171, 176, 178, 297–298
privacy, 30, 114, 117, 227
prototyping, *see* baseline implementation

refactoring, 107, 137, 151–153, 190, 238
registry, 120–121, 176
    artefact, 120, 121, 164, 271, 292
    container, 121, 122, 170, 264
    model, 121, 122, 183, 269, 270, 297
rollback, 105, 145, 173, 182–280

security, 30, 104, 114, 122, 137, 141, 167–168, 170–171, 236

technical debt, 98–99
    architecture, 104–106, 143, 177, 200, 222, 229
    code, 106–107, 133, 137–138, 151–152, 165, 170, 229
    data, 99–101, 119, 214, 218–219
    model, 101–103
    models, 219, 221–222, 281
technical documentation, 205–206
tests

acceptance, 142, 172,
  235–237
coverage, 107, 123,
  239–241
integration, 101–102, 142,
  222, 234–236, 259
property-based, 243
quality gate, 100
quality gates, 101, 118, 235
system, 142, 234, 236, 259
unit, 140, 159, 222,
  234–235, 259,
  300–301
trade-offs
  cloud computing, 28–30,
    32–33
  computational complexity,
    90–92
  data structures, 61–62
  editors, 251–252
  hardware, 26–28, 30–32
  machine learning
    platforms, 266–267
  variables, 56–61
trunk-based development,
  144–145, 148

ubiquitous language, 104, 110,
  136, 187, 199–202,
  204, 205
use cases, 209–211, 277–302

variables
  floating point, 40–47
  integers, 36–40
  strings, 47–48
versioning
  code, 97, 107–108, 116,
    141–146, 148–149, 151,
    183

configurations, *see*
  experiment tracking
documentation, 189
models, *see* experiment
  tracking